less Bid

Taming the Unreliable Price of Oil to Secure the Economy

Dan Dicker

WILEY

John Wiley & Sons, Inc.

Published by John Wiley & Sons, Inc., Hoboken, New Jersey.

Published simultaneously in Canada.

Library of Congress Cataloging-in-Publication Data:
Dicker, Daniel, 1960–
    Oil's endless bid : taming the unreliable price of oil to secure our economy / Daniel Dicker.
        p. cm.
      Includes index.
    ISBN 978-0-470-91562-2 (cloth); ISBN 978-1-118-03039-4 (ebk);
    ISBN 978-1-118-03040-0 (ebk); ISBN 978-1-118-03041-7 (ebk)
    1. Petroleum products–Prices.   2. Petroleum reserves.
3. Petroleum industry and trade.   4. Commodity futures.   I. Title.
      HD9560.4.D53 2011
      338.2'3282–dc22

                                                                2010053527

Printed in the United States of America

10   9   8   7   6   5   4   3   2   1

Contents

Introduction

The Oil Market Is Broken

This book is for anyone who has wondered why it costs $30 to fill a tank with gas one year and $75 the next.

Why have oil and gas increased in price six-fold from 2003 to 2008, only to plummet and rise again?

Why are we stripping our national wealth and handing it over to foreign oil producers, if the supply of cheap traditional energy is greater than it's ever been?

Where is the price of oil headed, and can we do anything to change its trajectory?

We've lost control of our oil markets—and it's become the biggest financial story of the decade. I've been an oil trader working in the center of the action, in the pits of the New York Mercantile Exchange, where I've been a member since 1982. I've watched the oil markets change dramatically over the last 20 years, particularly since 2005, when the idea of oil as an asset class, the invention of new financial products, and the advent of electronic access took a sleepy, club-like market into the national spotlight.

I was finally convinced to write this book while watching my screens in May 2008: I watched in amazement as the crude barrel spot price clicked to more than $130 a barrel. One hundred and thirty dollars? That's just nuts!

That's when I realized the oil market was broken, running like a train off its tracks, totally out of control. I had seen it getting worse and worse and moving into absurdity during 2005 to 2008, the last three years I spent as a floor trader at NYMEX—the New York Mercantile Exchange—the hub for oil pricing. Oil prices had stopped responding to normal economic rules of supply and demand, and by 2008, the market was busted. In its place, oil had become dominated by a new flow of money pulsing through it—speculative money from investors and traders who had no natural connection to oil at all.

The Oil Market Isn't Like the Stock Market

This wasn't the way it was supposed to work. Futures markets were never intended to operate this way, and that $130 price that day in May 2008 was proof of just how badly the market was buckling under the strain. Economists, oil analysts, company CEOs, pundits—just about everyone with an opinion—were weighing in with a different reason for this energy price spike. The explanations ran the gamut— from the falling value in the U.S. dollar, global economic growth, inflationary fears, or China's soaring energy needs. All of these expla- nations amounted to a bad alibi. Quite simply, a new set of players had come to dominate the oil markets and control them. Futures markets were designed to accommodate only a small group of hedgers—farmers providing raw products and manufacturers making finished products. Unlike the stock market or the bond market, the oil futures markets were never meant to accommodate investment, which it was now being forced to do.

Investment Banks Changed the Business of Trading Oil

When I entered the oil trading world in the early 1980s, the foremost actors trading oil were the Exxons and BPs and Chevrons and Shells. They used the futures markets as a tool only to guard the risks of their real physical assets. To them, trading oil was only a side note, helping their primary business of selling oil. Outside of these giants of the market, small trading groups and independent traders like me provided the grease to match their hedging needs and create fluidity. We were tiny players picking up the leftover crumbs—our participation was never enough to concern (let alone overwhelm) the capital and interest of the big oil players.

But since 2000 or so, and particularly the years leading up to that price spike in the summer of 2008, a new set of players had come to displace the oil companies and dominate the trading of energy. These were the financial players—mostly the large investment banks, but also new energy hedge funds and managed futures funds.

Feeding the profit trough for these new financial traders at the banks and the funds was a flood of dumb money (as we used to call it on the trading floor): billions of dollars of investment interest in oil, entering the game overwhelmingly in the form of commodity index funds, but also appearing from individuals through online futures accounts and with stock-like ETFs. I began to refer to these overwhelming influences on price as "Oil's Endless Bid."

Commodities just aren't stocks. Oil can't be traded or invested in like a stock, not without these wild and unwanted consequences. Oil's endless bid created a new financial market, overwhelming the old physical oil market. Oil's endless bid was investors rushing in to add oil to their traditional portfolios of stocks and bonds.

Moreover, nobody was trying to stop it. On the contrary, trading and investing in oil continued to be universally encouraged. Investors and professionals alike were told by the futures industry, the wider financial industry, the media, and our government that our markets were fine and would take care of themselves. Meanwhile, oil's endless bid drove prices higher throughout that summer in 2008 to an unfathomable $147 a barrel, with little fundamental evidence to support its rise.

When the bubble popped in July 2008 and the money fled from oil investment, everything was made crystal clear if there was even a lingering doubt: the oil market, for a brief moment relieved of much of the purely financial interest that had buoyed it higher, reflected true fundamental pricing for the first time in years. And it was trading at $32 a barrel. That was closer to what oil was really worth.

But it didn't take long at all for money to find its courage again and resume its domination of the capital markets: equities surged, treasuries ceased paying a negative interest, bond spreads began to come back from Armageddon levels, and, yes, oil, the newest capital market, began its march back up, reaching $82 in October 2009. In other words, the endless bid was back.

And it came back with a vengeance. The $75 median price of oil in 2009 was arguably even less defensible than the $100-plus prices we saw in 2008. Supplies were filled to the brim, reaching levels not seen since 1990, while demand was at generational lows, befitting the worse global recession since the Great Depression. The last time I had seen fundamentals as weak as these, oil was trading for $22, not more than $70.

Why Should You Care about the Volatility of Oil Prices?

I knew that 2009's price, indefensible as it was, was just a stepping-stone. Oil's wild moves were bound to get wilder, higher, and more uncontrollable in the not-too-distant future. The volatility of oil in 2009 and 2010 had been the equal of any year on record, following slavishly the wild swings in the stock market and the dollar. I knew that 2009's price was a springboard, and a powerful one, toward $150, $200, perhaps even $250 per barrel, as soon as even the slightest hint of recovery was felt and an even greater hunger to own oil returned. Figure I.1 shows the history of oil prices—and it's a scary picture of the future.

Looking at the price of oil since 1990, it is incredibly stable, as flat as a highway rolling across the center of Texas, until around 2003. Then all hell breaks loose—with the price increasing sixfold in five years, then losing almost 80% of its value in less than six months, only to immediately triple again.

Can the American economy, which is increasingly dependent on oil, ever be expected to robustly grow, with a crazy swinging price like that?

"Why should I care about the swinging prices of oil?" I hear many people say. "America is a capitalist society; we believe in the free

$/bbl

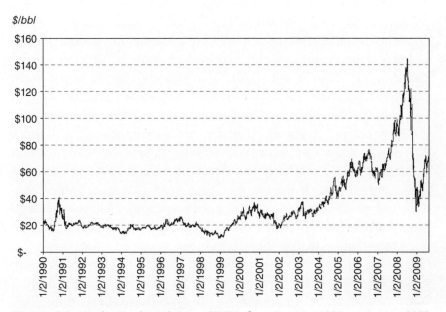

Figure I.1   Daily Crude Oil Price (WTI) from January 1990 to August 2009
SOURCE: Energy Information Administration

markets working; and we are always better off letting them take care of themselves." Indeed, the oil market in 2008 and 2009 showed a great similarity to other speculative bubbles where no one questioned the market's wild action, like the tech stock bubble in the Nasdaq of the late 1990s. The difference is that people choose to invest in stocks, therefore, they bear responsibility for their own risks and possible losses. But whether it is the heat in our homes or the fuel for our cars, even the foods we eat and the clothes we wear—just about everything in our lives is tied to the costs of energy. *We are all invested in oil, whether we like it or not.* Business is hardly exempt. More than 50% of the companies on the New York Stock Exchange rely on energy as their single largest input cost, and that doesn't even include the energy companies themselves (some of which were being put out of business by the high price of oil!)

Is there any single thing in the world with as much global impact as the price of the crude barrel?

The continuing high cost of oil causes everyone to suffer. Downstream costs of energy are passed on to the consumer, from airlines to railroads, from refrigeration to energy-dependent industrial products as diverse as aluminum, plastics, and pharmaceuticals. But the consumer is balking, under pressure from an imploding housing market and increasing unemployment. Economic growth is in reverse for the first time in a decade and a half. The high costs of oil helped force the global economy off a cliff in 2008 and ensures that the current recession will be more long-lasting and recovery from it slower.

Even for me, a career oil trader, little about the way oil trades now makes sense. Oil prices now incredibly chase the equity markets in lockstep: if the stock market rallies, oil now follows. For most of my career, the stock market and oil moved in opposite directions. That just made common sense that anyone could understand: a high price for energy is bad for most business.

More than a market or a regulatory issue, oil's high price has become a serious U.S. national security issue. With oil prices spiking, huge chunks of money, now more than $200 billion a year, is flowing from the pockets of Americans into the pockets of the OPEC cartel. That's happening now four times faster than even two short years ago. Talk about a war on terrorism! The modern oil pricing system now works to fill the coffers and sovereign wealth funds of the nations most likely to fund our worst and most diabolical enemies.

We have caused this; there is no one else to blame. We have inspired this disaster with lax regulation, a blind belief in free markets, and unfettered greed. The oil market has followed a similar pattern to other modern asset markets, becoming enmeshed in more and more complex derivative products that benefit mostly the people that sell them. We encourage and reward best the people who create and squeeze profits out of these new product markets, and we invite—no, warn—every investor to participate as well, lest they miss the latest and greatest money-making opportunity. The result of this avalanche of activity is clear, causing prices to boom, only to bust violently before beginning the cycle over again.

Is Anyone Out There?

But in Washington, Congress is slow to see the danger, confused as to the causes, and incompetent at understanding possible solutions.

Hearings called to figure out what was going on were dominated by industry spokesmen, derivative salesmen, and bank loyalists, all touting the advantages of increased liquidity and financial innovation. Congressmen used those platforms to pander to their constituencies and scream about rising prices with no apparent desire to understand why it was happening or how to fix it. The financial media lost an opportunity to seriously question the system and inform the public on causes and possible solutions.

When the banking crisis of mid-2008 hit its fever pitch with the failure of Lehman Brothers and the subsequent rapid deleveraging of all capital markets, it also violently burst the oil bubble and removed 80% of its traded value in less than seven months. I felt vindicated. Nothing proved a speculative bubble more convincingly than the rapid price collapse we saw then. But I knew that the fall of oil was only a side effect of a larger market collapse and did nothing to answer the question of how bad things were and how bad they were sure to get in the future. The price collapse had taken the heat off of investigating how the oil markets really operate.

In the midst of a greater economic crisis, oil's price drop ended the motivation to understand speculation as the cause of commodity inflation. This, I knew, was an awful, terrible mistake. The bottom line was that nothing, absolutely nothing, had changed or was likely to change in the way that oil was being priced, making it a sure thing that the boom/bust cycle would replay itself soon.

How had it changed? How did my sleepy, quiet, and insular market become this over-active whirlwind, in need of thousands of written articles and 20 CNBC hits a day? Three enormous changes rocked the oil markets forever, and Part I of this book describes these in detail.

Problem #1: The Assetization of Oil

First and probably most important, new institutional and individual investor interest in commodities, and particularly the price of crude, became the hottest game in town, and the world is rushing to play. Using commodity index funds and exchange-traded funds (ETFs), through dedicated energy hedge funds as well as individual futures accounts, the price of oil is now as easily investable as any stock or bond.

This is why the bid has become endless: although stocks and bonds have been around for centuries, oil has only been available as an investment for a few years. As an asset class, oil has a lot of catching up to do, and a lot of new money yet to assimilate. Chapters 2 and 3 describe the assetization of oil in detail.

Problem #2: Financial Finagling

Second, as I'll discuss in Chapter 4, there had been a rush for fresh financial innovation. Following patterns from similar derivative markets, the investment banks and energy marketers created and sold a whole new category of specialized and customized products to cater to every kind of energy client they could imagine, products that would help mitigate risks from differing grades of crude, of transporting and refining crude, and from the output products from crude and their final sale. This created dozens of new markets, most of them over the counter and designed to be closed to most investors and accessible only to in-house traders of proprietary accounts.

Commodity exchanges rushed to offer clearing of these side markets and get in on the new action. While West Texas Intermediate was the only traded crude product in the world when I first started on the floor, by the time I left it, the exchange was offering clearing on more than 75 futures and derivative of derivatives on crude with even more numerous and complicated products offered in refined products and natural gas. While the opportunity for profiting from the sale and proprietary trading of this unnecessary diversity grew, so did the nominally traded market in oil, now 15 times greater than the amount of real physical oil.

Problem #3: Electronic Access to the Oil Markets

Finally, as I'll discuss in Chapter 5, the change from the human trading floor where I spent my career to an electronic virtual world of price discovery destroyed many of the governors on price swings. While the world of on-floor trading that I experienced in the pits seems quaint now, it did provide as near to perfect a pipeline for orderly trade, forcing all the participants to transparently appear at one place to transact business. Universal access of internet-based electronic platforms to oil spurred massive increases in volume and open interest, but also created massive volatility and higher prices with it.

We Can Fix This

It's not too late to stop the continuing havoc that the modern energy markets wreak on the price of oil. The price of oil has become too violent, too high, and too unreliable. I want to see that highway-across-Texas price restored that had allowed business to grow steadily without being derailed by spiking costs. I want to see the consumer relieved of an energy burden that is killing the wallet. And I want to see our country become self-sufficient and quit pouring money unnecessarily into Arab hands.

To see this happen, some major changes would have to take place. The Federal regulating agencies in Washington charged with market oversight had advanced a number of possible ideas. Unfortunately, most of these measures have been watered down by lobbyists, and even those weakened ideas have little chance of passing through a partisan Congress anytime soon. Moreover, the first thing that needs to happen to see any substantive change in the oil markets will have to be a conviction on everyone's part—whether inside the industry or inside the beltway—that the mechanism is broken.

That's the hope of this book.

Oil's Endless Bid charts the changes that I saw and continue to see: Chapters 2 through 5 in Part I describe how the oil market was and how it worked and why it operated fairly and with respect to fundamentals; it also describes how and why the oil market changed and how it operates now. Chapters 6 through 10 in Part II explain why the price of oil is unfair and without respect to economic laws. Finally, Chapter 11 offers some solutions to what can be done about the broken oil markets ... Throughout this book, I give a taste of what it was like to sit at the nexus of oil price discovery for more than two decades—which was, without question, the most exciting, interesting, and intrepid job any person can be lucky enough to have, even for a day. Follow me and by the end of this book you'll know what's really moving oil's price and what you can do to prepare and take advantage of its wild swings. Toward the end, I hope my case is made strongly enough to suggest some rather progressive measures with which to deal with our financial energy crisis, by taking some of the profit opportunity away from the largest investment banks and hedge funds, removing a lot of the investor access to the direct price of the crude barrel, but also by restoring some of the smaller, independent traders and trading groups, who have been sidelined by recent innovations, back in their roles as legitimate market makers and liquidity providers. I think we can do it.

And I think we have to do it. Without serious reform, I believe our economy and we as individuals are destined to be routinely crippled, manacled to an oil price that whips around without warning like a roller coaster and cuts through our economy like a chain saw.

It's been a long, nearly 20-year process to see our oil markets destroyed and the price of energy become wholly unreliable. Some of the changes I track in this book are simple to understand and obvious, while others require at least a cursory understanding of commodities and how the oil markets work. But stick with me, and I promise as clear a description as I can muster—from the simplest hedge an oil consumer might use to the most complicated derivative offered from a broker's over-the-counter platform—and from the quickest scalp trade of a local floor trader looking to make $100 for rent money, to the multi-million-dollar bets that huge energy traders from Goldman Sachs or Morgan Stanley undertake. Although the mechanisms require some work to understand, the motives don't: it is, of course, all about money, and not about providing the most reliable and honest price for oil and oil products to business and individual consumers.

Before we can even dig into oil's endless bid, getting a flavor of how oil was traded in the good old days gives some perspective to how differently oil prices are arrived at today. Chapter 1 gives a little insight, from my own experience. However, if you know nothing about the futures market or want a practical refresher course, Appendix A offers a brief tutorial that I recommend everyone read before getting started.

Chapter 1

A Brief Look Back at the Good Old Days of Oil Trading

An old cliché says: "To know where you're going, you have to know where you've been." The oil markets have become broken, but they weren't always. In the first 20 or so years of my career as a trader, the oil markets worked much better—at least for consumers and the economy at large; it provided much steadier and generally much, much cheaper prices. Describing how things used to work will quickly show you why.

In my earliest days, from 1983 until about 2000, it was very difficult surviving as a day trader in oil. Statistically, only 15% of those who tried to be floor traders during this time period were able to survive for more than five years. Why was that? Well, simply put, it was about volume and volatility. Nobody outside of the oil companies and our small band of traders cared much at all about oil. So our days were an endless string of small volumes and small ranges. After all, if nothing much moves, how can you make money? It's tough, believe me. We'd wait for something to happen and take advantage of the

1

spurts of interest and motion. In those days, the trick was surviving long enough to see the good days ahead.

In the second part of my career, the world began to see oil as a financial opportunity, although they first struggled with how best to capture it. These were the golden days for us on the floor—from about 2000 until around 2006. Enormous daily volumes and movement began to come into our oil markets, and we finally began to live the dream that most people imagine when they think of oil traders. Opportunities, both to win and lose, arrived practically daily. Floor traders had their best years ever.

The final stage of my career began in 2006, when markets began shifting to electronic venues, and OTC markets began to really swell. But it was a confusing time for the career oil trader on the floor. Volatility, which was normally the lifeblood for profits, had never been greater. Volumes were astronomical and growing daily. And yet, there were no profits to be had. On the contrary, our honed skills seemed to be working against us, and the rules that we had learned were turned upside down by the financial market forces that now completely dominate price. But the story of energy futures trading on a tiny New York commodity exchange begins in 1979, and there, on the floor of the New York Mercantile Exchange is where I appeared, as a fresh-faced participant soon after, in 1982.

Who Grows Up Wanting to Be an Oil Trader?

Going through high school, I had little idea what I would do for a career. I had certainly never heard of commodities. I was ignorant of what that word even meant. *"Commodities? You mean like pork bellies?"* Why pork bellies always comes to mind when anyone mentions commodities (even today) is a cruel joke to anyone in the industry. But that's what I thought of whenever I heard talk of commodities on the news.

Meanwhile, my father ran a small hospital on the south shore of Long Island, NY, and he was keenly aware of the advantages to being an MD. *"You don't know what you want to do? You're good at the sciences—be a doctor,"* he told me.

Good enough. I headed off to college to undertake pre-med courses, with a couple thousand other smart kids whose fathers also thought that was a pretty good major—if you didn't have a better idea.

However, I quickly found out the work required to actually *become* a doctor wasn't so much fun. I was good at school, good at taking tests and retaining information, and I was a decent writer. But I hated the long classes and the arcane material—organic chemistry being a particularly difficult course to bear. I was far more of an instant gratification kind of guy, never happy working at something for weeks and months at a time for a grand result.

Besides being impatient for success and a bit lazy, something else began to take hold of my interest and thwarted my father's (and my) plans of me becoming a doctor. I fell in love with the horse races. I started going to Belmont Park almost as soon as I could drive and could legally bet. I loved that feeling of vindication and validation—of having taken the raw information of the arcane numbers and symbols in the daily racing form, and converting those to relative odds and a betting strategy. That process had just enough math, just enough analysis, and just enough exposure to real risk to create the perfect cocktail for me.

I knew I was pitting myself against the rest of the betting population in every race, that I was in silent competition with them. To continually make money at the track according to this system, the foolproof plan to follow was simply to be smarter than the rest of the betting public. I wasn't a genius, and I didn't come up with any grand new theories of assessing the abilities of horse flesh that gave me any kind of significant edge over the rest of the betting public. Like most other players, I wasn't a long-term winner at the track. But that didn't stop my passion. And 'a good score' (a nice payoff on a race) would go a long way to bringing me back again and again looking for that fantastic, validating feeling.

I remember my first $500 wager on Slew o' Gold, a four-year-old horse running against three-year-old contenders and winners of that year's Triple Crown races. At almost three-to-one odds, Slew o' Gold was clearly being overlooked, but Slew had been racing beautifully in other handicaps and stakes races. To me, he seemed to have only gotten stronger since his own Triple Crown campaign a year earlier.

That horse, on that day, represented to me an incredible and rare, maybe once-in-a-lifetime money-making opportunity, and I summoned the courage to put down more money than I really could afford to lose at the time, right on his nose. The feeling of elation and superiority I felt when Slew bounded across the finish line an easy two lengths in front has never been matched since, although I have continued to search and hoped to find equally validating money-making opportunities every day of my life. But there's something particularly special about the horses that even a good stock buy or a value sale of a long-term spread can't match.

I retained my love of the ponies deep into my trading career. It should come as no surprise that I was met on the floor by many others who had spent plenty of time at the track in their youths, and retained an interest. My early boss whom I clerked for, Mike Milano, was one. Another was Harry Bienenfeld, a legendary platinum trader who left the metals pit to take advantage of the exploding oil markets and ended up standing next to me for much of my career in the gasoline pit. I would see Harry at the old Roosevelt Raceway trotters track in the evenings after the markets closed, when I was still a clerk and only aspiring to become a trader. Another horse junkie from the floor was Joel Bush, a wonderful man who worked for various independent brokerage houses and represented his love of the track by his badge "HORS" (in those days, there were no five-letter badges). Some even owned horses, like Sandy Goldfarb, who had established his own very successful brokerage operation as well as a pretty well-known stable of horses over the years. And Leon Mayer, the godfather of the gasoline pit, who used to stop me when he saw me leaving the trading floor for the track. He'd reach into his pocket, draw out 4 crisp $100 bills, and tell me with his thick Yiddish accent, "*DANO, in the 3rd, 5th, and 7th race, give me the 1, 5, and 7 exacta box for $20. And the rest is for you!*"

But before finding myself among my own kind on the floor of the exchange, where gambling on the races was considered a useful skill and to be admired, I fought the tendency to waste my days at the local off-track betting (OTB) during my college days at the State University of New York at StonyBrook. In one particularly bad semester of procrastination and self-destruction, I spent most of my days trying to find the best-quality $18,000 claimer running in the fourth race at Aqueduct instead of trying to figure out the annealing point of phenols—a much more appropriate use of my energies then. Through a massive rationalization, I had managed to convince myself through much of that semester that I could make up all of the work I was missing until two weeks before final exams, when I had to admit that maybe I was in a bit of a fix. I needed to petition the academic board at the University to remove the semester of NRs (Never Reported) from my records for extreme circumstances. And I was on academic probation for three semesters after that, forced to submit every test score from every class to the committee to prove I was staying on the straight and narrow.

I never went back to the OTB during classes after that, doing well for the rest of my college career, but I had sunk any chance I might have had of going on to medical school. I wasn't sorry. Even now, I can't imagine how I would have been able to stand an additional four years of brutal graduate work followed by another four years of residency to complete a medical degree and finally be in a position to make some money. Whether I had sabotaged myself or not, it was clear how much I hated school. And it would soon become clear how much my passion for betting on horses would have in common with my ultimate career in trading oil.

The Family Tree of Brokers

After the OTB semester, however, not only did my grades improve. I was lucky to fall in with a group of guys who shared much in common with me: Jewish, with European parents, and a familiar upbringing. One was Mark Burnett, whom I met, in a great coincidence of serendipity: we both owned beat-up 1973 red Toyota Corollas, and he mistook his car for mine one day. We hit it off right away and became great friends and suite-mates.

During the time at college with Mark, I kept on hearing of the "neat" job his cousin had as a broker for heating oil in New York. And I kept in touch when Mark joined his cousin on the floor of the exchange, working as a broker after his graduation. After graduation, I had no thoughts of commodities initially; instead, I thought of using my facility in German, gained through school study and a summer spent in Frankfurt working for an import/export firm. In New York, I scoured the papers for jobs that would allow me to continue to use my language skills and give me some continuing international contact, since I had always enjoyed travelling overseas. But all the opportunities I encountered on graduating amounted to little more than secretarial and bookkeeping roles, and instead of being questioned in interviews about my world view or fluency in German, I was constantly being asked how many words a minute I could type.

After a few months of this, entirely frustrated, my father again had a bright idea.

"*Why don't you go see what Mark's doing?*" he suggested, not knowing the first thing about commodities either. "*It sounds fast, and you don't have a lot of patience anyway.....you might like it.*"

I went down to the floor. Mark introduced me to Drew Stein, who was working the phones at a small independent oil company brokerage, where Mark and his cousin were filling orders in the young heating oil pit. Drew knew everyone on the floor and helped me run around, looking for a start-up position I could fill. He had a good relationship with many of the locals and particularly one, Howard Hazelcorn, who had become frustrated with his daily position clerk and was looking for an excuse to fire him. I became the perfect excuse. Inside of a week, I started for Howie and his partner, Mike Milano, at a starting salary of $160 a week. Thanks to Mark and Drew, I was in the commodities business.

Over the course of my many years on the floor, I found out that my story of how I came to be on the floor was similar to so many others. It was almost impossible to get started on the floor of *any* exchange (not only ours) without the help of someone already there. I never heard a story of anyone who answered an ad or got a call from an employment agency for a position as a phone clerk or a runner or a broker's assistant. It seemed that everyone on the floor got there through the help of a relative or a friend. Like six degrees of separation, you could trace an almost incestuous family tree of members and brokers, all giving the leg up to someone else on the floor. It was a very, very closed group.

First Impressions of the Trading Floor

I don't literally remember the first day I walked onto the trading floor of the New York Mercantile Exchange at 4 World Trade Center (4WTC) sometime in 1982. But I do recall the first few months of my life there. Back then, the trading floor was shared by four separate exchanges at the same time: the Commodity Exchange (COMEX); The Cotton Exchange; The Coffee, Sugar, and Cocoa Exchange (CSCE then, ultimately renamed the New York Board of Trade, or NYBOT); and my NYMEX. This quartile arrangement placed the NYMEX at the furthest corner of the room. Our exchange had 816 memberships, or seats, that were allocated. (Each of the other three exchanges had a similar number of seats available.) You needed a seat to transact trades and each seat was in constant use. The support staff for each member either taking care of orders or trading his own accounts (or a little of both) was probably a little more than two other people: brokers required much more help than independent (or local) traders. Add to that population the exchange employees necessary to register trades, work the trade entry room, and administer to exchange business, and you were looking at quite a crowd on this shared, 20,000-square-foot trading floor. We had an intimate (if not ridiculously crowded) condition in which we worked, at least when I first started out on the floor in 1982, as a fresh-faced 22-year-old college graduate.

Even as I remember it now, the scene was incredible. I clearly recall attending my first baseball game, at the tender age of five, because of the impression those vast green fields and living crowds had on me. At age 22, the space carved out for the four New York commodity exchanges were nearly as impressive to me. Pricing boards, with hundreds of unfathomable numbers, ratcheted constantly on all four tall walls, which led up to the amazing 40-foot ceiling. These boards would be considered antiques today, but when I first arrived in 1982, they were a major upgrade from the handwritten chalk boards that had been in use in the previous exchange location at 15 Harrison Street (where NYMEX had moved from, into its new digs as part of the Commodity Exchange Center, in 1979). And they literally ratcheted, making a loud clicking noise when the prices changed. Represented in orange and green numbers, you could easily tell which were the most current (or last print) prices from the older traded prices.

Members of each exchange were easily recognizable from other workers and exchange employees. Each one of them wore a badge—a colored identification card that contained a trader number on top of the badge, which was assigned by the exchange, and a (usually) three- or four-letter handle underneath the trader number, which traders were allowed to choose for themselves. Each exchange had its own unique color that referred to the membership badges that were associated with it: green for COMEX, light blue for the CSCE, orange for the Cotton Exchange, and yellow for NYMEX members.

A membership entitled a trader access to all of the products each exchange had exclusive control over. A few traders owned memberships in more than one exchange, and that was represented with badges cut into two or three of the exchange colors. But I *never* saw four colors on one badge, which represented membership in all four exchanges. Why not? Because only a vaunted few traders purchased licenses to enter and trade in *every* product offered on that combined exchange floor: therefore, they received special badges: the Gold badge. I gave these trading monsters wide berth and spoke of them in hushed tones—as if the ownership of four memberships assigned some great success and reverence to the person wearing the badge. To a 22-year-old who knew nothing of commodities, it was pretty impressive to me.

As you walked back into the NYMEX corner, three trading centers or pits were evident: The first ring you came in contact with was the Potato Pit. Trading in Maine potatoes was a holdback from the earliest days of the exchange, when the NYMEX was first known as "the Butter and Eggs exchange." Its agricultural roots had all but disappeared, except for this last representation into the 1980s, with the potato contract. There was good reason that potatoes had survived to see the new exchange address at 4WTC. It had been the engine which had all but supported the exchange for many years, when other commodity exchanges floundered and disappeared. In many ways, the NYMEX really owed its life to this old and quaint marketplace.

But when I got to the exchange in 1982, although the potato contract had a few more tricks and turns to play out before it was delisted in 1987, it held little interest for me or other young traders breaking into the commodity markets. The traders who populated the Potato Pit were the remaining old-timers from Harrison Street, mostly over 60 years old. And in those days, on the floor of the rapidly growing commodities game, 60 years old was considered beyond ancient. The median age outside of the Potato Pit at NYMEX couldn't have been much more than 25.

The guys who didn't exclusively trade their own accounts in the Potato Pit were often the owners of the small independent brokerages that tended to the potato orders coming in from farmers and end users. It was a tight-knit group that few independent traders wanted to try to invade, mostly because it was a quiet, steady, and ultimately not-very-sexy market.

One of the first traders I met on the NYMEX floor was a 50-ish local trader in the Potato Pit. He never ventured outside of it, and he couldn't have been happier. With some patience, he often glowed to me how he could find a "couple of good trades" a day in the quiescent "spuds," often netting him $200 or *even* $300 in a day. "*Shhh.......don't tell anybody*," he would say, literally guilty about the great world he was a daily part of. "*What a wonderful business!*" he would crow. "*I can't believe I can do this for a living, as opposed to really working!*" Many of us over the years shared his disbelief and some of the guilt, but as a young man on the exchanges, I had no idea what he was talking about. And I wanted much more. As excited as this potato trader was about his small market, everyone else knew that the really great prospects on the fast expanding NYMEX were not going to be with the quickly unwinding and dying potato contracts.

One of the more likely sources of a future living was to the right of the small Potato Pit, the Platinum Ring. The platinum and palladium pit contained the most active NYMEX contracts at the time, populated by traders who wanted access to the only metals markets that NYMEX controlled. Metals were the most lucrative markets available to traders in New York in those days and had dwarfed trade in every other New York commodity market in the early 1980s. The huge bull market in metals and the Hunt Brothers' attempts to corner the silver market (which culminated in the "Silver Thursday" market collapse on March 27, 1980) were still a fresh memory. (If you're not familiar with this episode, the Appendix offers a summary.) Roiling from that fortune-making market move were still being felt when I entered the floor in 1982, and many thought that the next great bull market would be repeated in metals at any moment, so they wanted access. In hindsight, their expectations were misplaced. Although platinum touched over $1,000 an ounce in early 1980, it would be late 2008 before we saw that milestone price again.

Compared to the Potato Pit, however, Platinum was a power-house: it had as many as 100 or more traders wrapped around a very tight circle toward the right edge of our quad. Compared to the enormous COMEX Gold and COMEX Silver contracts, however, Platinum was a very weak sister indeed, and Palladium was even more miniscule. Still, the desire for exposure to metals during the 1980s was so strong that Platinum offered NYMEX members a very good trading opportunity and housed some of the most expert and successful NYMEX traders.

The upstart pit of the NYMEX offerings was the newly created #2 Heating Oil contract, begun in 1978, where all the young and fresh guns were heading to make their fortunes. Getting commercial interest from oil producers and users was the major hurdle to the initial success of energy contracts at our exchange—no one knew if any oil participants, let alone the largest oil companies, would even bother with the tiny financial opportunities offered by the NYMEX, a blip on their radars. But little by little, commercial participants began to use the contracts and get more and more involved, spurring a gaso-line contract to be listed to flank the heating oil in 1981, and finally inspiring what would become the flagship contract—West Texas Intermediate Crude Oil Futures—in 1983. Before the better part of a year of clerking had passed, I took my opportunity to become a trader by completing the exchange's training course, borrowing $25,000 from my father to open a trading account and signing a lease for six months for a seat with which to trade, at the cheap price of $400 dollars a month. In 1983, I walked into the New York Leaded Gasoline pit for the first time as a member of the NYMEX and as a bona fide oil trader.

How the Trading Floor Worked

Anyone who has seen the movie *Trading Places,* with Eddie Murphy and Dan Aykroyd, has some idea of what the trading floor looked like back in the old days of trading oil. Believe it or not, that scene was filmed on location, in 1983, at the NYMEX where I worked for 25 years, at the now-destroyed 4 World Trade Center building. I remember that traders were given the opportunity, for 50 bucks, to come back down to the floor on a Saturday to appear as extras in that film. Very few brokers accepted that offer, however—a reflection of the big money we were making, the exhaustion we all felt by the end of the week, and the horrible prospect of coming back down to the floor on a weekend. In fact, most of the people in that scene were clerks who borrowed trading badges from their bosses in order to briefly appear. Although that scene is probably the best known representation of a commodity trading floor captured for the general public, it is an entirely false one.

The sounds and rhythm of a trading floor in full flight is singularly unique and impossible to recreate with fake orders and symbols. Unfathomable to neophytes and outsiders, every sound adds a layer of information to those engaged in trade on the floor. To us, the noises of the floor were anything but chaotic. It was a perfect symphony of sounds, where every order bid on and countered with offers was an added note on that musical staff. Floor traders quickly get used to the rhythm and music of the noise on the floor, instantly subtracting the useless information and internalizing the important sounds. Many of the traders on the floor became adept at taking these waves of sound and turning them into trading decisions. On most days, I was one of these types of traders.

So there I was, standing shoulder to shoulder with another 120 sweaty, smelly traders, elbowing my way toward the center of the ring, so that I could be seen and heard by the crowd when I needed to be. These guys were my friends and my enemies. But everyone knows that once the bell rings, relationships will instantly change.

Everyone is alone in this crowded space, known primarily by the letters on the badge they wore. Traders sometimes referred to another broker by combining his first name with the badge symbol—*"you hear what happened to Johnny DEVO?,"*—but more often, the badge itself sufficed to name you, especially if it easily rolled off the tongue—*"Hey Freddo!"* (FRDO) or *"What the f*** are YOU lookin' at, DUBS?"*

I was one of these. DANO was my badge, named by my first employer down there when I was a lowly clerk. It was a reference to the 1970s TV show *Hawaii Five-O*, which shows just how old my boss was. But it stuck well enough that I used it when I entered the ring in 1983. I liked a single, recognizable name, like Cher, but far less famous (or successful).

I spent most of my career in the unleaded gasoline pit, a small sideshow to the larger and much more crowded crude oil and natural gas pits. But we had our cast of characters. Everything that was listed for trade in unleaded gas could be quoted and traded in that pit, and we listed 24 consecutive months as well as listing December quotes as far out as six or seven years. But 90% or more of the trading was done in the first four or five months listed, and probably two-thirds of that was confined to the first two months on the board. It's where a lot of the open interest was (contracts that weren't closed out by the end of the trading day) and where the most liquidity could be found.

The bottom line was always liquidity: it gave you easy access in and out of the market at prices that you could trust, at least relatively. Liquidity is a scalper's prerequisite: he provides some, but he needs it even more.

There are basically two types of trading a floor trader could apply himself toward in order to make a living: outright or spread trading. Let's take a look at each type.

Outright Traders

Outright trading was simple enough: you bought a contract and attempted to sell it at a higher price, or alternatively, you sold it to try and buy it cheaper. Your holdings could last as little as a few seconds or as much as a few months. Most floor traders preferred a large number of very short maturity trades to a few very long holds. As compared to the retail community, our commissions as floor brokers were insignificant and allowed us the great luxury of churning volume just as much as we pleased. You just never wanted to get into too many long-term trades. *Trade—don't become an investor.* This was one of the many maxims of the floor that we lived by. If you started playing the game like a retail customer, you were, in essence, voluntarily giving away the advantage you had in wearing the yellow badge.

Many traders on the floor were purely outright traders, and they tended to be the most colorful and explosive: they made big noises in the pits, waved the most, screamed the loudest, took on the biggest risks. They were the cowboys looking to intimidate the market and other traders around them to make moves in their favor. If you were making a movie, these are the guys you would want to keep the cameras on and highlight. Almost daily, their accounts swelled and contracted by huge amounts.

I considered them romantic figures, and I wanted to be like them, but I never had the courage they did. And I knew it, which was almost certainly a good thing. Yet, once in a while, I would take on that persona in the pit, trying to drive my measly 40 or 50 lot position to great heights (the true outright monster would own a couple of hundred at least).

"Quarter bid!" I'd scream.

Translation: I am willing to pay 25/100ths of a cent of the currently traded handle, on a so-far undisclosed number of contracts, on the spot month of the product we are currently engaged in, my fellow gentlemen.

"Quarter bid!!" I'd repeat, even more loudly, as if I'd buy 1,000 lots if they came in for offer. Most likely, I'd have choked to have to buy another 10. But I continue with the ploy, increasing the bid and, hopefully, the upward pressure on the market........

"Half bid!" ... ... *"HALF BID!!!!"*

"How many, DANO!?!" (Some either annoyed, hateful, or currently short local would scream at me.)

"Hit me and see ... ... HALF BID!!"

"A THOUSAND at even!"

Translation: You—DANO—you, I am reasonably sure, are a bulls★★t bidder, trying to bull up your position on nothing but hot air. I know it; you know it; and to prove it, I have just offered 1,000 contracts at the next handle up that I am daring you to buy. This is a trade that, if we complete it, will certainly ruin the day and almost surely the year of both of us; neither of us is capable of working a thousand lot position favorably, even a winning one. The bottom line is: I don't want to sell just as much as you don't want to buy the contracts you are currently bidding for. Now prove me wrong, you bulls★★ter...

Luckily, in this scenario, I can keep my manhood without committing the year to a stupid macho trick just by standing my ground and not taking this bait:

"Half bid!"

Translation: Of course, you're right—I am bulling my position. BUT, I also believe the market is going up and to a certain degree, YOU DO TOO, because you decided to call me out above the market as opposed to just hitting my bid and testing me immediately. Therefore, you have as small a pair as I do.

This type of posturing from outright traders went on all day in the pits, mostly to little effect. Markets will always go where they need to go, and position plays from outright trading locals serve to do little more than stir the pot and make the outcomes percolate a little faster.......perhaps. But traders are, of course, egotists: they need to believe they are right.

Part of the beauty of open outcry as a trade system is that it allows individuals open forums to declare their opinions on the markets in bids and offers and reinforce for themselves the value of those opinions. So much for the pure outright trader. The real ones, as opposed to the playing ones like me, would take those thousand-lot offers and risk their year in a macho fit of frenzy. They'd carry thousand-lot positions across several trading days, sometimes several trading weeks— probing, pushing, adding, and subtracting to positions and waiting for the big move to validate their incredible appetites for risk. In no way, shape, or form did I play on the same playground as they did—not the same universe.

Spread Traders

The other major way to make a living on the floor was through *spread trading*. Although the concept is simple, the application can get a lot more complex. Also, note that spread trading is unique to derivatives; a parallel concept does not exist in equities. Because of this, it is overwhelmingly popular with traders of commodities.

If you wanna trade oil, cowboy, you'll have to learn about *spreads.* Most people who think about trading oil think about just buying or selling it and waiting for a change in the price. But oil traders don't. Even oil traders who *only* buy or sell oil and wait for a change in the price—who are the outright traders I just described—have a keen interest and knowledge of spreads.

Why? Because spreads and how they function are one of the most obvious and telling difference between commodities—particularly oil—and other capital markets. If you want success in commodities, you simply can't ignore the spreads.

What are spreads? They are the price difference of two or more traded issues. For oil, they are normally the difference between two different trading months on the curve of prices.

The greatest oil traders I ever saw were dedicated spread traders. They could figure out dislocations between the various months of a contract (or even figure dislocations between other related contracts) and find the advantage in them faster than most other guys, including me, who had to rely on simpler trades to make money.

In general, the really good spread traders were the more wonky guys, guys with Ivy League degrees who were really fast with numbers. Although they tended to shy away from the super-fast and more excit-ing risk of outright positions (i.e., simply being long or short and betting on the direction of the market), they were hardly risk averse. Even relatively calm spreads that moved slowly could become very big risk trades, depending, of course, on just how many you had on and just how easily you could get into and out of a position. One of the most often heard jokes of trading was when a trader told you he had just hedged his outright position by putting on a spread, "and you know that there's no risk in spreads, right?" Absolutely right, no risk at all. Ha, ha. The truth is that spread trading only *reduced* the risks and most often the speed of your exposure. But that exposure could become quite dangerous too, if not quite as bad as a simple directional trade.

Two of the best floor spread traders I saw were as different in their approaches as could be. It just happened that both were named Rob.

Rob no. 1 was much more of a swashbuckling trader, even if he was a spreader. He had all sorts of positions, running over all three of our major oil markets (crude oil, heating oil, and gasoline), both outright and in spreads. The risks he took on his positions were overwhelming, but I never saw him put any position on, not one, without thought of the spread quotes in each of the three markets. He was convinced of the value he was getting, whether long or short, and he was far more willing to bank on that value in even very esoteric relationships. I'd see him run into my gas market and talk about—actually *effuse* over—his latest trade:

"The ocks in heating oil came in 75 bid, so I hit those out and hit the 2–1–1 crack bid at 12.45—all while the crude July/ock was still offered at a dollar forty! Against the Aprils, I KNOW I have at least 15 points in them—what dummies!"

Translation: A broker had an order to buy October heating oil contracts at what Rob figured was a pretty pricey premium. How did he figure this? He had found an esoteric crack spread that priced the heating oil directly against crude oil at a $12.45 differential. In essence, Rob was taking the heating oil sale he was making and rolling that sale into a crude sale instead.

Why did he want to do that? He also knew about a July/October crude spread quote at a differential of $1.40, and he was able to roll that October crude oil sale into a July sale, which had a rock-solid profit attached of 15¢, based on a near-month spread relating to April, which was far closer to the front of the curve, a lot more liquid, and the prices therefore more reliable. Simple? Of course not.

Moreover, to put a topper on it, this one complicated trade gets more complicated still. In Rob's quick explanation of the trade, he forgot to mention a gasoline position in October that he had coincidentally initiated, implied by the mention of "a 2–1–1 crack." Besides dealing with the relationship of heating oil to crude, that crack had also introduced a trade of a gasoline relationship to crude as well. This piece of this fairly complex puzzle didn't seem to bother Rob at all, as he didn't even bother to mention it. Still, Rob felt sure that his trade was a solid guaranteed winner—how could that broker, or the buyer on the other end of that order for the original October heating oil contracts, not see how much he was overpaying? What dummies!

Rob no. 2 was a different kind of spread trader. A Penn graduate, Rob had started out in the heating oil pit, trading that market exclusively. Slowly but surely, Rob's grasp of the spread values set him apart from many of the other local traders, even though he was flanked by a group of very smart guys. But Rob always seemed to have a better understanding of the curve in heating oil as a continuous whole, instead of just a group of spreads moving up and down. Rob traded crack spreads of heating oil contracts against crude oil contracts, but he also began to put on other, much more difficult spreads to assess and maintain—with contracts very far out along the curve. As you move further out in time, the relative values of prices become much more difficult to see: after all, how does anyone know what will happen in a year and a half?

That didn't seem to bother Rob. He made quotes anywhere in the curve, even going out to the maximum limit, which was 18 months forward at that time. Rob had so much success in making markets in these illiquid and obtuse months that other locals began to follow him and use his quotes for themselves, believing in Rob's ability to see where the value was in markets seemingly so difficult to know.

Rob finally had had enough of the traders in the pit using his hard work to find value in the deep back months of heating oil, although he was always publicly pretty generous with his ideas. But Rob had found a different game in which to put his great spread trading ability to work—in the heating oil swaps market.

When the over-the-counter (OTC) markets first began, and oil trading began moving outside of the pits of the NYMEX, crude oil was the most obvious place for it to start. The European Brent crude benchmark was the first newly created market outside of the regulated NYMEX exchange that gained traction. Slowly but surely, however, OTC markets emerged to satisfy a wealth of new hedging (and betting!) interests, and eventually, they came to the heating oil pit. A host of new heating oil products were designed to allow both producers and end users to fix their prices for heating oil far, far into the future. These products could take the form of forwards (a futures-like contract, but they had a specific physical exchange of real product), or they could be strips (a combination of delivery dates to hedge a six-month or full-year period).

Both types of OTC contracts needed market makers to become liquid enough to trade and provide steady access to customers. These markets were housed almost exclusively at the trading desks of Goldman Sachs and Morgan Stanley, and their traders were most eager to be able to make those markets and the profits from trading them.

But in the early start-up days of heating oil swaps, even the traders from Goldman and Morgan weren't quite as astute in back-month spread trading as Rob was. For a few years at the start of this new market, Rob was a consistent market maker for heating oil swaps, in direct daily contact with the Goldman and Morgan Stanley desks. Even with his great skill, Rob, as a single trader, just didn't have the capital to make liquid markets himself in these esoteric contracts. As those markets began trading, the Goldman boys got quite a good and free education at the feet of Rob, whose quotes were equivalent to a fine watchmaker disassembling his works in front of you to see how he did it. Rob's gift of the bargain, of course, was in the huge pile of money he was raking in: essentially, he was able to be the bank at a proprietary desk, without having to work for them.

After a time, Goldman figured out the spread markets and stopped needing Rob for those quotes. But for a few years, one local spread trader at NYMEX held court on the entire OTC market in heating oil, and he made quite a good living at it. Rob was one of the few spread trading geniuses I met during my time on the floor.

However, few traders on the floor were smart enough to do eso-teric spread trading. You needed not only huge capital to retain the various outside-month and weird spread positions that were left over from such varied trading; you also needed a fantastic memory of where a few dozen quotes in each market were going at almost every moment in the day, a super quick mind for arithmetic, and even faster conviction that the calculations you were making were correct. For all that work, you'd get a less risky trade with a much better-than-average chance of making some pretty good money. But I for one was never up to that challenge—though I admired the ability of the truly great spread traders.

The Trading Mistake that Almost Ended My Career

I was never an excellent trader, but I was steady. But there were plenty of guys who lived big, both in the ring and outside of it. These were the guys people think of when they imagine commodity traders and even more specifically, oil traders. These guys bet big, held huge positions, and watched their accounts move by five figures every day, with not uncommon equity swings of the legendary six-figure day. These guys were swashbucklers, they swaggered in and out of the pits, and they were admired and respected by all the other traders on the floor. They cut a wide path, and they lived their power when the markets were closed and when they were open.

I once saw one of these guys, Neil from the crude pit, walk into my local swanky big money jewelry store (where I was getting a new battery for my watch). Neil was dressed precisely as he came to the pits: designer jeans, untucked polo shirt, and a three-day beard, in the style of Antonio Banderas or George Clooney. He was quite a sight among the fancy Chanel- and D+G-clad group from the North Shore of Long Island, but the statement was clear: *"F*** it, I've got the money to do whatever I want."*

I stood by the repair counter, and Neil never noticed or recognized me. (In fairness, I was an unleaded gas trader and did very small volume in comparison to him; he ran with a different tribe of trader.) But I watched as he told the saleswoman that he needed a "knockaround" watch for a deep-sea fishing trip he was planning. He tried on a couple of Rolexes. He couldn't decide between two models, and after a minute decided to take them both. I imagine those watches carried a retail price of $8,000 to $12,000 each, maybe more, and this luxury shop on the miracle mile in Manhasset, New York wasn't in the habit of discounting much. Neil plunked down his American Express Platinum card, turned around, and walked out with both watches. He couldn't have been in the store more than 10 minutes, tops. Another big swinging dick in the Natural Gas pit was a guy named Simon. Every year, Simon took a group of guys who stood near him and were his pals down to the Kentucky Derby. He chartered a big jet, complete with stewardesses and a full bar, and he and about 20 of his crew headed down for a weekend of revelry. I was never lucky enough to be included on one of these trips, but the damage that these guys did to their health (and some of their marriages) during these weekends was the stuff of legends. For Simon, this yearly event was part celebration, part pay-off, and part just because I can. And he could: the $100,000 that Simon parted with every year to create this bacchanalia was a small price, compared to the daily swings his account saw in the natural gas pit. And, of course, Simon depended on the guys he treated annually to keep rolling those swings in his favor. Did Simon see that obscene yearly expense as an investment with a positive return? Lots of us on the floor did, and we whispered about it every year in April when the Derby approached. But we mostly groused because we were just jealous that we didn't get invited. I know I was—a bit.

Simon and Neil were two of a handful of maybe two or three dozen traders who were the most fearless among us, who took on huge positions, who made big and sometimes lost big.

I was not one of these guys. For me, a big losing day could destroy my year—or worse.

It was on one such day in January 1991 that I made a simple mistake and ran into a freight train.

It was a crazy moment for oil. Iraq had invaded Kuwait to kick off Gulf War I on August 2, 1990, pushing prices from $21 a barrel to over $28, in just a few days. I know this sounds tame considering the movement of oil in 2008, but in those days, this represented a historic and quick run. As an aside, the history of oil prices prior to the Iraqi invasion caused much suspicion on the floor: oil prices had been languishing in the mid-teens for most of the year, but managed to rally almost 25% in July 1990, right before the invasion. For most of us on the floor, we were convinced that various inside Middle East trading shops had taken advantage of some inside information to capitalize on Saddam's not entirely secret plan.

For me, it was a time to be careful because the new volatility of an invasion into Kuwaiti oil fields brought great opportunities for trading, but also lots of new chances to get caught and lose a bundle. Those months between the Iraqi invasion in August and the U.S.-led coalition strikes of Desert Storm in January of 1991 gave us a market that we had never seen before (and would not see again for another 12 years).

Through August 1990, the initial surprise of the invasion gave way after a few days to a selloff, but when the question of whether the enormous Saudi oilfields would be the next target for Saddam was left unanswered, the market really started to move higher. Then-president George H.W. Bush's famous "this aggression will not stand" speech on September 11, 1990, to the joint session of Congress signaled clearly that not only would the United States use its military to defend interests and the ruling sheiks in Saudi Arabia, but that he was issuing an ultimatum to Saddam that Kuwaiti occupation would not continue to be tolerated.

However, throughout the fall and winter of 1990, it wasn't clear when or if Saddam was going to back down from American threats and withdraw voluntarily, or even if he was crazy enough to continue his push into Saudi Arabia, where American and other coalition forces stood waiting. Oil prices pushed higher, to over $34 in September—an almost unbelievable level to us on the floor, because oil had been closer to half that, at $16 only three months earlier. Talk of $40 a barrel oil dominated trading conversations. The latest strike price in the options pit—for forty bucks—was receiving a lot of volume. It was the big bet that winter, figuring out just when a counterstrike would come, or whether it would be necessary at all.

The rest of the fall and winter of 1990 was a great time for trading. We saw volatility and opportunity we never could have imagined before. It was our first real experience at fast markets, the kind that the metals markets had seen in the 1980s. Whether a spread or outright trader, we all watched the ticker for fresh news flashes that would bring avalanches of buying or selling. Every perceived comment from Bush and Saddam and every new deployment of troops from United States or other coalition force brought a quick new move in the market. Even with this volatility, oil prices were signaling that Saddam would eventually have to give up on his dreams of conquest: oil had retreated from an almost $40 high in October 1990 to trade in a violent but lower range of $26 to $30 at the start of 1991.

On one Friday in January of 1991, the bell rang, signaling the last two minutes of trading for the day—the close. I spotted a huge amount of selling entering from the left side of the pit, and with barely two minutes left in the trading day, I sold a 30-lot piece to a broker standing close to me, more than a normal shot for me, but not outrageous. Two other brokers were selling their lungs out on the other side of the pit and I had, at least theoretically, a 50-point profit on the sales I had just made in seconds.

I jumped and yelled and waved my arms and tried to get the attention of either of the two brokers—it seemed like they had hundreds of lots for sale and couldn't find a buyer. But I was a buyer and couldn't get their attention. I was frustrated, screaming and cursing and jumping around like a madman. Finally, with less than 20 seconds to go in the session, I figured my only chance was to physically get to them. I started to bully my way through the circle around the pit, elbowing and squeezing through traders and brokers, all screaming and sweating like me.

I reached the first selling broker and screamed "*buy 'em!*" in his face, but he said he was out—finished with his selling. Just as I reached the second broker, the bell rang, but he also claimed to be long finished, cleaned out of all the selling he had. Once his sales had evaporated, the market had quickly returned to where I had sold my 30 lots. My expected profit was certainly gone, but worse, I was holding a short position going into the weekend.

I felt sick. I was stuck.

I scrambled around to see if any selling at any price, in any market, was available. I managed to get seven crude lots to partially offset my shorts in gasoline, and I went home and waited to see the outcome of a long weekend with my 23-contract short position.

I actually slept well that weekend and wasn't that worried: it was the kind of anti-intuitive position that tended to work out. No one wanted to be short in that market, with all the crazy things happening then in the Gulf; therefore, from a trading standpoint, that's precisely what you needed to be to make money. The market was going to come in lower on Monday, I convinced myself; it would all be OK.

I was wrong.

Monday morning greeted me with very bad news: UN Secretary General Javier Perez De Cuellar had abandoned his attempts with Saddam to find a diplomatic solution to the Gulf crisis, saying "only God knows" if a war was imminent. With the end of diplomatic talks came a fresh statement from Saddam, convincing the world that either this was one crazy bastard or he had a real death wish. Not only was he in no way going to retreat from Kuwait, but he gave every indication that he was preparing a fresh invasion, spoiling for a fight in Saudi Arabia with the American coalition, as the self-proclaimed leader of Arabs worldwide.

The world took him seriously, at least for the moment. Crude oil reacted with a $5 spike in price, setting a record then for the largest opening spike ever in crude oil, as war seemed now unavoidable.

I reacted to this news in a daze. I had caught a double whammy: not only had I walked in that morning stuck on a position (which, for me, was incredibly rare), but I had caught the worst possible news and was in line for the biggest single price spike in the history of crude oil. And I was on the wrong side.

There was nothing to be done. I watched the market open, saw my life slipping away, and covered my position. As if to add insult to injury, gasoline opened up much stronger than crude, because it was perceived that the refined products would be in even greater demand than crude if war were to break out. Even my seven hedges were big losers, but still nothing compared to the 23 naked shorts I had carried in that day.

I gave my trading pad to my clerk and went home. Silently, I walked into my apartment, where my wife was sitting with our seven-month-old son. I stepped into the bedroom and shut the door. I calculated my loss: $131,000, give or take a thousand or two. I was finished.

I sat on the edge of the bed and cried.

■ ■ ■

Of course, I wasn't finished, although it felt that way at the time.

The next day was busy with recriminating thoughts of how I could have managed my risk better, of how God might be punishing me for some unknown transgression against my fellow man that week, and just wondering how the hell I could be so damn unlucky. I mean, 23 contracts overnight was a couple more than I tended to carry when I went home with an outright position, but for many of the traders I knew, it was a piddling nothing. That such a tiny exposure could lead to a $133,000 loss was inconceivable to me. And yet, here I was.

Oh well, they say you never make it big until you go broke at least twice. This felt bad enough, along with another very poor year in 1989, to count as making the quota.

I really didn't have many choices. I knew well enough that the only way out of this hole was to trade my way out of it. So I set on the task of recapitalization, otherwise known as begging for dough.

The clearinghouse was by far the best candidate. I was hardly the first trader who had blown up—a euphemism for taking a big loss. The thing to avoid was being blown out—a similar euphemism for a big loss, but one that resulted in the end of a trading career. The difference between the two was usually the amount of the loss—and the politics of the clearinghouse relationship. Their reticence to take on fresh clients and the strange bipolar arm's-length/best-buddy relationships they maintained with their current clients is best grasped by understanding a little about leverage in the futures game. So bear with me as I interrupt my story about my career-threatening hit to explain how I thought I could survive it.

How the Clearinghouse System Works

So much has been written recently in regard to the banks and their wide—until 2008—use of borrowing to supercharge their incredible trading and profits. The key word of leverage was used to describe this borrowing power, but borrowing is not unique to the banks. Indeed, when you take out a mortgage on a house with a 10% down payment, you've employed a quite nifty 10 times leverage. Of course, banks are much better equipped than we are at convincing various governments, investors, and other banks about the quality of the assets that they are being loaned money on, which is why we have heard tales of mortgages, student loans, car loans, and commercial real estate portfolios being run at upwards of 40 times debt to equity—very heady leverage indeed.

But this is all child's play compared to the oil markets.

The traditional clearinghouse system makes it possible to have practically unlimited leverage, at least for futures participants. The clearinghouse system, as it operated then, is the most democratic, self-regulating, and marvelous system of monitoring the participants inside the commodity markets. It is the reason that commodity defaults have been so rare—and the few that have happened have been resolved internally and without outside help required.

The mechanics are simple: every clearinghouse is directly responsible for every market participant that clears through it. Therefore, every trade that a clearinghouse customer does is, to some degree, the clearinghouse's trade: the clearinghouse is ultimately liable to make good on every trade that comes through the house. And when a clearinghouse gets permission from an exchange (the NYMEX or any other exchange) to clear its products and become clearing members, it becomes part of an even larger network of houses committed to ensuring that no default takes place. It becomes partners, to a certain degree, with every other clearinghouse, ultimately sharing responsibility as a whole for every participant in the pool.

The clearinghouse system does not entirely prevent the rare rogue futures trader from often taking on far more risk than he should. But it does put a level of mutual responsibility for all the participants in the system that just doesn't exist in other, less-regulated markets. In my early days at the exchange trading oil, such lax margin requirements lent us incredible leverage in our overnight trading and practically unlimited leverage in our day trading.

That kind of leverage, combined with the outsized volatility that the oil markets were experiencing as I was having my blow up, made the clearinghouses far more guarded with their absolutely necessary and golden guarantee that every trader needed. Exchange margin requirements have changed often during the years and continue to fluctuate up and down, depending on the current barrel price and recent volatility, but I recall per-contract margins of crude oil in the late 1980s at $750 a lot overnight. Even with $20-a-barrel crude in those days, that represented more than 26 times leverage for even the smallest trader with very limited capital resources. And these margin requirements were actually requested of the *clearinghouse*, not of the trader—it was the clearinghouse's total positions of all of its customers that elicited exchange margin deposits, deposits that were more than likely overnight borrowing of the clearinghouse itself using its access to bank or repo rates.

Moreover, for intraday trading, which consumed most of the day traders' efforts (including mine), margin wasn't ever an issue at all. Unless you were a clerk of a local reporting to the clearinghouse during the day as positions accumulated (a practice I imagine went on, but I never actually saw), any local on the floor with a badge and an account could in theory establish any position during the day they wanted—no matter how large or risky. In those first days of wild activity for oil, some of those local intraday positions were getting frisky in a hurry. Toward the end of my days on the floor, margins increased astronomically—today, the exchange exacts margins of $4,000 for an outright lot of crude, $400 for a spread.

With the amount I normally maintained in my account, I shouldn't, in theory at least, have been allowed to accumulate many more than 12 lots either long or short during the day—a laughable restriction, even for me as a small guy. Clearinghouses had gotten used to carrying this risk on individual accounts for the most part—until the market really started to swing wildly. It was impossible to measure and monitor individual positions during the day, and it was entirely up to the trader to keep them in check and not go overboard—a system that worked out incredibly well over the years. Although there were many traders who managed to get overemotional and overextended, most of these outcomes were well controlled by the clearinghouses that accepted their trades.

Those kinds of good results only happened with a lot of work from those houses that dealt with local traders and their consistently honest relationships: most clearinghouses had their own special methods of monitoring and reining in their most swashbuckling traders. At Pioneer (where I cleared), Neil Citrone ran the clearinghouse and kept tabs on his stable of locals in between hours of trading in the pit himself: he would sit in his office and talk to rogue guys, exhorting them to lighten up on positions that were in danger of falling off the desk with a thud. Geldermann, another clearinghouse, had a guy we used to call the enforcer: Harry Marshall, an ex-marine who had served in Korea, still an imposing figure while pushing 60, would stand by the triple doors into the main trading floor, the only way in or out, looking for the locals who had entirely overstepped their limits on margin and positions. I'm not sure Harry had any other job in the company besides this one, designed obviously to intimidate guys 30 years his junior into liquidating accumulated positions or adding cash to their accounts or both simultaneously. Mark Fisher, the owner of the largest clearinghouse of locals at NYMEX, the self-named MBF, would in a case of an extreme margin miscreant in his ranks appear on to the floor himself wearing his badge. Mark, who had started as a brilliant trader but had moved into his office to trade and run the huge clearinghouse years before, was a rare sight on the floor, but when he appeared, we knew someone in his house was in trouble. He'd walk straight into the pit where the offensive position had been initiated and begin liquidating the position himself. Of course, whatever he traded for you was yours—if he needed to come downstairs, you didn't complain about the prices for the trades he executed on your behalf.

The hierarchy of risk assumption was simple: of course, the trader's accounts were the first to be at risk on all his positions. But then the clearinghouse would be on the hook. Finally, if the clearinghouse was unable to make good on losses from rogue clients, other clearing members were brought in to clean up the mess. If this still wasn't enough, talk would run to default, threatening the integrity of the exchange itself. Defaults killed exchanges, and without exchanges, there was no business for anyone; therefore, this democratization of risk made a lot of sense for everyone.

Let me explain with a couple of stories:

One enormous gasoline trader we all knew, named Jeff, had huge spread positions almost all the time, often creating large positions in less-than-liquid back months and creating obtuse relationships between commodities. His risk profile from this style of trading was very bad, although everyone in the ring admired his courage. For his clearinghouse, he was a double-edged sword as a customer: although he generated massive commissions, he also always carried positions that required added margin loans and ran constant risks of blow ups. That often frightened clearing officers because the clearinghouse has to guarantee all the trades of every client it carries. If something goes terribly wrong with a trade, the clearinghouse ultimately must stand behind the trader and bankroll the losses.

An old trading joke has a desperate trader putting 5,000 long contracts on at the end of a trading day, before a clearinghouse could possibly monitor and stop any one individual from initiating such a massively risky trade. The trader then runs out of the building and heads to JFK airport to hop the next flight to Rio (or some other fantasy South American paradise). If the market comes in higher the next day, he calls from Rio and has the position unwound, returning home at his leisure to collect his money and retire in style.

And if the market goes the other way? He doesn't call.

That's an old and long-running fantasy story, and we never heard of anyone actually blatantly running out on their positions, at least not *that* way to a South American hideaway. But it points to the responsibility of the clearinghouse in the trading process. In many ways, the clearinghouse was a partner of every trader on its books. It would measure the value of a client by risk as well as success. The clearinghouse had to view him not only in terms of the commissions he generated, but also by the *agita* he could generate with his risky positions.

With Jeff, we often heard of his jump from one clearinghouse to another, as the margin managers grew tired of monitoring and managing his positions and would ask him to find a new home. As if it were playing a vicious game of musical chairs, one of the clearinghouses was left holding his account when Jeff blew up—for almost a million dollars.

An old saying goes: "owe the bank a thousand dollars, and the bank owns you. Owe the bank a million dollars, and you own the bank."

The clearinghouse had no choice with Jeff. As collateral, it took his seat (which was then worth far less than a million dollars), and it continued to bankroll him in the ring. That was the only chance it had of getting any of its money back. Jeff became an indentured servant to the clearinghouse for much of the rest of his career on the floor.

The shared responsibility of the clearinghouse system didn't always work flawlessly, however—and once I can recall when it ended tragically. In all my years at the exchange, I can recall only one example where other clearing members were needed to help fix another's problems—with Mocatta gold. One partner in the firm had made enormous sales of metals options, adding to call sales as the price rose, waiting for a respite. One particular spike day forced covering of the entire position, outstripping the firm's capital by a great deal—they lost everything first, while other houses were forced to pony up small amounts to make up the difference.

One of the partners of that firm was John Chadonic, who ran the floor operations. John was a terrific guy, living on the upper west side with his two kids, and he had come from nothing. He wasn't a trader, but a decent operations guy who had forgone much of the bonus money due him through the years—as many in the firm had—to continue building up equity. In his mid-50s at that time, John was looking at a nice cashout on his 25-plus years of work within another five years when the disaster struck, destroying his entire life and career on the trading whims of one of his partners. The way John told it, the most senior men still managed to get equity out of the firm before it folded, while he and other junior partners watched their life savings disappear, practically overnight.

For a few weeks after the event, we still saw John, smoking incessantly and playing pinochle with us at lunchtime while he tried to figure out how or why he'd want to create a second career after all this. He didn't need to worry long. We heard of John's death a few months after that, most of us convinced that the incredible disappointment and frustration of a life's work gone south had been too much for him to bear—but we never asked, and his family kept the specifics of John's death to themselves, as they had every right to do. We mourned John, a good guy who was just another part of the commodity system. That system, like it or not, linked us all together. You had a responsibility to be responsible in your trading—not just to yourself and your own family, but to everyone else tied into the system—which was everyone.

The $50,000 Loan that Saved My Ass

Running a clearinghouse was a serious risk and a tough job because every client represented a risk/reward equation for the house and the system at large. I knew that, but I also knew that my situation was nowhere like Mocatta's or even anything as bad as Jeff's. My deficit was piddling in comparison, and I had something else far more important going for me. I was a steady trader, most of the time. I had never given the clearinghouse much to worry about: this loss I had just taken was as close to a one-time fluke as it got for me and my particular style. It wouldn't happen again, and everyone who knew me knew it. I wasn't a big money maker for the clearinghouse, but I was a good client—$20,000 to $40,000 a year in commissions generated, with very low risk attached.

I went confidently to Geldermann, Inc., my clearinghouse where I had started trading and had given them my exclusive business for the last nine years, and I asked for a $50,000 loan to get back into the ring and back to work.

They turned me down flat.

They claimed that the big guys in Chicago had stopped extending loans to traders. (Geldermann was, like many of the big futures clearinghouses, based in Chicago, with most of the big futures markets.) The two chief managers of the New York office, Stanley and Fred, who had taken my money and laughed and smiled with me for years, now shook their heads and feigned sorrow at being unable to help me out. These two f***ing guys who spent their days using high-powered binoculars to check out the skirts walking through the WTC plaza (high summer temperatures and a stiff breeze made for the best sightings, they advised me)—now were ready to see me blown out and on the street. F*** them. No, really, really f*** them.

No—really—F#%& THEM.

I moved on to the next logical clearinghouse. Although Geldermann had been my home, it was a pretty large house, based in Chicago, with lots of commercial clients and lots of bureaucracy. Surely, I thought, I'd do better with a New York-based clearinghouse that specialized in locals and had few if any commercial customers.

So I went next to a clearinghouse that catered exclusively to locals where most of their traders were Jewish, like me. I found the owner of the house, an orthodox Jew named Schlomo, on the floor. I made my case: I would guarantee my seat as collateral, I was a steady trader, a family guy, and had been around more than a few years. . . .

He also turned me down flat. The new market volatility caused by the impending Gulf War had made all the clearinghouses very leery of added risk: They were trying to get used to the larger risk and equity swings from their current crop of traders, and they didn't have much appetite for new traders at the moment. I was scared, wondering whether in this new environment I would be able to find a new home.

But I needed a new home, and quick: the trading was good, and it represented my only chance to claw back to even.

I had only a few more places to try. I walked across the street to the office of another New York clearinghouse that only worked with locals: Pioneer Futures.

Pioneer Futures was a clearinghouse born out of an interesting partnership between two very dynamic and different guys: Russell Rosenthal and Vincent (Vinnie) Viola. Both were stellar traders. Both had cut their teeth in the gasoline pits (where I was trading), and both had made massive money. Both were far more talented traders than I ever was, but they both stood near me in the pits, and they knew me and my style.

After forming the clearinghouse, Russell continued for many years to concentrate on his trading, moving to foreign and OTC markets as well as the NYMEX markets. Vinnie, on the other hand, managed the Pioneer office and would ultimately buy out his partner Russell, but was engaged in other far-reaching business as well. Vinny had made brilliant investments in Houston banks when the oil market was particularly depressed, for pennies on the dollar. He was reaping the benefits of those investments when I visited him in his office on that January day.

I walked in looking beaten, and without much hope, I simply said, "*Vinnie, I'm stuck.*"

Vinnie held a law degree and was a West Point graduate, reaching the rank of Major in the Army reserves. He was fit and chiseled and handsome. (Vinnie would also rise to become Chairman of the NYMEX in 2001 and later start one of the first and most powerful algorithmic trading groups, foreseeing and taking advantage of the electronic revolution in futures trading far sooner than almost everyone else.) His response to me that day still amazes me:

"*Whatever you need, you got it.*"

"*I think $40,000 will get me going again.*" I said. "*I'll sign over my seat to you.*"

"*No need to do that, Dan,*" he said. "*I know you. I've stood next to you and seen you trade. I'll put 60 grand in an account; I know you'll get it back to me when you can.*"

I looked him straight in the eye and began to cry. I was saved.

The rest of the story is pretty interesting. Two days later, in the early morning on Thursday, January 17th, American troops crossed the border from Saudi Arabia into Kuwait, thus initiating "Operation Desert Storm." Overnight, markets touched $43 a barrel for oil briefly, but by the time the morning came, the war was essentially over, as Saddam's troops surrendered in droves.

The market opened $9 lower and went down from there, ending up more than $12 lower for the day. My positions from three days earlier, if I had held them, would have made a greater than $200,000 profit. But I neither would have had them nor held them. I was not that kind of trader.

But the lesson was clear—timing *is* everything.

The leftover volatility of the quick war during the following months of 1991 allowed me to make back a lot of the money I had lost, while still supporting my family. I managed to get my accounts back to even and pay back Pioneer by the end of the year.

I never forgot Vinnie's generosity and confidence in me. Despite countless minor squabbles with Pioneer over the years and offers to move to other clearinghouses offering discounted commissions, I remained loyal to that house for the remaining 15 years of my on-floor trading career. I also proved to be a good investment for Vinnie, but I always gave him credit and my undying gratitude: at that moment in my life, he was the only one willing to take the chance on me. Of the people in my life who emerged at key moments and helped me to succeed, I always remember Vinnie as high on my list.

I never had another blow up incident during my career on the floor, although like most traders, I would have particularly bad days amounting to small five-figure losses once or twice a year. That was just the nature of the beast. Luckily, I missed another confluence of bad events that could threaten me, and I managed to slowly increase my risk appetite while maintaining my conservative trading style. And I slowly increased my yearly take. In other words, I was doing OK as a trader, and although the risk represented a daily stress, I liked it.

But fantastic change in the oil markets began to take place as the calendar brought a new millennium. They brought me significantly better trading profits and ultimately delivered the windfall of my NYMEX membership, which increased in value over my career more than 200-fold. What can possibly cause an asset to balloon in value like this?

Most obviously to me, oil changed—not the oil you'd find being pumped out of the ground in Texas or Saudi Arabia or Nigeria—but *financial* oil, the only kind I dealt with, and it changed in three distinct ways. First, it changed from a tool that participants used to help efficiently run their oil-related businesses into a complex capital market resembling stocks and bonds—what I call the assetization of oil. Next, the financial engineers, investment banks, fund managers, and traders took full advantage of this change to game the system and derive obscene oil profits on the backs of the consuming public. Finally, helping these new players gain their edge was a huge influx of new technology, allowing full and unrestricted access to these once-closed and shielded markets. The results of all three of these changes resulted in an energy price that is overwhelmingly unstable, fundamentally too high, and for the sake of our larger economy, unsustainable.

Part I explains those changes.

Part I

OIL'S ENDLESS BID: WHAT CAUSED IT?

Chapter 2

The Assetization of Oil, Part 1

Commodities Aren't Stocks

C ommodities aren't stocks. Oil isn't a stock. You'll hear me saying that over and over, like a mantra, throughout this book. I keep saying it, because it is the key point to take away from this book, the one point that 99.99% of the public and probably 90% of even the best informed investors don't understand. Throughout my long career trading oil, when a stranger would ask me at a party or conversationally what I did for a living, I would answer "I'm an oil futures trader." Nine times out of ten, the response from the stranger would be "Oh, you mean like *STOCKS*?" Yes, I'd nod—but only to be polite; to you, the reader, I instead shake my head most vigorously and scream "NO!"..........."*NOT* like stocks!"

But almost all people now lump financial oil with stocks for good reason. Oil trading has changed because now *anyone* can trade oil—

and the media is encouraging *everyone* to do exactly that. Oil is now viewed as a financial asset, like any other—that is, like stocks, bonds, mutual funds, index funds, exchange-traded funds (ETF), even real estate. But *commodities are not stocks*. And they shouldn't be traded like stocks. To understand why, let's take a closer look at what I call the "assetization" of oil, in this chapter, which shows how commodities aren't like stocks, and in Chapter 3, which shows further the problem with investing in commodity index funds and commodity ETFs.

Beware of Investing Your Hard-Earned Money Based on What You Hear on TV

Am I about to burst the bubbles of the people most likely to be reading this? I am sure most of you are reading this book because you're interested in the oil markets—and you're equally interested in knowing how to *invest* in the oil markets. Instead, I am going to tell you *not* to invest directly in the oil markets—at least not with the derivative instruments that are available to you today. Don't do it with futures, don't be convinced by your financial advisor to put your hard-earned money into a structured or indexed product for oil, and for God's sake, if nothing else, please stay away from futures-based ETFs.

It's obvious, however, from the incredible growth that all three of these vehicles have experienced that no one is about to take my advice. Everyone wants to make money, and oil is moving rapidly, enticing investors looking for a quick buck. For the people selling the access to commodity price swings, marketing plays a huge role in luring investors into playing this game. I'm as cynical as I can be, watching this carny pitch day after day, as TV and the Internet continue to deliver a fresh army of financial oil buyers into the derivative markets.

In fact, CNBC is on behind me in my office right now. It's always on while I'm trading, but it fades into the background and I rarely look up at the TV screen, unless something hits my ear that sounds interesting or controversial. Nothing is particularly new today—but it's this new normal that has me turning around and watching. CNBC produces individual segments where their very talented show hosts interview financial experts. No matter what the topic, each segment tries to drive home a forceful answer to the same exact question: *"Where should people put money to work today?"*

Tell someone what to buy or sell, whether it is a good time to be in bonds or stocks or a good time to be out of the markets altogether and in cash, and you've made the segment actionable. Actionable advice is what viewers overwhelmingly want to see and what attracts the strongest audiences.

But there is a new steady stream of actionable advice on CNBC these days, advice I rarely if ever saw even a few years ago. Instead of touting stocks or fixed-income investments, more and more actionable segments are about *commodities*. And that actionable advice and exploding investment in them has changed the commodity markets—particularly the oil markets—into a whirlwind of vicious motion and higher prices. Which makes me want to scream at the television:

"COMMODITIES AREN'T STOCKS!"

But no one is listening. Over the last few years, oil and other commodities have been assetized—turned into facsimiles of other traditional investment vehicles, using all the varied tricks in the financial engineer's book. These days, no one even questions the difference between investment in the price of a barrel of crude and, let's say, investment in the price of a share of Chevron stock.

Don't believe me? Let's take a look at a few recent segments I saw on TV (see the sidebar, "Tired of Regular Investing? We've Got Something New …").

"Tired of Regular Investing? We've Got Something New …"

Two analysts are talking about where to put money since the bottoming of the equity markets in March of 2009. Every one of them is talking about commodities: *"They're right for a weakening dollar,"* they say, and *"in an inflationary environment."* *"We've advised*
(*Continued*)

"Tired of Regular Investing? We've Got Something New . . ." (*Continued*)

our client to allocate [5 or 10 or 15 or 20%—the number changes, but it hardly matters—] *to dollar-denominated assets."*

Man, if that hasn't been the daily dose on financial television, I don't know what has—a universal agreement among not just asset managers, but just about anyone and everyone who gets three-and-a-half minutes of fame on-air: "Buy oil!" "Buy gold!" "Buy commodity indexes!" "Buy commodity stocks!"

And these stocks have been responding. For example, look at Freeport-McMoran, a copper and gold mining company. Since the suspension of its dividend in 2009 (right before the benchmark Standard and Poor's (S+P) stock index hit its very spooky, but purely coincidental, low of 666), Freeport traded a low price of just over $26. By the end of 2009, however, the huge copper and gold miner will stop just short of trading $90 a share. Figure 2.1 illustrates the rise. That 3.5 time increase is, of course, a function of the rise of gold and copper prices, but it's much more a

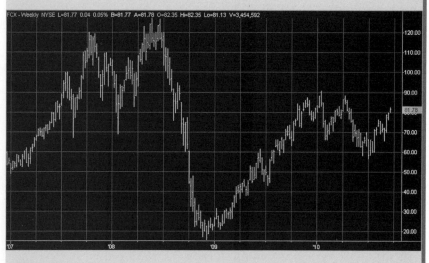

Figure 2.1 Tracking the Stock Price of Freeport-McMoran Copper from 2008–2010
DATA SOURCE: Tradestation

"Tired of Regular Investing? We've Got Something New . . ." (*Continued*)

function of the frenzy of managers and their clients to get in on the commodity rush.

Even TV Commercials Are Promoting Investing in Commodities
CNBC ends their segment and breaks to cut to a commercial: A handsome European gentleman in his early forties smiles from a set stage, where he is seen making a phony television commercial, surrounded by a phony director and phony production staff: "I'm Christian Baha. Have you considered managed futures? My Superfund is for average in-*wes*-tors, looking for their own hedge fund!" Then the phony director interrupts: "No, Christian, it's in-*ves*-tors!" This cute poke at Baha's Austrian accent is particularly galling: the Superfund is a European phenomenon, but it has been recently growing by leaps and bounds here in the United States. Baha is a college dropout and an ex-Viennese policeman—the perfect combo, I suppose, for wrestling with hundreds of millions of "in-wes-tor" dollars engaged in the complex world of the futures markets.

I guess I shouldn't be so hard on the smiling Baha. After all, what real qualifications did anyone have, or need, to engage in the trading of commodities? There isn't a school for it, and even if there were, graduating from it couldn't guarantee success. Even on the floor where I lived, the success rate for more than five years was dismal, some estimating that only 15% of those who tried the floor survived.

So I suppose Christian Baha was as ready as anyone to offer a *managed* approach to futures, which is very different from an indexed approach. Indexes only try to match the performance of the underlying asset, whether good or bad. For example, if you bought an index in commodities and oil, and then gold retreated, you lost money. If commodities went up, you made some. (I say *some*, because the index approach to oil and other commodities

(*Continued*)

"Tired of Regular Investing? We've Got Something New . . ." (*Continued*)

has plenty of problems in really capturing the gains of price when they happen, but I'll talk about that at more length in Chapter 3.)

In contrast to the indexed approach, *managed futures* approach commodities differently. When you invest in managed funds, you essentially make an investment in a trader, or a trade methodology being run by a trader. Precisely as with other hedge funds, investment in managed futures is a bet on the greater insight of a man or a system to find the best opportunities—whether long or short, in oil or gold or grains, in spreads or intramarket relationships—and make you consistent money. You might expect, as with any other managed fund in any asset class or sector, that most of the time is spent finding assets to *buy*, as opposed to sell, and with managed futures, this is mostly the case. But the critical decisions of what to buy and sell, when and how much, is still entirely up to the fund managers. And they don't ever need to disclose to anyone (particularly their clients) how they do any of it. *Discretionary* is Wall Street gobbledygook for trading systems that are secret and usually not as impressive as you might hope.

Yet there's little argument that Christian Baha had done really well at it. Superfund's most advertised product, the Superfund Q-AG, has achieved a stunning 14.53% per-year profit since its inception in 1996, making it one of the best performing managed funds worldwide. Uh, the problem with this fund, however, is that it has been closed to new investors since 2002. In fact, Baha's company offers five classes of funds, labeled A, B, C, Gold, and Garant. In each of these classes, the funds that are open for public investment are all sharply *in the red,* most with double-digit losses.

Nevertheless, it seems Mr. Baha is very good at something. With its spectacular growth, Superfund now supports a Formula One racing team, directed by world-class Austrian driver Alexander Wurz, with fantastic-looking 'brolly dollies' to shade his delicate pate during pit stops. Futures trading is sexy stuff, and Christian

"Tired of Regular Investing? We've Got Something New . . ." (*Continued*)

Baha has grown his business drawing on this appeal, but the bottom line is clear: trading oil and gold and other futures for profit consistently is very, very hard, compared to marketing successfully the funds that attempt to do it, which is a lot easier. Money continues to pour into the Superfunds.

Cut to Commercial #2: "Why Not Trade Commodities?"
"Having trouble trading stocks? Why not try commodities? You can trade Coffee, or Gold, or Oil..........things you really UNDERSTAND." And 'Ling-Waldman' can help you start.

I bristle. My 25 years of trading oil has convinced me of how little about oil trade I really understand. Yet futures discount brokers like "Ling-Waldman" are lining up to sell their services and access to people on the belief that if you put gas in your car, or put corn flakes on your breakfast table, you've got the insight into commodities to be successful at trading them.

Everyone wants a piece of the new commodity action. It's hard for anyone with money to invest to watch an oil market increase six-fold or watch gold go up almost five-fold without feeling the urge to try and get in on some of that easy money. That understandable urge has spawned a new industry of discount commodity access for that class of investor who has always made his own investment decisions and done his own trading. But commodities aren't stocks, and these new traders have been learning the extra tough pitfalls of commodity trading the very hard way. It hasn't stopped the huge increase in the number of personal commodity trading accounts.

It has become all too commonplace to see commodities and particularly oil spoken of in the same breath and under the exact same umbrella as stocks and bonds by asset managers and brokers. They're not. When I was a newly arrived member of the New York Mercantile Exchange (NYMEX) in 1983, the oil market was a small and insular group of players and we never—never, EVER—dreamed that access to those markets would ever become available to anyone outside of our small oil world.

It is worth the time to discuss at length the changes in all three of these new instruments of the modern investor—indexes, managed futures, and ETFs. Each one of these has contributed its share in increasing the volatility of oil and do only one thing to price—drive it unnecessarily higher, and that's my point in this chapter and the next. I've said it before, and I'll say it again, throughout this book: *commodities aren't stocks*. To understand what is so destructive in the attempt to turn oil into just another investment—oil's assetization—we need to examine the important differences between commodities and stocks.

You Can't *Invest* in Oil; You Can Only *Bet* on the Price

Oil is a lousy investment. Oil, represented financially through contracts and bought and sold through the derivative markets, wasn't ever designed or intended to be used for investing, although that's the way most people now use oil derivative contracts. The financial world—including investors, brokers, money managers, and the financial media—has foolishly lumped oil (and most other big commodity markets) in with other, more traditional capital markets. They talk about oil as if it were a stock or a bond. And because of that, most all people—including smart, financially savvy people—tend to trade and invest in it as if it were a stock or a bond. This is a big mistake, and it's the single most diabolical source of our pricing problem with oil.

Oil is a lousy investment because *it isn't an investment*. It's just a *bet*—and it's a bet with a ticking time bomb attached to it. It doesn't look, feel, or act like a stock or a bond, and you shouldn't apply the same rules of investing to it that you do with other capital investment instruments. Let's see what goes wrong when you do.

When investing in a stock, you exchange your cash for a certificate that represents a small percentage ownership interest in a company.

For a bond investment, your cash outlay is exchanged for an obligation to return your money at a set interval (normally a very long-term timeframe), with an added interest payment attached for having the use of your money.

In contrast, what do you get in return for your investment in oil? Nothing—unless you intend to burn it yourself. You get no partial interest in the ownership of a greater valued entity, no debenture that needs to be repaid. Instead, you are trying to profit from an outright bet on *price direction.*

There's nothing wrong with that, of course. Most of us buy and sell stocks and bonds without really worrying about the underlying value of the companies much. But even if we don't worry about it, the *value* of the underlying companies is what makes stocks and bonds so suitable for investment. What have you got when you try to apply value to the bet you have just made in oil prices? There are no metrics to be applied to oil as there are to a stock or a bond. There's no price-to-earnings (P/E) ratio, no growth projections, no inventory or fixed or variable costs, and no sales.

What can you look at if you're trying to fathom the movement of oil and make a profitable bet on the price? There are only very non-specific supply-and-demand estimates to suffice for metrics. Stockpile numbers. Demand statistics. And guesses on where those numbers will be in the future, both domestically and worldwide. Add to those relatively calculable factors the far less reliable factors of weather, geopolitical unrest, strikes, and terrorism. Then you have interconnections with other markets, including currencies and domestic and international equities. At different moments, it seems clear that certain factors will have more importance in valuing oil than others.

With a stock, you use established metrics to value the price. Company A has a small price-to-earnings ratio or a safe dividend or is registering consistent growth. The success of investors in the stock market shows that there is consistent opportunity in using these established metrics. But try and value oil this way, and you're in for a surprise. Deep supply and weak demand does not translate necessarily into low prices. Either the factors that combine to make oil price are so complicated that even the savviest oil analyst can't explain them, or the established metrics have less value than for any other kind of asset.

Price itself becomes oil's one and only worthwhile metric. It's as if you stepped up to the roulette wheel and placed a bet on red, or a column of numbers. In fact, in oil futures, you've taken the analogy of the roulette table one step further: You've generated a time limit on your bet, where you have a limited time with which to assess the value of your wager. Like a spin of a wheel, your contracts have an expiration date, and your decisions about that bet must definitely be considered with that expiry in mind.

So that's the first difference, and it's an important one between oil and stocks: Metrics are difficult to rely on as a measure of value.

And there's a reason the metrics for oil are less reliable: the transfer of a stock is a literal transfer of value—a piece of a company. But the transfer of a futures contract is designed to be only a transfer of *risk*—the wager of price movement.

Take a stock or bond certificate and stick it in your bureau drawer and you can forget about it, if you want. That's an investment. But if you take an oil contract and put it under your pillow, sooner or later, someone will come looking for you. Stocks don't have expiration dates. Bonds do, but in a good way—if you wait them out, barring an uncommon default, you'll at least get your money back. That's hardly the case with oil.

So, if oil doesn't work like a traditional investment, how do people make money trading oil? And if people *do* make money, what's wrong with trying to get in on the game?

So How Can You Make Money Trading Oil?

There are numerous ways to trade oil for profit, each one with its unique pitfalls, none of them like any other capital market, and none of them really appropriate for the typical investor.

Buying and Holding Oil

Trading real, physical oil is as close to making oil act like a stock as you can get. Buy barrels from one source, sell them to another for a profit. But very few people can contemplate buying and selling physical oil. And if you *are* engaged in the physical trading of oil for profit, chances are you aren't an investor but more likely in the transport business or the physical brokerage business. If you engage in physical brokerage, you will want to be free of the oil in a hurry, and it's better still if you can work an arrangement where it doesn't come into your possession at all, not even for a moment. This is because if you have it, you are very soon confronted with *storage*, which is a profit-dissolving problem.

It's obvious, then, why gold and other precious metals have long been favored as long-term commodity investments, rather than oil. If you are trading or investing in metals, the worst that can happen is you are forced to take delivery of a few 100-ounce contracts of gold and obtain storage yourself; for that, a family-room lockbox will suffice nicely. Be careful with the silver, though: each contract of silver is 5,000 ounces, which equals 312 pounds, so taking possession of even just a few silver contracts requires a lot of closet space. Compared to oil, however, you would much rather have been trading silver, because a couple of contracts of 1,000-barrel oil delivered to your home can crowd out the TV space in your family room in a hurry.

Physical trading of oil is the closest thing to value transfer like stock trading. But you don't want to build tank farms in your backyard or lease space at the local oil storage port. You think that China is growing, so you wanted to bet a little of your mad investment money on rising prices, right? But, if the physical product is closed to you, what else can you do to invest in oil?

Buying Derivatives of Oil

If you have to forgo physical trading, you must look at derivatives of the physical product. Derivatives has become a scary word recently, but understanding what they are and how they work can take some of the fear away.

As the name implies, a derivative has no true value of its own; instead, its value is derived from the value of some other real physical thing—which could be a share of stock, a corporate bond, or a barrel of oil. When a derivative is created, any financial variable can be attached to it: It all depends on the intended purpose of the instrument.

The important point to remember is that *derivatives have no inherent value of their own*. A stock option has worth based only on the price of the underlying shares. A credit default swap similarly is valued by the price—and therefore the credit worthiness—of the underlying corporate bonds. Commodity futures are a very specific and in some ways even more complex kind of derivative. As their name implies, oil *futures* derive value from barrels that are *yet to be priced*.

How strange is that? It's an impossibly weird idea to comprehend, but it's also a brilliant financial construct. Because the value of futures is derived not only from underlying commodities but also so closely intertwined with *time*, futures don't act like any other kind of financial instrument. Investment in futures gets much trickier than the storage problems you encounter trading physical oil. There is no exchange of a physical item for cash. With futures, you exchange *promissory notes* to either buy or sell a fixed amount of oil sometime in the future, at a fixed location, for a variable price.

The key point again is that futures contracts do not, therefore, represent an exchange of *value*, because they refer to an unknown— something that hasn't even happened yet. Futures instead represent a transfer of *risk* only—protection, insurance. This is the most important and unique trait of futures.

Let's take a simple example. A farmer wants to rid himself of the *risk* of lower prices for his crops next year, so he sells futures a year out. The price of those contracts should represent a price for his crops that he can rely on. Let's say corn is selling 12 months from today on the CBOT for $4 a bushel. That price agrees with our farmer, so he sells an equivalent number of contracts to reflect his probable crop. When the year passes, we look again at our contracts, now ready to expire. Let's say that the cash, or prompt, market is trading at $3.50 and the contracts that our farmer sold are also trading at $3.50. This is a commodity market fundamental called convergence, where prices for expiring futures and physical traded products will ultimately match. [As an aside, financial interest in commodities has made convergence an industry joke, particularly in the grains markets, but for our example, we'll assume the old tools still operate as they were intended.]

As our farmer's contracts are ready to expire, he will engage the cash market to sell his mature crop, realizing $3.50 a bushel, while simultaneously retiring his futures positions, gaining a 50¢ profit per bushel as well. Together, the farmer has realized the $4 price target he set for himself when he originally sold contracts a year ago. Similarly, you can see that if the markets were higher, selling let's say for $4.50 a bushel, the farmer would lose 50¢ retiring his futures position, again realizing the $4 price target he agreed to.

But let's go back to our futures market investor, who does not have any intention of ever engaging the physical market as a farmer would.

The Problem with Investing in Oil Futures Is All about *Time*

Because they are instruments of *risk transfer* and not *value transfer*, using futures as investments opens up a whole new set of problems. As mentioned above, the first problems are time problems. If you invest in futures contracts, your investment has (by definition) an expiry date attached to it. You've taken on contracts in a certain month or a strip of contracts that will be expiring either in your favor or against it, at a certain moment in time. If you are aware of these limitations and well acquainted with them, this can be a perfectly acceptable strategy.

(For example, all options have an expiration date and are wonderful financial tools. It is interesting to note here that the world of finance has never made a similar mistake with options—which are by far the most common derivative—by imagining them as assets by themselves, as they have with derivative oil.)

Most people who are looking to gain exposure to anything they perceive as investment (whether stocks or bonds or other true assets) expect and will normally demand the ability to decide as the time moves along whether they will keep, add to, subtract, or totally rid themselves of the investment. Achieving this goal becomes difficult and sometimes nearly impossible using derivatives, particularly oil derivatives, because of their inflexible storage demands. Most investors also think in terms of many months for investments (as they should) and even years. In contrast, if you have an investment in oil using futures, you've got some new and interesting wrinkles to deal with that you won't find with any stock or bond.

The first problem, obviously, is when your futures contracts get close to expiration. You'll have reached the end of the investment's half-life, and you'll have to decide whether to get out of your investment, find some way to extend it, or go into the oil transport business. For the physical participants like the oil companies we've already met who dominated oil trade in the first half of my history of trading, the issues surrounding expiration and delivery weren't a problem. They understood the nature of futures, and most of them had some physical assets or at least easy access to those markets. Of course, they rarely wanted to make or take delivery on futures contracts either, but at least they were much better equipped and capable of operating as easily in the prompt markets as in our rings, unlike someone like me, for example. If you want to know how tough it can be, read my true-life experience, in the sidebar.

How I Lost $11,000 One Day

Nothing came close to the disaster I had during Gulf War I when I lost six figures overnight, but on one particularly bad day, I learned about how the cash markets work—the hard way. It was on the last day of the expiration of the June 1998 contract. I was trading the spot month spread, scalping the differential between the June and July contracts. This was relatively risky, but it was also a very lucrative strategy, because a small number of participants in the spot month always chose to wait for the last minute to decide what they wanted to do with their positions. The limited remaining open interest in that month and the need for so many to liquidate made the days leading up to expiration and particularly the final day extremely volatile. In that volatility, locals like me could make wider markets and try to take advantage of very quick trends.

For example, if a lot of weak players were long the spot month, they might cause a small avalanche of selling. If you caught the vibe of this onslaught of get-me-out selling as it was happen-

How I Lost $11,000 One Day (*Continued*)

ing, you could *scalp the spread* and make a quick buck. Essentially, you would sell the spread, therefore making you short the spot month and long the second month in. Then, when you saw the selling in the spot month pour in, you would first sell out your longs in the second month, where there was greater liquidity and competitive bids. That would now make you outright short the front month, just as all that lovely selling was coming in, shopping for a bid. If you timed this whole thing right, often you would be one of the only players willing to buy at that moment. It was dangerous, but you could make an easy 25 to 50 points a spread ($100 to $200), and sometimes more—if you had the guts to wait out the panic until the very end of the day.

I was admittedly a small-time player and looked to catch only 10 to 20 of these spreads a couple of times during the day. It wasn't always there, and it didn't always go my way, but when it was working, that trade alone could net $2,000 to maybe $10,000 or more on that last day of expiration. That's if it was working. If you got stuck the other way, however, the lack of liquidity could quickly hit you hard the other way—it was easy to lose that same $10,000 getting out of poorly timed scalping of spot spreads. Forget about the timing of this trade for a second, though, because the more important trick was making sure you had no leftover spot contracts in your position, either long or short, at the end of that last day.

Anyway, I had probably had a bad night the night before this last day of expiration because I thought I was having a pretty good day scalping spot spreads going into the close. I had almost exclusively confined my day to this trade because I had caught it right: selling spreads, lifting my leg by selling my longs in the second month and buying back my spot shorts for a profit. I think I had scalped more than 200 spreads on the day, both on the long and the short side—not a very big amount in volume, by the way, but significant for me. With a bit of a remaining hangover and some

(*Continued*)

How I Lost $11,000 One Day (*Continued*)

hubris, the bell went off, signifying we were in the close (i.e., the last two minutes of the trading day), and I continued to rapidly scalp spreads until that final bell rang, ending the trading day and forever ending trade on the June 1998 contract.

I gave my last sheets to my clerk and sat down around the ring, waiting for confirmations and checking trades. Fifteen minutes later, my clerk finished counting me up and found me still short 12 spot contracts—not her fault, as I had literally lost count of my legs in those final moments of the close and miscounted. I thought I had made myself flat (with no position). But I hadn't.

I looked over the last couple of trades that had hit the board before the final bell rang, and I figured I was still in the money on the shorts I had on, if only I could find someone to take them from me. I ran around the ring whispering (because it wasn't really legal to trade after the close), trying to see if there were any orders left unfilled, where a broker might be able to call a customer and offer my contracts up to help complete the order. Everyone was either completely filled or had no interest in buying anything after the bell. I was stuck.

If someone wants to trade oil futures or spreads on oil futures or options on oil futures, they're playing in my world. But if you're a futures trader and you find yourself with contracts in a month that's just gone off the board, you've now entered someone else's world, and you're up the river without a paddle. I was about to learn just how much of a disadvantage it is to be stuck in someone else's market. Miscounting on the last day of spot wasn't an impossibly rare event: it had happened to local traders in the past, and the clearinghouse was the first and best source to help you get out of the remaining contracts.

So I informed my clearinghouse about my mistake, and it got to work calling the three or four possible sources that had attachment to physical assets and would offer me a market on my 12 lots. There are a few days between when the spot market goes off the board and final allocations of remaining contracts are made for

How I Lost $11,000 One Day (*Continued*)

delivery, so although the participants had narrowed to a precious few, I still wasn't in much danger of seeing oil trucks trying to deposit gasoline shipments on my front lawn.

On the afternoon of the next day, my clearinghouse gave me the results of all its calls: my best offer turned out to be 2.2¢ per gallon higher than the final settlement price reached the previous day. (And the market was down the next day as well!) I was told by my clearinghouse that this was a very good offer, very much an accommodation, and much better than the few other offers my clearinghouse had managed to find. I had little choice. The liquidation of my 12 lousy lots amounted to an $11,000 loss, entirely erasing my good work of the previous day and turning it into a pretty sizable loser.

I refrained from trading spot ever again into the close, and I counted and checked my spot trades very carefully, if I even ventured into trading that month on the last day. But most important, I learned how tough it is to play in someone else's sandbox.

My point is that expiration is a touchy and tricky business, for locals (like me) who were just trying to make a day-trading buck, but even more so for a longer-term investor deciding what to do with his expiring contracts in oil.

Let's turn back to our long-term investor, using derivatives, in this case futures, for exposure. As we catch up with him, his contracts are nearing their expiration date: they're ready for delivery. The stamp on his milk carton says it's either time to drink the stuff or find some fresh milk. What can he do?

Well, he can extend his investment further into the future, by retiring his contracts and initiating a new position, further out on the curve. Now things aren't so simple anymore. Although you'll never have to reinitiate a stock position (unless there is a tax advantage to do so), *oil contracts continually force you to renew and regenerate your holdings*. If futures are your choice for exposure, sooner or later, you'll need to roll. *Rolling* a position simply means you are retiring your previous contracts and initiating a new and equivalent position with a later expiration date. And although that may sound like a simple procedure, again, you're going to encounter problems you won't find with any other asset class.

- First, if the positions you were holding were in your favor as you retired them, you created a generated profit with a tax liability, even if you planned on having the entire investment run for a very long time.
- Second, you're in for a fresh round of commissions and fees, not on one trade but on two: Getting out and getting back in somewhere else on the curve.
- Third, you're going to have to engage the market in two places simultaneously—which means two opportunities for you to be taken advantage of by brokers and locals like me.

Now, wait, you're wondering. Why can't I make my investment so far out in the future, so far out on the curve that I don't have to worry about rolling it at all? This is a good idea, but unfortunately, you are faced with tough lessons about the curve of prices: in general, the market will have the best liquidity and therefore tightest and truest prices the closer it is to the spot market—that is, the closer it is to expiration. If you try to invest with a contract well out on the curve, you're very likely going to pay a terrible premium just getting in and another on the way out the door.

But there is a more interesting problem with going so far out in the future: The further into the future your investment goes, *the less your investment becomes tied to the commodity itself.* You no longer become engaged in oil investment and more and more give that up in favor of betting on the movement of the spread of prices of the curve itself.

For example, let's assume that oil is on the upswing. Although oil may be rallying spectacularly and getting daily discussion on CNN, that rally is primarily going on in the front months. And while the fronts may be rallying, there's absolutely no guarantee that the backs, where you are invested, are rallying as strongly, or at all. Most likely, your investment is experiencing a much, much smaller percentage move. That's been the history of the oil curve and the action of oil spreads: on a percentage basis, the front months have historically out-performed the back months on the curve, both on the upside and the downside.

Too bad that idea doesn't work out well for us as investors, because it is a good one—going far out on the curve to try and reduce as much as possible the time factor from futures investment. The only problem is, the further out you go, the less is known. What are the demand and supply, geopolitical, weather, dollar, and other factors going to be 18 months or even two or three years from now? No one could possibly know; consequently, you get a thin, untradeable, uninvestable, and often contrived market.

So if you are determined to use futures to get investment in oil, you have to deal with the very short-term limited front months and figure out ways of managing their quirks.

Luckily (for the financial services industry), financial innovation has brought a whole set of instruments to help investors and their managers avoid and ignore the inherent differences between oil and other traditional asset classes (i.e., between commodities and stocks). Managers who want to deliver asset-class diversity and direct com-modity exposure to clients, and who don't want to face the hassles of investment in futures and other derivatives have turned overwhelm-ingly to *managed futures products*. These include index funds (which I'll discuss in Chapter 3), commodity trade advisors, and dedicated com-modity hedge funds.

Individual investors have also become increasingly interested in gaining the same kind of exposure to oil and other commodities that wealth managers and other institutional brokers deliver to their afflu-ent clients. After all, no one wants to be left out of a market move as exciting and seemingly profitable as oil has looked for the past five years. However, faced with high minimums and other hurdles of hedge funds and managed accounts, this army of investors and their avalanche of money have turned to ETFs that are specific to oil (as I'll describe in more detail in Chapter 3). Individual investors' assets may be smaller than the clients of wealth managers and other institu-tional investors, but their influence has been no less important.

Oil Is a Zero-Sum Game

There is one more critical way that oil is not like a stock. Because oil is ultimately priced as a commodity instead of as a company, trading oil is a zero-sum game: in financial terms, the total amount of money in oil does not change much over time. A zero-sum game in an asset market is like a game of poker between a group of guys having fun on a Saturday night. One guy might pay for the beer, but if you count the amount of money that everyone brings to the table at the start of the night, that amount doesn't change at the end of the night—it just separates itself into different pockets. The most important point of a zero-sum game is that there is a perfect *exchange* of capital, not *growth* of capital. Similar to a poker game, an equal amount of money exchanges hands from the participants in the oil markets every day: For every winner, there must be a loser.

This is far, far different from how the total capital pool operates in other asset markets, particularly stocks and bonds, which continue to grow in the size of their real value and therefore can deliver far more winners than losers. In fact, it is possible that *every* investor can be a winner in stocks over time. But in oil, this is not the case. If I'm making money trading oil on the floor, and investment banks are making money upstairs at their desks, and oil companies are net winners in their trading divisions, then someone is throwing a lot of money into the pot and not collecting at the end of many hands— maybe none at all. In the final analysis, someone has to pay for the profits that oil traders make trading oil.

Notice I did not say that someone has to pay for the profits that oil *companies* make *selling* oil. Of course, that is true—but there is a product being delivered for the price that consumers pay. I'm talking about what we might call an exacted fee that is financial and far more specific—there is a price that is being paid for the profits that financial participants are taking out of the oil market. As oil continues to become more and more financialized, that price has grown, not only through the enormous growth of the oil market, but with the continuing number and nominal value of derivatives on oil being created and traded over the counter and at exchanges. All of the new marketplaces are supporting profitable trading, and that profit has to necessarily increase the burden on the price of the underlying commodity, and on the industries and consumers that have no choice but to buy oil and gas. Although everyone who plays can theoretically come out ahead in stocks and bonds, in oil, that just isn't the case: Someone has to lose. Overwhelmingly, that someone is ultimately and inevitably the consumer.

In *Stocks for the Long Run,* his definitive book on buy and hold investing in the stock market, Harvard professor Jeremy Siegel makes the case that investing in U.S. equities historically far outpaces any other asset class in existence. Professor Siegel takes little time in making that point in his diligently researched and rigorously written bible of stock investing. He waits until all of page 6 of his 370-page opus to show the definitive chart of his investigations, shown here in Figure 2.2.

With one look at this chart, we are reminded of the (perhaps apocryphal) story of Hillel, the great scholar of the Jewish Scriptures,

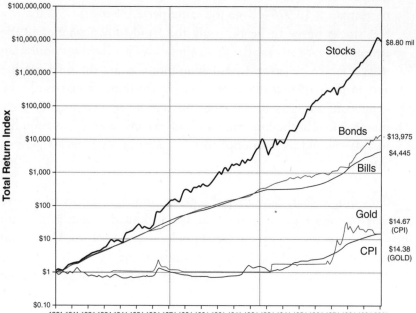

Figure 2.2   U.S. Stocks Outpace All Other Assets Since 1800
SOURCE: Siegel, Jeremy J. *Stocks for the Long Run, Fourth Edition.* (New York: McGraw-Hill, 2007.)

who was asked by an arrogant young student to explain the entire meaning of the Torah while standing on one leg. The scholar calmly replies with a negative variant of the Golden Rule, "That which is hateful to you, do not do to your fellow. The rest is all commentary— now go study it!"

Indeed, the rest of Dr. Siegel's book is nothing more than commentary after showing this chart (although it *is* fascinating commentary). The chart follows the investment trajectory of one measly dollar, invested in each of the following five asset classes from 1801 to 2001, including the compounded returns of interest payments (in the case of bonds) and dividends (in the case of stocks): gold, the Consumer Price index (CPI), treasury bills, treasury bonds, and U.S. domestic stocks. The results are stunning:

- A $1 investment in gold or the CPI returns only a $14 profit after 200 years.
- Treasuries fare better, delivering a $4,455 return on a buck.
- Longer-term bonds return more than three times that amount— more than $ 13,975—over the same period.
- But stocks prove to be not only the hands-down winner in the investment race over time; *they entirely blow out every other asset class without breaking a sweat.* Even taking into account the stock crashes and corporate bankruptcies that one might think would be stocks' derailment to success, the stock market as an investment barely notices them in the long run: a measly $1 invested in U.S. equities in 1801 would have multiplied to *a whopping $8.8 million profit in 2001!*

This simple chart has inspired a generation of investors to believe and rely on long-term investment in the stock market and, along with index investment champion Jack Bogle (creator of the Vanguard funds) in the buy-and-hold theory of investment.

I'm not about to argue with professor Siegel's logic, even if the stock market has delivered two crashes in the last 10 years, wiping out gains from at least one decade and, depending on whether your stocks were well-diversified or not, perhaps even two decades. I believe there are modern influences on the stock market that will test

Dr. Siegel's chart in the future, although I believe it will still stand up over the long haul.

Instead, what we need to understand is: How is this possible? How can stocks as an investment so far overtake the profitability of every other asset class over every period in history?

And what does this mean for commodities, and particularly oil, as an investment?

Understanding professor Siegel's chart gives us all we need to know. Each asset he mentions has a specific model for delivering returns, and understanding those differences tells us quickly why stocks beat all other investments over the long run. Let's take a closer look at each asset class.

The Bond Markets

Bonds seem like the best place to start, because they are the easiest to understand how their profits are gained—through compounded interest. Both the U.S. Treasury bills market and bond market have delivered historically low rates of return. As with all investments, there is an inverse relationship between risk and return—and if there is such a thing as a riskless investment, the closest to it must be U.S. sovereign debt. Both long- and short-term treasury debt followed almost exact payment schedules for the first 120 years of our 200-year chart, but the Great Depression forced the U.S. government to finally pay more for longer-term debt to entice investors. For the years 1928 to the present, short-term U.S. debt has averaged a 3.79% rate of return, while longer-term bonds have delivered 5.24%. Because of this, longer-term bonds have steamed away from U.S. treasuries as investment vehicles, causing the more than three-fold better final return over the full 200-year period, although it is only the latter 80 years that have made the difference.

The Consumer Price Index

Next, we come to the CPI, a collective index of the prices of typical goods and services, recorded by the U.S. Department of Labor. The CPI is derived using very complex formulas, but it really does its best job tracking commodities and the prices that people pay for them. Although the CPI does not measure only price fluctuations in commodities like a Commodity Research Board (CRB) or Goldman Sachs Commodity Index (GSCI), its results are very closely matched. That is why there is such a high correlation between the CPI on the Siegel chart and everyone's favorite benchmark commodity, gold. Both of these asset classes have failed utterly to keep pace with any other investment on Siegel's chart: If you take a dollar's worth of gold in 1801 and put it in your desk drawer, after 200 years you have barely (but only barely) kept pace with inflation.

The Stock Market

Finally, we come to the most superior investment vehicle by far: U.S. stocks. Over the 200-year period that Professor Siegel surveys, U.S. stocks outperform U.S. sovereign debt by more than 600 times and commodity prices by more than 50,000 times.

The reason for stocks' overwhelming advantage is clear: The economy continues to grow. In no other asset class can you get a representation of growth as you can in the stock market. The inevitable growth in population, spurring an inexorable rise of consumption, continues to force new companies to form and old companies to expand to satisfy growing needs.

Charting the Dow Jones Industrial Average (DJIA) for the last century, as shown in Figure 2.3, delivers an impressive, if not equally powerful picture to Siegel's chart. Even considering the Depression wiped out 30 years of wealth in the stock market, since that time, the index has grown more than 200 times. But that hardly tells the entire picture of investment goodies to be had by concentrating on stocks. Add onto that continuing engine of growth the reinvestment of dividends gained by owning stocks, historically equal and often greater than the return on U.S. treasuries alone, and you have a supercharged vehicle that literally blows away everything else. You need not be an economics professor from Harvard to understand why stocks are by far the best vehicles to invest in.

This is the first, and perhaps slightly facile reason why commodities and specifically oil, are an incredibly inferior investment: there is

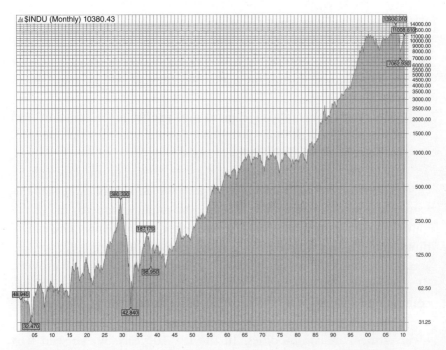

Figure 2.3 Growth of the Dow Jones Industrial Average, 1900–2010
SOURCE: stockcharts.com

no growth to be seen in a commodity, no inexorably growing market cap that must expand to take care of an ever-expanding population and standard of living. There are no dividends or interest payments received from owning oil, nor is there a way to reinvest profits and compound returns. *There is simply the profit to be gained by an increasing price of oil.*

Even this simple outlining of the differences in these three asset classes makes for a very interesting comparison of the relative merits of each investment:

- *Bonds,* whether short- or long-term and no matter who is issuing them, have only one engine for profit: The return on capital through interest payments that are either stated on the coupon if purchased at par or implied by the price you pay for the bond during its lifetime.

- *Commodities* have price as their engine of reward only. And although it is likely that commodity prices will go higher over time, they have historically had long flat and even short deflationary periods, and during those periods, they reward investors little, if at all.
- Only *stocks* deliver both engines for profit: price inflation and return on equity through dividends. Even if you miss on one side, the other will continue to pay you.

Modern economists are engaged in daily debate on whether the nature of economic growth is changing to such a degree to infect the inevitable superiority of stocks to all other investments. Growth is finite in all things: nothing can expand forever, and some economists argue that the U.S. stock market has seen its best days of growth; therefore, domestic stocks will no longer be able to return the massive compounded profits that the last 200 years have historically seen.

If you compare Figures 2.4 and 2.5, you can see the new theories of investment in commodities. In the last 10 years, we've seen two massive equity bubbles explode, destroying most all of the stock wealth accumulated previously. This has been known as the lost decade for stocks, where the benchmark DJIA has barely moved from where it began in the last decade. Dividends on stocks have still made sure of a better return than U.S. treasuries during this period, but just barely.

In comparison, gold prices have managed to increase four-fold during this period, for the first time in history annihilating the returns on stocks for a 10-year period. Oil has followed a similar trajectory of price inflation as gold has in the last 10 years, and except for its mini-bust in 2008, has been almost as impressive. To the new economist analyzing returns on capital and correct allocation of assets, Professor Siegel's chart is dead, a dinosaur not befitting a new age of investment priorities. Hard assets will trump paper, and commodities will now dominate on positive returns, in the way that stocks previously have.

I'm not so sure. Stocks have had rough periods before, remaining flat from the start of the twentieth century to the prices reached at the depths of the Depression in 1934, a period of more than 30 years.

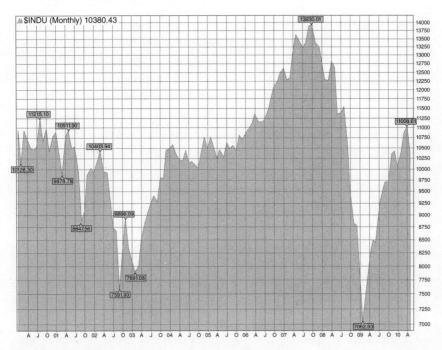

Figure 2.4   2000–2010: The Lost Decade for Stocks
SOURCE: stockcharts.com

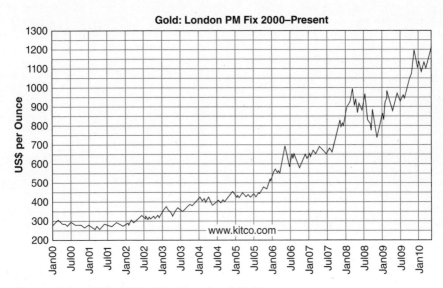

Figure 2.5   2000–2010: The Decade of Gold
SOURCE: www.kitco.com

During the worst moments of the early 1930s, it must have seemed that stocks were finished as investable assets, never to be worthy of a saved dollar's trust again, and yet they came roaring back practically unabated for the next 80 years. The stock market's last 10 years will not write away 200 years of accumulated wealth so quickly. And that is again because of the dual multiplying force of stocks to generate wealth—both through dividends and through growth. That mechanism of profitability cannot change, no matter what the economy is doing at any particular moment. It's just got to be easier over the long haul if you've got two batters taking swings at the ball, as opposed to just one, no matter how curved and unexpected the pitch might be.

Stocks clearly hold an investment advantage, but because stocks have had a rocky decade from the start of the millennium, oil has gained greater and greater interest from investors. Despite the fact that its zero-sum nature ensures that it cannot ultimately accumulate wealth as equities can, more and more money has been finding its way into oil and other commodities. Let's look at the most widely used investment vehicle for investing in oil price and see how it skews what American business and American consumers are forced to pay for energy: Commodity Indexes. For that, turn to Chapter 3.

Chapter 3

The Assetization of Oil, Part 2

The Problem with Commodity Indexes and Exchange-Traded Funds

Concurrent with financial oil's metamorphosis to a capital market (i.e., to being treated and priced like a stock, described in Chapter 2), new instruments began to emerge to play it like a stock as well: commodity index funds and commodity exchange-traded funds (ETF). To make oil trading even more viciously volatile and pricing less reliable, a brand new group of investors prepared to grab the dice for a pass at the table. But one group's new influence began to become overwhelming and stunning, so let's begin this chapter by taking a look at them.

A New Group of Oil Investors:
Index Speculators

Beginning at the turn of the millennium, but with a rush starting in 2003, a new army of participants that no one expected entered the oil markets, started trading, and began unwittingly manipulating prices higher. Who were they? America's working people.

They did it through their pension plans and when they entrusted their investments and retirement accounts to outside managers. Some of the most financially savvy working folk did it knowingly, but most who were involved did it oblivious of its effect, through new and specific commodity index funds. Billions of dollars were thrown at the commodity markets for investment using indexes, causing unprecedented price inflation of oil and virtually all publicly traded commodities. Higher prices from index investing showed up in corn and wheat and coffee, but because the indexes are biased toward the energy markets, giving the energy components of the index more weight, the effect on oil was outsized.

I marvel at the irony of this story: on the one hand, the people most affected negatively from higher energy costs are these working people of America, the ones most likely to own a piece of large, institutionally managed public pensions. These are also the most likely managers to diversify into commodity indexes, which drive energy prices higher, to the detriment of their members.

It was astounding to watch this new flow of capital appear and begin to work its influence in the 2000s from my perch on the trading floor. Everything we thought we knew about how our oil market was supposed to trade and what should affect it lost its value, because this new group of participants came to trade oil for the purpose of investment only—and was therefore a type of participant we had never before seen, nor the market was ever designed to cope with.

Much of the data I quote from in this next section comes from the fine work of Mike Masters, a hedge fund manager who has invested hundreds of hours and many more of his own dollars compiling data on this new group of participants. For that reason, I grudgingly use his appellation for the group: *index speculators*.

The reason I dislike this name is the word speculator implies motive and intent. The first word that springs to mind when you see the word speculation is manipulation, as in using the mechanisms of the market to fool it just long enough to make an outsized, but phony, profit from it. As an oil trader, I cringe when that term is used to refer to me: I am a *trader,* adding liquidity and taking risk to profit from market dislocations and inequalities, not a *speculator* in the instant connections one makes with that word and the likes of the Hunt brothers and Enron. Because the majority of investors in indexes are deriving profit without premeditative motive to manipulate (in fact, most are personally burdened by it), I prefer the term index investors. Yet, because the investments of this group have no doubt been the most influential single manipulator of price, even unknowingly, we'll stick to Mike Masters's *index speculators.*

Disappointment with Stocks Led Ordinary Investors to Look Elsewhere

To trace the roots of these index speculators, we need a quick overview of the equity markets in the late 1990s, particularly the disaster that the exploding tech bubble had on portfolios in early 2000. Traditional long-term investment described the purchase of stocks and bonds only. The standard formula for investment typically used age as a guideline. Your age approximately matched your investment percentage in bonds, about 10% of your money was allocated to cash or treasuries, and the rest was prescribed for investing in stocks. Historically, stocks have proven a riskier yet more profitable investment in the long run (although the lost decade from 2000 to 2010, when stock indexes ended close to where they started, might have many reassessing their formulas). For example, using this crude formula, a 40-year-old investor would put fully half of his retirement fund in stocks.

Outside of some cyclical setbacks, the stock market had experienced two decades of phenomenal growth and returns. But the tech bubble explosion in 2000 ended the fantasy of a stock market that mechanically delivers outsized double-digit returns year after year. Personal fortunes invested in Nasdaq stocks disappeared in 2000 as the tech index lost 70% of its value. Big-board stocks of established blue-chip companies fared much better, but even the benchmark Dow Jones Industrial Average (DJIA) lost almost 35% of its value in two years. Two years is a long time to withstand negative returns on investments, particularly in stocks, which was where the majority of investor money was allocated. Many investors and their managers of large corporate and pension portfolios cried out for other places to invest money that would help increase returns, but at the very least, would put portfolios at lesser risk of future bubbles, big setbacks, and negative returns.

The Rise of Hedge Funds

That's when alternative asset classes began their ascendency, and the most popular form was the equity hedge fund. Hedge funds had been around long before the Nasdaq crash of 2000, but almost all investors now felt they needed to look at them for protection and diversification, so the number and size of hedge funds grew astronomically. Traders were given gobs of money to invest, using any system or methodology they chose, because consistent profits (not risk) was the only important metric.

Like traders in any market, hedge fund managers sought to find spread values and other dislocations in equities, able to go long or short any particular stock or sector. A good hedge fund didn't necessarily rely on the steady march upward of stock indexes to be profitable; therefore, a hedge fund was a useful diversifier to a traditional portfolio of stocks and bonds to increase total returns. Managers of funds who put together several years of better returns than benchmark indexes became famous rock stars, and they had investors beating their doors down to contribute to their funds.

Many investors became so enamored with the returns some funds were delivering that they fed a greater and greater percentage of their portfolios to these alternative investments, thereby destroying the concept of using hedge funds for diversification purposes. Those whose greed overcame their better judgment and put most of their eggs in one hedge fund basket paid the price in 2008, when many of the top-performing funds had disaster years. Still others learned that outsized historical returns are often too good to be true, when *$50 billion* of wealth disappeared under the fraudulent custodianship of one huckster fund manager named Bernie Madoff.

Interest in Other Alternative Investments

For a small but growing group of investors, alternative investment meant being entirely removed from stocks and bonds, even if these equity hedge funds did not track the motion of their underlying indexes. A new appetite for financial innovation in fresh asset classes was recognized, and the financial services industry hopped to the ready to satisfy it. An explosion of new investment vehicles for real estate, sovereign debt, emerging markets, and (of course) commodities began to be offered. The idea of this diversification was sound enough, if the end result turned out not to be so: it was thought that greater diversification into as many varied asset classes as possible would spare portfolios from the kind of cataclysmic shellacking they received in Nasdaq stocks back in 2000.

Tracking the prices of commodities through indexing had been around for years, but they had been created for academic purposes. That changed in 2000, with the passage of the Commodity Futures Modernization Act (CFMA) under President Bill Clinton and then-Fed Chairman Alan Greenspan. The CFMA opened the road for new commodity swap instruments to be created away from the regulated exchanges and over-the-counter trading (which I'll discuss in more detail in Chapter 4), and also paved the way for the sale and marketing of commodity indexes as an investment. Many competitors began to devise instruments to capture the price motion of commodity indexes.

The Goldman Sachs Commodity Index

As money began to flow into them, it wasn't surprising to see one index product separate from the crowd to become the benchmark: The Goldman Sachs Commodity Index (GSCI). During the early years of my career on the floor in the 1980s and 1990s, the only well-known and reliable commodity index that was ever referenced was the Reuters-created Commodity Research Board (CRB) index, by far and away still the best recognized index in 2000 when the CFMA was passed. Yet when commodity indexes became investable and big money, the index from Goldman Sachs was quickly able to dominate and dwarf the older and better-established CRB.

The CRB was the benchmark reference point for commodity prices. Calculation of the index was done in an academic way, using the first nine months' average prices of 28 different commodities. The CRB has been constantly updated since its beginnings in 1957: commodities have been included and removed, their percentage weightings have changed, and the months used in the average calculations have changed. All of these tweaks have been done more to correctly represent commodity influence on the U.S. economy, and less to accommodate a commercially traded product. Today, energy components of the still-alive CRB make up 33% of the index. The CRB has failed numerous times to become a viably tradable index, although it is today listed on the New York Board of Trade (NYBOT), a part of the Intercontinental Exchange (ICE), where it languishes in obscurity.

In contrast, the GSCI, created on the heels of the CFMA, was always intended to be used as an investment alternative to commodity futures. It is traded publicly on the Chicago Mercantile Exchange, but swaps on the index directly with Goldman are a more common way for index fund managers to gain access. Two very different methodologies are employed for weighting the market-leading GSCI and the CRB and other commodity indexes with proportions of individual commodities.

The Goldman Sachs index employs something the company calls economic weighting: it tries to measure the total impact that any one commodity will have on the economy at large and relatively weight each one proportionally. As Goldman Sachs explains it, "production weighting is not only appropriate but vital" and "investment performance" can only be correctly represented by the amount of capital committed to holding each asset. In essence, the GSCI measures the interest in each commodity, both physical and financial, in order to arrive at their weightings, as shown in Table 3.1.

Table 3.1 Comparative Weightings of the GSCI

Energy	70.88	Industrial Metals	8.66	Precious Metals	3.14	Agriculture	12.58	Livestock	4.74
Crude Oil	37.32	Aluminum	2.66	Gold	2.80	Wheat	2.71	Live Cattle	2.64
Brent Crude Oil	14.85	Copper	3.84	Silver	0.34	Red Wheat	0.54	Feeder Cattle	0.46
RBOB Gas	4.80	Lead	0.49			Corn	3.02	Lean Hogs	1.65
Heating Oil	4.57	Nickel	0.95			Soybeans	2.24		
Gas Oil	5.79	Zinc	0.72			Cotton	1.22		
Natural Gas	3.55					Sugar	1.80		
						Coffee	0.72		
						Cocoa	0.35		

SOURCE: Goldman Sachs, www.goldmansachs.com

In contrast, the CRB uses a far different methodology, shown in Table 3.2. It is based on liquidity of the underlying futures markets. The CRB categorizes commodities into four groups: petroleum, liquid assets, highly liquid assets, and diverse commodities. No single group can hold more than 33% of the weightings. (The much smaller but recognized Dow Jones-AIG commodity index uses a similar methodology.) The real point of this weighting system is to try to capture the broad movements of commodities as a group, irrespective of individual components. It is less likely that a big move from a single component of the index will move the CRB or the DJ-AIG much, instead representing a general benchmark of commodity price trajectories.

The bottom line, however, is that the GSCI index is weighted overwhelmingly into energy commodities, comprising more than 70% of the index as of February 2010. In addition, the GSCI is nominally twice as big as all other commodity indexes combined. Their dominance allows this particular index game to work like an endless circle: overwhelming interest in oil fuels a deeper weighting into petroleum products, which subsequently adds more interest to and investment money into oil. It's a tidy trick. Goldman Sachs and its index managers can sell a sexier product and make a tidier profit by promoting their weightings more deeply into the most volatile commodities, and no commodity has recently been more volatile than oil. Suspicious or not, an investment in commodity indexes tied to the market dominating GSCI is going to act pretty much like a straight up bet on the price of oil.

How does the GSCI make these bets on oil and track the price?

How Indexes *Should* Work—Stock Indexes

Let's look quickly at how a stock index fund would work: a manager trying only to mirror the movements of an underlying index would simply buy the individual stocks in that index, hopefully in the same proportions as the index uses. There might be a few mistakes in execution, and of course, you'd be adjusting your positions daily based on the inflow and outflow of capital, but you'd get very close to approximating the movement of the purely mathematical index.

Table 3.2 Commodities Included in the Thomson Reuters/Jefferies
CRB Index

	Commodity	Index Weight	Contract Months	Exchange
Group I	WTI Crude Oil	23%	Jan–Dec	NYMEX
	Heating Oil	5%	Jan–Dec	NYMEX
	Unleaded Gas	5%	Jan–Dec	NYMEX
	Total	**33%**		
Group II	Natural Gas	6%	Jan–Dec	NYMEX
	Corn	6%	Mar, May, Jul, Sep, Dec	CBOT
	Soybeans	6%	Jan, Mar, May, Jul, Nov	CBOT
	Live Cattle	6%	Feb, Apr, Jun, Aug, Oct, Dec	CME
	Gold	6%	Feb, Apr, Jun, Aug, Dec	COMEX
	Aluminum	6%	Mar, Jun, Sep, Dec	LME
	Copper	6%	Mar, May, Jul, Sep, Dec	COMEX
	Total	**42%**		
Group III	Sugar	5%	Mar, May, Jul, Oct	NYBOT
	Cotton	5%	Mar, May, Jul, Dec	NYBOT
	Cocoa	5%	Mar, May, Jul, Sep, Dec	NYBOT
	Coffee	5%	Mar, May, Jul, Sep, Dec	NYBOT
	Total	**20%**		
Group IV	Nickel	1%	Mar, Jun, Sep, Dec	LME
	Wheat	1%	Mar, May, Jul, Sep, Dec	CBOT
	Lean Hogs	1%	Feb, Apr, Jun, Jul, Aug, Oct, Dec	CME
	Orange Juice	1%	Jan, Mar, May, Jul, Sep, Nov	NYBOT
	Silver	1%	Mar, May, Jul, Sep, Dec	COMEX
	Total	**5%**		

SOURCE: Energy Information Administration, www.eia.doe.gov

The GSCI tries to work the same way, by buying underlying futures that represent the prices of commodities in the proportions of the index, but as you know by now, *commodities aren't stocks*, and it doesn't work the same way. But the GSCI still tries to do it—by buying futures contracts as if they were stock certificates.

As discussed in Chapter 2, the number of contracts available in any traded futures contract is not fixed, as a stock is. Although a stock has a fixed quantity of shares, you can create an infinite number of future contract shares of oil. Therefore, there are no limits at all on the amount of money and the number of participants able to enter any commodity market. This is the first difficulty in indexes trying to track commodity prices through the purchase of futures contracts: The supply of shares in oil continues to be a moving target.

Instead, there is a constant creation and destruction of shares. For the creator of a commodity index, this is a very tough problem to overcome. How do you correctly represent the price of oil, when not only is the number of shares changing constantly, but the investment itself self-destructs every 30 days? You do it by rolling your positions forward. Again as described in Chapter 2, rolling is a key term in futures investing, and it has become a very important part of how commodity markets trade, precisely because of index funds. Rolling refers to retiring a position in a month about to expire and reinitiating it in a month further out on the curve. It is the only way for index funds to continually try to represent an investable price for oil. (We'll see how unpredictable rolling can make long-term investments with the story of Metallgesellschaft, in Chapter 7.)

But more recent rolling of positions by indexes has made a total catastrophic mess of the futures markets. When rolling happens in small bits, nothing much is affected. However, when index managers with several billions of investor dollars have to roll thousands of contracts trying to maintain positions, it can make for a very big difference in the prices that the market represents.

As if the outright buying of futures by index managers from ever-increasing investment didn't add enough upward pressure on prices, a steady rolling of positions forward imbalances the price of the market upward even more. That's because as positions are rolled, second month prices get artificially inflated just as they're about to assume the front-month position and become the benchmark for quoted prices to the actual physical market.

This creates a price curve called a *contango,* where prices continue to rise as you move further out in time. It is a most unnatural condition of futures markets, and it was an incredibly rare occurrence in oil before 2006. Today, however, it is the norm. I discuss the contango at length in Chapter 7 and show how much of a mess it makes out of the market, but for now it is enough to know that the presence of a constant oil contango is proof enough of the massive power of index speculation.

Index speculation is a *one-way* street. Investors come in looking for exposure to commodities. That means that they want to *buy* and only *buy* contracts. Again, commodity markets were never designed to expect this kind of participant. Those engaging in the oil futures markets, even if they were speculating, needed to release the trade before expiration. Only the rarest participant in the traditional futures market wanted anything to do with delivery. In contrast, index investors *never* want to release their position. They only want to stay long, keep their investment, and continue to roll contracts forward. Some have referred to this as a stockpiling of financial oil—investors just continue to hold contracts representing future deliveries of oil with no desire to either end the positions or receive physical delivery.

There's been massive growth in the size of investment in index funds: more than $200 billion from 2006 to 2008 alone. That amount of investor money has made index investors the most influential group of participants in the oil market today. The Commodity Futures Trade Commission (CFTC) keeps records of two types of participants in the futures markets using their Commitment of Traders' (COT) reports: commercial and noncommercial, and I'll discuss the COT reports in more detail in Chapter 11, but these two classifications are supposed to draw a line between hedgers with physical assets (commercial) and speculating (non-commercial) interests. It does a miserable job at that, but it's the only benchmark from the regulatory agency, and it's the best we've got. Even using this crude tracking model, non-commercial interests in oil have increased from 20% of the total of oil interest in 2002 to more than 50% of oil interest in 2008, as shown in Figure 3.1.

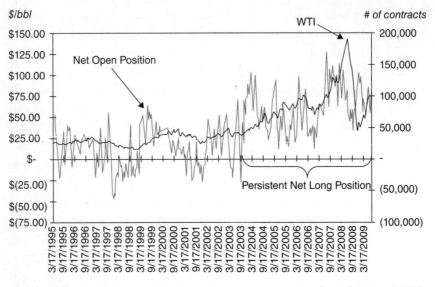

Figure 3.1 Noncommercial Open Positions versus Crude Oil Price (WTI), from 1995–2009

SOURCE: Energy Information Administration, www.eia.goe.gov

Besides increasing in overall amount of investment to become the dominating group, this graph shows just how *one way* this investment pressure is. Money seeks to buy, and only buy, oil through indexes. The other natural side of the futures trade is missing. The only way you can encourage people to sell something they really don't want to sell is to offer an outrageous sum for it. Looking at Figure 3.1, our noncommercial participant hasn't been net short the oil market since 2003, although he ventured to be short several dozen times for the 12 years before then. Indeed, even while staying persistently long since 2003, it is clear how deeply oil prices would drop when speculators of all stripes wanted to get a little less long as in late 2006, or get much less long, as in late 2008 and early 2009. There's little doubt: the price of oil is largely controlled by these forces.

A little more than $300 billion of indexed investment has been documented when oil was at its peak in July 2008. Most of this money never hit the futures markets, because most investment banks make better profits keeping them in-house as swaps, but even a moderate percentage leaking out to the underlying crude pit will have a big impact on oil prices. Open interest in West Texas Intermediate (WTI) traded at the New York Mercantile Exchange (NYMEX) sits at approximately 1.3 million contracts today. Even using the heady (and mathematically easy) net price of $100 a barrel for crude, the total value of open contracts—in other words, the market cap of oil—is only $130 billion.

That $130 billion may sound like a lot, but it's not. For example, the market cap for Exxon/Mobil, the largest American consolidated oil company, is more than $350 billion. Take the top four oil companies of Exxon, Royal Dutch Shell, BP, and Chevron, and you've got a total combined market cap of about three quarters of a trillion dollars.

Ok, let's throw the net wider. Let's add in all the financial oil represented on the ICE and throw in all the oil cleared through the NYMEX swap mechanism, Clearport. We've still only managed a bit more than $250 billion of market cap. The obvious point is that oil is a comparatively small and delicate market. Therefore, *even a few billion dollars of new interest can be incredibly destabilizing and make the market move wildly.*

Another example: suppose you wanted to invest in the health care and drug sector of the New York Stock Exchange. You'd have a lot of choices in companies, including Merck, Pfizer, Novartis, Eli Lilly, Bristol Myers—plus a load of other small and specialized stocks. The market cap on these five alone totals almost $450 billion. But let's say instead of having your choice of companies in which to invest, you instead were forced to buy only Pfizer. That's the only choice for everyone: Pfizer or nothing, with its $140 billion market cap. Also, let's say that the ability to even invest in the drug industry became available only a few years ago, using a special drug sector investment vehicle. That vehicle has gained a lot of interest, increasing in size four times in the last four years. You would expect the shares of Pfizer to command quite a premium, wouldn't you? Well, that's what index investors are doing in oil.

While the effect of index investment is felt in the price of oil, that investment capital makes a few stops before landing in the futures markets. Nearly 80% of investment in indexes is accomplished through swaps, a contract with an investment bank to do the work of replicating the performance of the index for you. These swaps became necessary because most managers are not normally permitted to engage in commodity trade. Huge price fluctuations and less predictable returns have made commodity investment imprudent for managers. Ironically, much of what this book discusses attempts to prove these prejudices to be true and those old-fashioned ideas to show intelligent merit. But never let prudence stand in the way of the progress of financial instruments. The creation in the early 2000s of index swaps permitted managers to sidestep their regulations and caveats by securitizing them. In essence, if one could represent commodity investment so that it resembled a stock, it wasn't a commodity anymore – or at least according to the overseeing boards of directors. This is how swaps on commodity indexes have been marketed and sold, and four major investment banks have pioneered their sale to institutional managers: Morgan Stanley, Goldman Sachs, J.P. Morgan, and Barclays.

Besides collecting healthy fees for offering derivative alternatives to fund managers, these investment banks also benefit from the flow of orders in the futures markets mandated by their swap contracts. If an investment bank desired, it could engage in arbitraging the index swaps with the underlying commodity markets, and they often did. But more often, the banks kept and offset much of the index trade in house. Index swaps became a new and useful paper flow for the oil traders at the big investment banks.

Figure 3.2 compares the amount of money invested with index speculators in commodity funds with the overall price of the index over those years. From 2003, when index speculation appeared to begin in earnest, until July 1, 2008, the amount of money invested in indices exploded from $13 billion to $317 billion—*an increase of more than 25 times!* The coincident increase in the prices of the commodity indices shows the results of all that new, big money chasing some very small and capital sensitive markets. Commodity prices have increased on average more than six fold.

One notices only one of these three concentric circles growing across time in the very descriptive Figure 3.3—that of the index speculators' positions. As the balloons get larger, so they move higher, to higher spot index prices, which are composed overwhelmingly by oil.

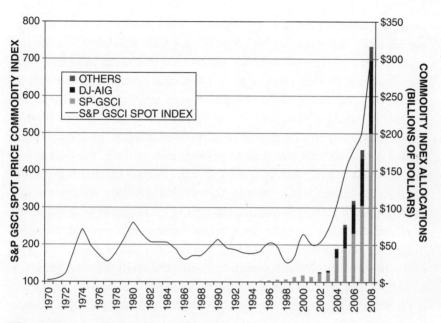

Figure 3.2   Standard & Poor's GSCI Spot Price Index versus Index Speculator
Assets
SOURCE: Bloomberg, Goldman Sachs, CFTC Commitments of Traders CIT Supplement

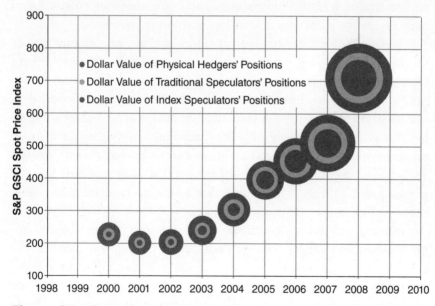

Figure 3.3   Comparing the Commodities Futures Market Size with the
Standard & Poor's GSCI Spot Price Index
SOURCE: Bloomberg, Goldman Sachs, CFTC Commitments of Traders CIT Supplement

If a picture is worth 1,000 words, Figure 3.3 should end all arguments: *index investment makes oil much more expensive than it should be.*

The most recent financial fallout has included disasters from markets as diverse as mortgages, CDOs, and credit default swaps to sovereign debt, commercial real estate, and more. In all of these, the pattern of disaster and destruction remains the same: Somehow, a group of very smart, very well-paid people manage to create a new financial product that seems to have great potential for allowing investors to grow their money in a new way. These smart people enlist some other pretty smart people to sell that product to anyone and everyone with money lying around to invest. They are very successful at selling the product, often to the point that they need not really sell it anymore: customers are beating their doors down to get in. This influx of new dumb money then becomes the engine for a brand new set of people who is perhaps the smartest of all, usually under the same roof as the other two sets, to trade very successfully this new product that the *customers* really don't fully understand—but they (the smart people) do, of course.

In oil, the overwhelming fuel for the profit engines of the smart-people traders and the most significant single cause of volatility and high prices has been investment in commodity indexes.

The public and institutional investors in indexes that buy oil are the source of the endless bid. If we're looking for the ultimate villains of unnecessarily high oil prices, we might just need to look in the mirror. No one has been more at fault for commodity inflation than our own investment hunger, our need to find the next great thing to bet our retirement money on. The problem is we've invested in oil the same way we've invested in other assets—buying them. Oil isn't a stock, and oil futures aren't oil barrels. You can't just buy them as if they were. Further, it's because this asset class is so relatively new, that this bid to buy has become endless.

But even if index investment in oil was more than a mere five or six years old wouldn't change the fact that the buy-and-hold theory of investment just doesn't work with oil. An investment in a commodity index is not like a share of Kraft or Johnson and Johnson that you're supposed to hold on to through all market conditions. Doing so creates unnecessarily high prices, extreme volatility, and panic selling, as we saw in late 2008, when everything from stocks and bonds to real estate and oil collapsed, all at the same time.

The problem with oil is only going to grow from here. The bid has just begun to prove just how endless it can be. The market for traditional investments in stocks and bonds was approximately $100 trillion in 2005. In commodity futures, the market in 2008 totaled about $830 billion, up from $150 billion just four years before that. Now, a more than five-fold increase in market size in four years is impressive growth. But even with that growth, the futures market is less than 1% the size of traditional investment markets. It is very, very clear that investment in oil is only now in its infancy and that most investors haven't even begun to catch on to this great new alternative opportunity.

Or, rather, they *have* begun to catch on—which is how we arrived at oil prices of $150 in 2008, $80 in 2009, and $92 in 2010, even in the midst of the greatest recession since 1932. What happens when the rest of the investing public decides that exposure to oil is as important to their portfolios as exposure to municipal bonds or technology stocks?

The price of oil will be very high indeed.

The sidebar tells a personal story of the unrelenting and sometimes unfathomable buying caused by index managers and how even good trading sense can be thwarted by the power of these powerhouse funds. Slightly less influential, but no less unfathomable, is the explosive growth of futures-based ETFs and their incredible effect on the oil market. The next section after the sidebar charts their rise.

Why Oil Traders Hate Oil Index Funds (How I Lost $11,000 in 30 Minutes)

In the spring of 2007, I was working to make the transition from trading on the floor to trading electronically. Rentals on seats for the floor were pretty high, close to $20,000 a month, so renting my seat allowed me the luxury of taking six months off the floor,

(Continued)

Why Oil Traders Hate Oil Index Funds (How I Lost $11,000 in 30 Minutes) (*Continued*)

turning on my computer in the office, and trying to learn how to make money using this new medium.

I'm trading lightly. It's a Wednesday, and it's early in the day. The market is waiting on its weekly Energy Information Administration (EIA) report of changes in stockpiles of crude oil and other products, and so am I.

In advance of the report, I have on a small position of crack spreads. A crack spread consists of two trades: a trade in crude oil and an opposite trade in one of the refined products, either gasoline or heating oil. If you buy the crude oil while selling one of the products, you are said to be short the crack; alternatively, if you have sold crude while buying products, you are long cracks.

I am long gasoline cracks, less than 20 of them, an interesting amount—enough to make a tidy profit for being right, without putting the bankroll at risk if I'm wrong. The cracks have been pretty cheap for a while. I've noticed a minor turnaround in the last several EIA reports that hopefully will harbor a move up in the cracks and a profit for me.

The new report hits the tape a little after 10:30 a.m. and shows a small decline in gasoline stockpiles, less than 500,000 barrels, but a very large increase in crude stockpiles of close to 6 million barrels. I smile. Actually, I hoot. The gas report was only slightly bullish, but the crude report was very bearish. I should be solidly in the money.

As I check back at my screens, the markets are reacting as expected and looking pretty good for me: crude has backed off almost 50¢, and although gasoline has followed it, it's not down nearly as much as crude. I'm up almost 25 points on my spreads right away, or about $3500. Not bad, but I'm looking for more: I'm feeling smug about my genius and considering adding to the position, holding for a few weeks, and perhaps riding a turnaround in gas crack spreads.

Why Oil Traders Hate Oil Index Funds
(How I Lost $11,000 in 30 Minutes) (*Continued*)

However, at precisely 10:40 a.m., something happens to wipe the grin off my face. The very deep crude market suddenly gets swept of all its offers in a 15-point range. Just like that, buying has come in and swallowed it all up in an instant. I can't tell precisely how many have traded, but at least a couple thousand contracts of crude oil are gone, and crude is now trading about 12 points higher. Gas doesn't follow at all, and my paper profits in my cracks are now nearly gone. But this report is so bullish for cracks that I mistake this for an opportunity: I can now put on *more* cracks at nearly the level they were at *before* the report came out—surely a great bet. I add another 20 cracks. And now my position is getting uncomfortably risky.

At precisely 10:50, it's the same wild phenomenon: out of the blue, like a whale swallowing plankton, all of the offers are gone, and crude is trading another 15 points higher. I'm out more than $6,000 now.

I'm getting the picture but not fast enough—at 10:55, there's a smaller rush for contracts, but still a rush.

I don't wait until 11AM. Cursing the index managers who are now obviously causing this, I have to compete with a couple thousand other cursing day traders who are all trying to get out of what should have been a winning position. I buy back my crude oil and wait until 11:00.

Sure enough, a solid wave of buying appears again at 11AM, forcing the gasoline contract, which I am still long to only feebly follow, cutting my losses only slightly. I sell that part of my position, and now I am out of this genius trade, now gone horribly wrong. I total up my losses—nearly $11,000, in less than 30 minutes.

Nothing proves a point to a trader better than losing money. Previously, I had been only peripherally aware of index funds and

(*Continued*)

Why Oil Traders Hate Oil Index Funds (How I Lost $11,000 in 30 Minutes) (*Continued*)

their influence on my oil market, but that day convinced me of their power—power they could wield only in an electronic marketplace.

That loss also convinced me of the stupidity of the way these funds operated: It was clear that the managers of those index funds had a slug of money that they needed to put to work in the oil market that day. They were doing it methodically, mechanically, at five-minute intervals, without any regard for any fundamentals or the price at the time. Nothing could have made crude oil rally that day, that closely to a very bearish report, except the mindless price-insensitive buying of the new commodity index funds. They needed an average, and they got it, taking the market up with it.

And sinking me.

ETFs and the Common Man

The endless bid has found an especially one-sided and relentless fuel for growth with a very recently created new product: ETFs for oil. With ETFs, investors have been given access to oil futures in a form that looks just like a stock; however, they may look like stocks, but they don't act like them. That small fact hasn't stopped investors from accessing them in droves. They have invested in these ETFs in precisely the same way as they always have with stocks, by buying them to hold. The result of their investing behavior has been clear: continually buying ETFs for investment has unnecessarily forced prices for the crude barrel ever higher.

ETFs are a rather new phenomenon for all asset classes. The idea behind them is simple: try to capture an entire sector of investments in a single and investable stock-like price. ETFs were cleverly designed to mitigate the risks of investing in only one or perhaps two stocks of a particular sector. Investing in just one or two representative stocks does not assure one of capturing the performance of the entire group.

For example, let's say you are convinced that the United States will experience especially strong economic growth, requiring greater and greater energy supplies to power it. You might consider investing in the oil services sector, which is surely a cyclical sector that benefits most in periods of outstanding growth. Although you like the idea of investing in the oil services group, you may not be as sure of which oil services company to invest in. Should you go for a big multi-national company, like a Halliburton or a Schlumberger? Or should you concentrate on on-shore drillers? Or is the best opportunity in off-shore drilling specialists, like with a Transocean or a Diamond Offshore? Well, if you decide you want exposure to *all* of these companies at once, you could invest in the Oil Services HOLDRs ETF (OIH), which is by far the biggest oil services ETF. OIH simply buys shares in each of these companies in relative amounts. The exact percentages of each company's shares that comprise the ETF are proprietary decisions of the fund manager, but the largest-market-cap companies almost always make up the largest percentages of the fund's holdings, unless there is a special need for specialty stocks. For the OIH, the distribution of shares is very straightforward and intuitive: 18 oil services companies are contained in the investment, including the four large-cap stocks I mentioned earlier, as well as Baker Hughes, National Oilwell Varco, Noble Energy, and 11 others in smaller percentages.

Although you have to be a little careful with ETFs and make sure that the stocks that the managers choose to represent their fund are truly representative of the sector strategy you're trying to capture, for the most part, the ETF industry has been a boon to average investors, allowing them to capture entire sectors with one easily accessible, stock-like price.

It's certainly proved to be a popular form of investing and trading: since the SPDR emerged in 1993 (this was the first ETF, and it tracked the S+P 500 index), the number of actively traded ETFs has exploded. In fact, it's hard to keep track, as funds open and close all the time, but recent estimates guess at 900 ETFs that are viably traded at various U.S. stock markets. And the variety and scope of these ETFs have obviously gone beyond just sector concentration in equities: ETFs have sprung up in every diverse asset class under the sun,

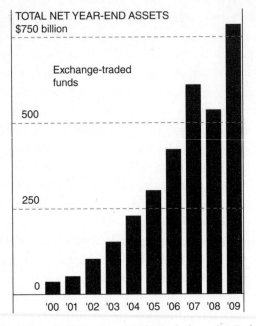

Figure 3.4   The Rise of ETFs since 2000, Including the Rebound of 2009
SOURCE: Morningstar

including emerging markets, bonds, the dollar, and indexes both long and short. For individual investors, the rise of ETFs has been the most significant new product in a decade, as shown in Figure 3.4.

And yes, the ETF market hasn't restricted itself to stock or bond sectors. A few intrepid funds have attempted to capture commodity prices in this stock-like form. It can't be done, because *commodities aren't stocks*, but that hasn't stopped a few from trying.

And it is genius, really—if investors and traders are unwilling, or unable, to understand the many important and nuanced differences between commodity futures and stock issues, an ETF stands waiting, telling them they don't even need to try. For example, the United States Oil (USO) Fund (which is the biggest oil ETF) packages a combination of futures and swaps contracts in crude oil and represents them in one fluid price, just like a stock. For USO, the appeal of this approach has been rewarded: Its fund has twice increased shares and now sports a $2.53 billion market cap of exclusively buyers of energy. Every avenue for involving investors in the world of oil has been covered by the financial industry. If diversity is the goal, and owning oil is deemed equally worthwhile to owning stocks, the index fund market is available. If you tend to like the added risks of putting your money in the hands of other traders, Commodity Trading Advisors (CTAs) and managed futures funds stand ready to assist. And, if you like to mix your own martini, access directly to the futures markets is offered by virtually every broker, both online and on the phone. Don't have the time to figure out futures, with all of those confusing expiring months and weird contract specifications? No problem. You've now got a whole menu of stock-like ETFs to keep you happy.

Oil Made to Look Exactly Like a Stock

Of course, almost inevitably, someone figured out a way to apply the ETF idea to commodities. This has been a disaster, both for the investor truly trying to capture the price motion of the underlying commodity, but particularly for oil, which has been delivered another onslaught of buying pressure for investment purpose only. We'll talk about just how really bad oil ETFs are as investments later in this chapter and how investors in them get played for saps, but for now let's see how the oil ETFs affect the price of oil. For our benchmark case, I'm again going to look at the largest oil ETF out there, the USO, which was rolled out in 2006.

Replicating the performance of a sector of stocks as an ETF is a fairly straightforward business: once the manager has chosen his representative family of stocks and his best guess at allocation percentages, the rest is pie. He can represent a composite share price using the share prices in his family adjusted by the allocation, remove his fee for his good work, and set up automatic, computer-driven buying and selling of shares dependent on the movement of his ETF and the movement of the sector shares. His job is to balance what is happening in the sector with the price representation of his fund. It sounds complicated, but in the new world of instantaneous computer transactions, once the program is set, a manager can almost literally stand away and collect his fee for as long as investors like and continue to use his product.

However, for oil ETFs that are based in futures, there is more difficulty. Futures contracts continue to expire monthly, unlike stocks, which is the first major problem. USO's prospectus intends to replicate the price motion of the spot price of crude as it is represented on the NYMEX. It makes sense to try and do this because the spot price is closest to the market price for physical crude oil. However, it is also the month soonest to expire. It is almost always the most liquid month too, but even being this liquid, the fund has to find a special mechanism to engage the futures market for both buying and selling contracts. In fact, they must use outside purchasers to buy or sell baskets of futures contracts to each represent 100,000 units of the fund. This is not such a terrible thing, but it does go to show how much more difficult it is to replicate futures prices into an ETF, as opposed to an ETF of stocks. A stock ETF, outside of its small fee can exactly represent its sector prices. However, by using a basket approach of futures, the USO cannot guarantee such a result. In many ways, USO and most other commodity ETFs can act a bit like closed-end funds, running either a premium or discount of its share price to the underlying value of the holdings in its fund. Simply put, a greater demand from investors can drive the share price higher than the hopefully corresponding price of crude. When the USO prices like this—at a premium—it has only one way to continue to try and replicate crude prices—by issuing more units. To do this, it needs SEC approval, and it has gone through that process three times since its inception in 2006—an indication of USO's popularity with investors.

The process for USO to replicate oil prices using futures is already complex—it needs specialty purchasers, it cannot fully guarantee exact or even very close correlation with crude prices, and it must use the spot price in the futures market and that contract almost exclusively when adjusting the rapid changes both in the oil market and in the number and enthusiasm of investors both coming and leaving the fund.

But the final straw, of course, comes when the spot contract of crude comes close to expiration. Fund managers must execute a monthly rolling maneuver of contracts which we have described previously in regard to index investment. Sometimes the fund will engage in some swaps trading and even some options trading to try and cushion the blow of this rolling to represent the correct Net Asset

Value (NAV) of the USO fund. But with the consistent contango that I've already described that has been generated by index investing being exacerbated even more strongly by ETF investing, it becomes practically impossible for the USO to maintain its NAV consistently near the changing price of spot crude. Between the constant draw of fees, brokerage charges, exchange fees, and the inherent difficulties of rolling positions, the USO is fighting an uphill battle they will eventually have to lose: as time continues to move forward, *the fund almost necessarily has to lose money.* Even in the few years that the fund has been in existence, this has become very clear:

- In 2006, USO caught a small downdraft in crude after its inception and *lost 23% of its value* from April to the end of the year.
- In the big upmove of 2007, the USO fared better, earning 46% for investors. This was however a disappointing result if you looked at spot crude prices, which nearly doubled that year.
- In 2008, the fund *dropped 54% of its value*, while crude dropped less than 46%.
- It was an even worse story in 2009: The USO gained less than 10%, while spot prices on the year nearly doubled again.
- Finally, as of this writing, 2010 has seen crude prices spike into the mid 80s as of April, while the USO has barely moved at all since the start of the year.

Clearly, in all cases, USO is a poster child for horrible investing: Whether oil goes up or goes down, you end up a net loser as an investor, and ultimately as a holder of shares in this fund. Even Figure 3.5 from the last year, which compares the performance of USO with outright oil price, shows just how bad ETFs are in tracking commodity price changes.

It would seem that this kind of underperformance, with contango and futures rolling and just the general costs of the fund, should make it a fantastic long-term short play. I am sure that there are a number of funds doing just that, but considering how good it looks, the numbers are surprising: The short interest in the USO has been fairly low for the first three years of its existence, not outside the range of most other ETFs out there. Lately, however, the funds seem to be catching on: Short interest has been rapidly increasing in the USO

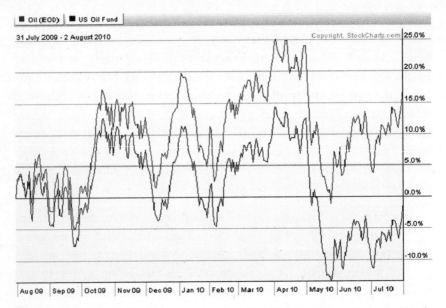

Figure 3.5   Contrast between Investing in Crude Oil and Investing in a Crude Oil ETF, over One Year: The ETF Always Underperforms
SOURCE: stockcharts.com

and other oil ETFs. As of April 29, 2010, short interest was just under 25% of the total of outstanding shares at close to 11 million. The bullseye seems to have been drawn around the USO, and I don't imagine it will survive much longer with its consistent underperformance and short pressure from other hedge funds.

No worries, however, for the fund managers: Their prospectus allows them full and unilateral rights at liquidation and settlement at their sole discretion. When things get bad enough, they can simply settle out the accounts, split up the money that's left with whomever is holding the awful shares, and go home—or start another oil fund. Wall Street is wonderful that way.

The bottom line is, if you are a long holder of the USO or any of the other oil ETFs based in futures, you are being played for a sap and siphoned of money to the benefit of fund managers and smart short/arbitrage players.

And all of those saps have had a not insignificant effect on the price of oil for the privilege of investing in bad ETFs like USO and

OIL, and we are collectively paying for it at the pumps: With a combined market cap of $3 billion, these two ETFs alone push almost $2.5 billion of money exclusively buying spot crude oil on the NYMEX every single month. Compared to the index investing described at the beginning of this chapter, this is a much, much smaller amount, but it is dynamic and significant. Remember that index investing can get split into various forms and does not always appear solely at the NYMEX in spot month purchases. Not so for these ETFs, whose prospectuses almost mandate their entry solely in this format. The market cap of the spot month for NYMEX crude might be grossly figured by multiplying the number of open contracts by the average price per barrel. Spot crude contract open interest hovers somewhere near 350,000 contracts. Even taking an optimistic, 2010 high price of $85 a barrel, we come out with a spot month market cap of about $30 billion. It is clear that $2.5 billion of buying every single month like clockwork will have a significant effect on the price, although admittedly, it's hard to put a dollar number on the influence.

One thing is for sure: If you were hoping for a low price for your home heating oil or gas to fill your car, this kind of speculative, investment buying into futures isn't going to help.

Correlations between the S&P and Oil

I'm watching the television as Sharon Epperson, CNBC's latest full-time reporter from the oil pits at the NYMEX, is trying somehow to explain oil's decline today of more than $4. That completes a move for today alone of more than 8% to around $46 in the May 2009 contract.

8%! From the days in the 1980s and 1990s when I roamed the pits with my friends and fellow traders, an 8% move could easily make or break most of our careers. We'd have been stunned by it, searching the news tickers and wondering how many funds had just exploded. Did someone find an unknown source of oil about to cascade on the market that no one ever expected? Perhaps OPEC has just made a surprise increase of quotas for all of its members? Or perhaps the

Israelis and Palestinians have just signed a 99-year peace agreement backed up by the nuclear powers of the United States, Europe, and Russia? Those would be events that might—*might*—trigger an 8% move in the days that I traded on the floor.

And Epperson is valiantly trying to draw on big macro ideas to explain today's selloff: demand numbers are down, stockpiles are up—but these are trends that have held steady for months, even while oil has rallied the previous four weeks from $45 up to $55 a barrel before falling out of bed like it has in the past few days, culminating in this barfing today. I'm feeling sorry for Sharon: she's got a tough job—appearing eight or ten times a day trying to find reasons for daily swings in the oil markets that traders like me wouldn't have imagined could ever take place on a regular basis. And today's 8% move, although significant, is nowadays hardly unusual.

But the answer, of course, is staring her in the face—as it's staring at me and everyone else with CNBC playing as background music in their places of work. It's in fact running across the top line ticker as she is speaking: the stock market is also off a significant amount today—by 250 Dow points and 60 S&P points. Aha. The connection couldn't be clearer, and it's a shame she can't fill all 12 of her daily spots with that easy explanation. But no one wants to admit the disaster that the oil markets have become.

Dumb, dumb, dumb. It is intuitively obvious to a child of 12 that the price of commodities and the price of the stock market should not run in tandem. Although both are subject to inflation and currency risk and both over time will naturally move upward, big moves in commodity prices, in either direction, should be a catalyst for at least a short-term move of stocks in the opposite direction. This should be particularly true in the case of oil. Oil prices decline and less is spent in raw material costs for transportation, refrigeration, chemicals—not to mention even energy shares themselves in refining and land-based oil services—margins and profits are helped and share prices should improve. Only a few stocks might be hurt (or helped) by an oil price decline (or rally)—perhaps a few integrated stocks perhaps some rig operators—those few issues that have shown correlation with the price of the crude barrel. But there can be no argument whatsoever: Business is helped by a lower price for energy and harmed by a higher one. That obvious truth should be reflected in the price action of equities, right?

To the contrary, the diametric opposite has been the case since the advent of the endless bid. Since the deleveraging process began after the fall of Lehman and the height of oil was reached in the fall of 2008, you could draw the charts for both oil and S&P side by side and without labeling them be entirely unable to tell the difference between the two. Previously, oil price and stock price would much more often act inversely as they should, but since late 2008, they have instead closely mirrored each other.

A cursory look at Figures 3.6 and 3.7 (where I have used the slightly less-than-accurate United States Oil Fund (USO) to represent a continuous oil futures price) shows a healthy correlation between oil and stocks in the last 24 months, but with increasing correlation in the last 12. This is a pattern that has been gaining strength almost continually since 1990, as further correlation is shown in Figure 3.8.

Figure 3.8 is a correlation chart of the Standard & Poor's (S&P) 500 index against six-month trailing oil prices as quoted at Cushing, the delivery point for NYMEX West Texas Intermediate crude. A correlation chart measures the movements of two assets and puts a

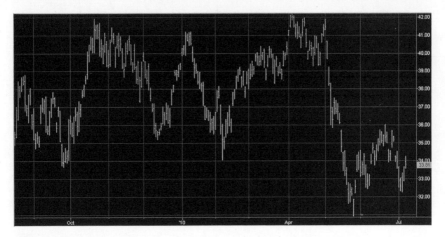

Figure 3.6 Tracking the Performance of USO Daily (ARCX, the United States Oil Fund) from October 2009 to July 2010
DATA SOURCE: Tradestation

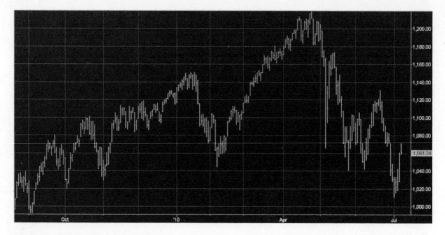

Figure 3.7 Tracking the Performance of an S&P 500 Index Fund from October 2009 to July 2010
DATA SOURCE: Tradestation

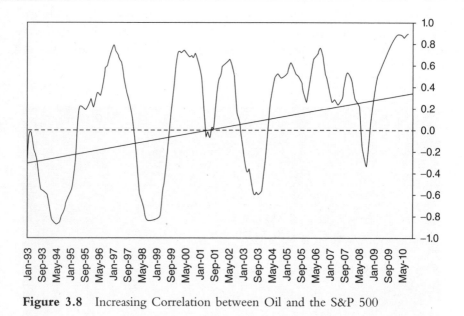

Figure 3.8 Increasing Correlation between Oil and the S&P 500

number between negative one and positive one on the similarity of their motions. A correlation of 1 would mean that the assets move always and equally in opposite directions on a percentage basis. A correlation of +1 would mean that they move in lockstep, not only in direction but also equivalently.

Correlation studies are an excellent tool for hedge funds, looking to find two assets, usually stocks, that they can play against each other: a fund might find what it thinks is a value stock and buy it, often selling another stock, usually in the same sector, with which to hedge their original bet. Correlation trading is how hedge funds got their name, although fewer and fewer hedge funds engage in true correlational trading anymore. A good example of strong correlations might be with Chevron and Conoco-Philips or with Pfizer and Merck. Even these shares, as tightly linked inside sectors, have far from perfect correlations. That's because finding any two assets that will move either perfectly together (or perfectly out of sync) is hopeless and thankfully so—there'd be no real business in trading stocks if correlations were always perfect.

And over the history of the oil trade since 1990 or so, there has seemed to be little correlation between the stock market and the oil market. We find that the correlation moves between −0.2 and +0.2 for a large portion of the time, moving outside of that range only on brief occasions, the most notable being the run-up to the Gulf war of 1991, when oil spiked toward $40, while the stock market understandably swooned. Here, correlation spiked downward to a very negative 0.56, which lasted only for a very brief few months.

But the wavy correlation line doesn't tell the whole story. I've drawn a smoothed-average correlation line that charts where correlation has headed in the last two decades and that line makes the trend very, clear: Oil and the stock market have been moving more and more in lockstep, moving over the zero mark of correlation not surprisingly at close to the turn of the century. This is not a surprising timeline: I have noted again and again in this book how the financialization of oil began to have significant effect on price as we entered the twenty-first century. Of course, much more notable is how the correlation of stocks to oil has accelerated, particularly in 2010, when it reached an incredible 0.6 correlation—amazing how positive correlation has recently exceeded the negative correlation caused by a Mid-east war!

A little more thought and explanation needs to be used to explain the particularly strong reciprocity in the last year. Certainly, hedge funds have found it increasingly easy to trade oil against stocks, as I've noted. Further, there is little doubt that allocations into oil from asset managers have tended to happen in tandem with allocations into equities more and more. Capital left on the sidelines after the crash of 2008 and 2009 has slowly made its way back into the stock market while it also continues to percolate into commodities. Even with all of this, the correlation between oil and stocks has been unbelievably and historically close. If you doubted for one moment the strength of this frankly absurd connection, this next chart from 2010 will certainly convince: see Figure 3.9.

There is an astounding question that a new, super-correlated oil and equity market forces us to ask: Is success in the equity market now directly tied to super-heated and astoundingly high oil prices?

It is a scary prospect that we have to consider, but with correlations between equities and oil getting increasingly tighter, we have to wonder if progress in the equities market must now naturally be accompanied by unnecessarily higher and higher oil prices. What kind of oil price might now be associated with the S&P regaining the highs it once held in October of 2007 at 1576? Could it be $150 a barrel, $200 a barrel, perhaps more? An increase of 65% in the S&P index from the lows of March 2009 to the beginning of March 2010 has been accompanied by more than a doubling of the price of oil. By

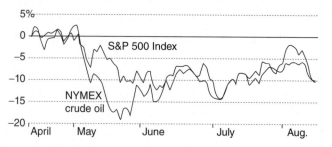

Figure 3.9   Tracking the Increasing Correlation of Stock Prices and Oil Prices from April to August 2010
SOURCE: WSJ Market Data Group

that reckoning, a move back to the previous highs in the S&P would be at the least equivalent to a $125-a-barrel spot oil price.

But don't we run the risk of derailing any kind of sustainable recovery and continued growth with an ever increasing price of crude? It seems that the financial connections between equity and oil prices could force a real recovery off the tracks, before it has even had a very long time to take hold. Can the stock market rally concurrently with crude? It would seem to be a difficult additional headwind to have to overcome, and overcome unnecessarily.

The conclusion is unfortunate but clear: Oil has been reduced to another capital market, no longer representing a commodity but just another investment vehicle. As money moves in and out of the markets, little differentiation is being made between instruments that were designed to be used for investment—like stocks and bonds—and others that were intended for quite another use entirely. And the results of this blurred purpose are very bad indeed.

Conclusion

I keep repeating over and over that commodities just aren't stocks. Oil just doesn't work as an investment for so many reasons. Because they are priced using futures, they don't have only one price; instead, they have a curve of deliverable cash prices that are spaced out over time. This is in contrast to stocks, which have a single, universally traded current price the world over. Plus, oil is tough to store; it hasn't got metrics with which to measure value (except for some very arguable supply-and-demand figures); and it has hundreds of different grades and access points. But because oil has been financialized or assetized—that is, made to look and be traded like a stock—it has been subject to all of the pressures of other investments like stocks, to the detriment of the price of the final products that you and I are forced to pay.

Assetization of oil hasn't hurt everyone, of course. In a few cases, the change of oil into a product ready to be molded and maneuvered like any other financial instrument has benefited some. It's easy to point fingers of blame for the mess that our oil market has become, but in the case of the investment banks, it's practically impossible to avoid doing it: No one single group has derived a more direct and ever-improving stream of profit, in good times or ill, from financial-ized oil than the engineers and traders inside the major Wall Street houses. Although they may not have single-handedly fed the problem, they have managed to optimize the profits to be gained from it. Chapter 4 explains.

Chapter 4

The Rise of the Investment Banks and Their Financial Finagling

There are lots of stories of oil companies that tried to become trading companies. As the process of pricing oil became less about the physical product and more about how it was represented financially in futures and other derivative instruments, oil companies had to become more and more adept at trading the stuff, as opposed to just selling it. This chapter includes my stories about Coastal and Northville, two relatively smaller oil companies that I came in contact with that tried to change and derive more from trading oil than finding and selling oil. The smaller you were and the less your physical assets were worth, the more tempting it was to get into the trading of oil, where the profits to be had were outsized compared to the effort.

But as I also show in this chapter, even the gargantuan integrated oil companies couldn't ignore the financialization of oil. BP, Exxon, Shell, Conoco, Hess—just about all of the big boys owned seats on the New York Mercantile Exchange (NYMEX) and were very aware of the changes in the marketplace. Although these big guys didn't abandon physical oil to the degree of many of the smaller independents, they certainly had to become a lot more committed to the trading side of the market to prosper, and remain to this day as significant participants. Simply, the financialization of oil affected everyone on the physical side of the equation.

And on the other side? While oil companies scrambled to keep up with Wall Street, there have been a few cases where Wall Street companies have actually entered the oil business.

Why would an investment bank want to sell oil? The answer is obvious: to make more money trading.

In the days before electronic trading re-leveled the playing field (or actually slanted it permanently toward those with the fastest server speed or newest algorithm), the advantages you had trading on the floor were admittedly huge. Part of my resentment and anger toward the investment banks/hedge fund/trading house cartel that I express is really envy: Admittedly due to their systematic ingress into markets that exchange members and traders hoped would be permanently ours. After 2003, we watched powerlessly as our advantages eroded and ultimately transferred to them. On the floor, those few active years before their influence destroyed our edge were exciting, wonderful, and very profitable. Being at the nexus of order flow (and being able to see nearly every order pass by you on its way to being executed) was a measure of information that allowed me and others with NYMEX memberships to profit from the risks we took far more often than we lost.

In fact, the rise of the investment banks as direct participants in the oil markets has been the amplifier for oil's endless bid. The unbelievable volatility and the unreliable prices we see currently are a direct result of the changeover of the primary players that now engage in the trade of oil. To fully understand and appreciate that change, you need to know something about how oil *used to be traded*.

Back in the Old Days: The Major Players Were the Oil Companies

In the days when I first entered the floor in the early 1980s, the oil companies understandably created much of the volume that would come through our pits: As mentioned in the Introduction, the major players were BP, Exxon, Chevron, Shell, and the like. But from about 2003 until 2008, my last five years of observation on the floor, virtually none of the volume I saw would come (at least directly) from the same oil companies that had dominated trade at the start of my career. Instead, paper flow from the likes of Paribas, Smith Barney, and Goldman Sachs became the most important and powerful to watch.

The results of such a switch of the primary participants were massive, if initially difficult to understand. Why should it matter who's involved in oil trade? In the end, oil undergoes the open outcry process at the exchange, a price is found, and prices will converge to real and tangible cash markets where real products are exchanged for money, right? What could (or what should) it possibly matter *who* those people are in the middle of the process? Market forces should still apply, shouldn't they? And if they do, the prices that are arrived at should be the same as well, right?

But in practice, the difference in who is trading oil makes for very real price differences. To put it simply, that's because the participants who are now primarily engaged in the modern oil markets *don't really care much about the price of oil.* Price does not matter one whit to their core business. And when price becomes unimportant, it can move in unexpected and radical ways.

The member lists of the NYMEX tell the history of the participants of oil trade clearly. As the exchange grew and established itself as the benchmark for oil price discovery, those involved in the buying and selling of oil found it important to buy and retain seats on the exchange. Although individuals tended to come and go as seat owners in the exchange, the companies that purchased seats tended to stay, right through the initial public offering (IPO) and merger with the Chicago Mercantile Exchange (CME).

Looking at that list, we can map the biggest players in oil trade during the 30-year history of the exchange. Of the 816 seats available, the number belonging to oil companies who wanted exposure to the exchange and traded futures is significant:

- Chevron: 4 seats,
- Amerada Hess: 2
- BP: 2
- Conoco/Phillips: 2
- Exxon/Mobil: 2
- Marathon/Ashland: 2
- Shell: 2
- Sunoco: 2
- Total of France: 2
- Valero: 2

It was important to own at least two seats, because two membership were required in order to become clearing members of the exchange and take advantage of lower exchange-clearing fee schedules. Other oil companies that engaged in futures trading worked through independent brokerages, their volume not significant enough to warrant a two-seat investment. But from the floor, Chevron, BP, Conoco, and Exxon dominated trade in the 1980s and early 1990s. For us on the floor, that was a fact upon which our very livelihoods relied: the sidebar tells more.

Where's the Money? Traders Always Know

For floor traders, there are virtual wars that can take place over where you stand in the pit. Although all should be equal among traders, in the pit, it was seldom so. Positioning yourself near active brokers who were executing constant and impactful orders was a tremendous advantage for a local. Therefore, the brokers who attracted the greatest crowds were the ones with large and complex orders—the kinds that could move the market, at least temporarily. If a broker (particularly a dedicated oil company's

Where's the Money? Traders Always Know (*Continued*)

broker) continued to get several hundred- or thousand-lot orders all day long (thereby biasing the market, temporarily, upward or downward), the second or two of added insight by standing close by, as a local, could make a huge difference to your bottom line for the day.

Of course, you also had the added advantage of being a lot more accessible to the broker, if you wanted to participate in any of this river of order flow. In essence, a good spot near an active broker gave you a consistent right of first refusal on orders. Orders can be juicy and worth climbing over other guys to get at, or they can be deathly—if you're selling first into a broker with several thousand contracts to buy, it doesn't matter if you're right or wrong in the end—for the moment, you're wrong. Either way, in figuring out the difference between a juicy and deathly order, it helps quite a bit if you're standing right next to the guy filling it.

In the Chicago pits, a pecking order of size was common: smaller traders stayed on low steps nearest the ring, and bigger traders stood higher up the staircase. The brokers executing paper for the biggest commercial clients all stood on the top steps, for instantaneous access to their runners and clerks.

But in New York, it was less organized: although brokers still occupied the very top steps, locals weren't barred from sharing that space with brokers, as they were in Chicago. Nor were you necessarily banned from moving high up the steps based on your volume and risk tolerance, although the biggest traders still tended to be closest to the paper. The lower down on the steps you found yourself, the worse your access and results generally were. In New York, one of the hurdles to becoming an independent trader involved finding a good spot in a ring. Breaking in to a ring was always touchy. Higher up the steps was always better. Starting out, you looked for a gap to make a spot or fought for a spot, and you established your position through daily elbowing combined with

(*Continued*)

Where's the Money? Traders Always Know (*Continued*)

some grousing and negotiation, until after a few weeks, your spot could no longer be challenged.

When I first came into the pits in the early 1980s, the really good spots next to the biggest paper brokers had long since been spoken for—and not surprisingly, they were next to the guys who did the Exxon, Hess, and BP paper. You may not think this is a very scientific study, but it couldn't be more telling. Oil traders are the best scientific measure of the most important people trading oil. Their livelihoods depended on finding the best money-making opportunities they could. If you walk into any pit and see a crowd of traders standing around a particular group of brokers, you can bet that the paper that those brokers are executing represents the most powerful participants in the game.

During the day, brokers were very close-lipped about the sources of their orders, but after the bell rang at the end of the day, they were less secretive about it. We learned who was most likely to handle the big outright and spread orders from the big oil players, although the oil companies often liked to mix up their brokers and use several at the same time. They continued to return to favorite brokers, however, and the locals crowded around them. We all knew who handled the important paper, and we watched every move they made during the day closely.

When the Big Banks Took Over

In the mid-1990s, the participants and performance of oil trading slowly started to change, and by 2003, the dominating forces in oil trade were no longer with the oil companies. The list of NYMEX seat owners again shows just how deep the change was. Right before going public in 2006, only 22 seats (although there had been about twice that many) remained in the hands of the oil companies that had direct involvement in the buying and selling of oil and oil products. But a much more significant percentage of seats were owned by companies that ostensibly had nothing to do with the buying and selling of physical oil—compare this list to the previous one:

- BNP Paribas (the French bank): 9 seats
- AIG: 6
- Merrill Lynch: 5
- Bank of America: 4
- Barclays: 4
- Citigroup: 4
- Deutsche Bank: 4
- JP Morgan: 4
- Morgan Stanley: 4
- UBS: 4
- Bear Stearns: 3
- Goldman Sachs: 3
- Lehman Brothers: 2

That's a total of 56 seats owned by investment banks! (And yes, I include the American Insurance Group, (AIG), which was an enormous booker of bets on oil too, not just in famously bad mortgage swaps.)

Of course, the most important purpose for some of these firms to own seats was to execute orders for clients, some retail, but many commercial clients who were being sold on the importance of risk management of energy costs. And during the years from the mid-1990s through 2005, this made for a legitimate increase in the volume of crude. But commercial growth of risk management programs was a happy appetizer for the quick rise of the investment banks in the trade of oil. Oil companies that tried to maintain a presence and dominance in trading began to be overshadowed by the volume and influence of trading from these banks and their clients.

For the traders on the floor, the biggest among us started to gravitate toward the paper brokers wearing the specialty colored jackets of the big investment banks: orange for Paribas, blue for the Smith Barney group, and an annoying azure with neon orange piping for the boys from Goldman Sachs. Aside from pure brokerage shops like Carr Futures and the enormous Man International, the investment bank brokers continued to get and pump out the biggest and most steady flow of influential orders, and we started watching them and what they did with a hawkish eye during the day. We needed to know what they were doing. What is it about the investment banks and what they do that made them the most important players in oil trade? We need to go inside the banks and understand just how they make money with oil to understand their rapid rise to preeminence.

Investment Banks Change the Game

Stock markets are the ultimate democracy—everyone gets their say on the value of any issue, voting on it with their bids and offers. Everybody's vote counts, and their opinions (and size of their wallets) are equally valid in creating a legitimate assessment of worth. In contrast, oil wasn't intended to be priced in a democracy; instead, the commodity markets were designed so that producers and end users could walk into a room, close the door, and argue over price with each other. That fight between physical participants alone was supposed to produce an honest price for oil. But when the investment banks entered into oil trading, the honest price for oil that the futures market was previously able to deliver to consumers and the world disappeared.

I'm not averse to making money off of oil trading: how could I be? I owe my life and my livelihood to the trading of oil with an edge, where I daily used my advantage of access to make money. Since the general stock market collapse and economic crisis of 2008, the investment banks have come under a fusillade of fire for their rapacious behavior in other markets, particularly in the neat tricks they managed in repackaging and securitizing mortgage notes into collateralized debt obligations (CDO) and with the huge expansion, trade, and dangerous activity surrounding Credit Default swaps (CDS). Oil, somehow, has missed the scrutiny of the media, which continues to shock me.

Maybe it's because the CDO market is connected to less-affluent people, with the advantage taken of them in sub-prime mortgages. When we see pictures of homes being locked up and foreclosed on by local sheriffs, we are naturally angry. When the camera swings to those less-than-savvy people whose homes were taken and lives destroyed by mortgage obligations their issuers knew they had no ability to repay, we immediately search for villains. *Who allowed this to happen?*

Similarly, when the federal government is forced to give close to $200 billion of taxpayer money to AIG to backstop bad bets in CDSs, we naturally ask: *How in the world could a financial instrument we never even heard of before put our entire financial system on the brink of failure? Who invented these things, and who is profiting from them?*

It's because these two formerly unknown financial instruments made such a mess and attracted such widespread attention that we were forced to learn about these markets and their dangers—dangers we never thought about or knew existed before. In contrast, oil trade inside the investment banks is far less known and admittedly much smaller than other, more famous markets; nonetheless, they have followed a similar trajectory: There's been a rapid increase in the creation and trade of complex derivative instruments and swaps, much like CDOs and CDSs.

The reason for this is obvious: They make a lot of money for the banks. And the more complex a product gets, the more potential profit gets unlocked. I'll begin to explain the workings of a few of these instruments and invented markets, how they look to service clients, and (without intending) how they move prices of oil in strange ways that are untethered to the fundamentals of supply and demand. But the similarity between the effect of oil derivatives and the other two more visible derivative markets (CDOs and CDSs) are ultimately the same: Money made in these markets ultimately comes out of the pockets of consumers and taxpayers. The outrage of common people toward Wall Street is understandable, and with oil, it's well-founded.

Over-the-Counter Oil Markets: Profit Drivers for Traders

When we look at oil prices on TV or in the newspaper, we're quoted prices from my old home, the NYMEX. But as already explained (in

Chapter 2), that price is for West Texas Intermediate (WTI)—which is a very specific grade of oil delivered to a specific place at a specific time. However, *in the real world*, pricing and slavery to that one grade of oil is not much practical use to anyone. There are literally hundreds of grades of crude oil, and both producers and end users don't necessarily abide by a once-a-month schedule for oil.

For all of those other grades, all those other delivery points, all of those other schedules, the over-the-counter (OTC) market was born (and as you'll read later in this chapter, I had my own encounter with the OTC oil market in one of my job interviews in the 1990s). It should be made very clear at the outset, of course, that *much of the OTC market in oil was invented and is sold, traded, and cleared by the investment banks*. So although the oil markets were always complex, it is only in the last several years that oil trade somehow needed the wide diversity of offerings this market now provides.

OTC contracts follow a similar pattern to regulated futures. If you understand the workings of futures, it's a small step to understand OTC derivatives. They are designed to be like regulated futures, with defined amounts, grades, delivery points, and price. But they describe different specifications than the benchmarks like NYMEX WTI and Intercontinental Exchange (ICE) Brent crude. They can be widely traded and more common, or specifically designed with many moving parts (although these are rarer). Many of the dozens of standardized OTC contracts are cleared through regulated exchanges like the NYMEX but more particularly ICE. But with the overwhelming majority, OTC contracts are bilaterally cleared meaning that the guarantee for delivery and payment on the contract rests solely and entirely on the two parties that enter into the contract, as opposed to the safer and more transparent general clearing pool of regulated commodities.

But no matter how complex or simple an OTC contract appears, there are two qualities they all share: they are almost all *cash-settled* as opposed to *physically settled*, and they all ultimately rely on a benchmark like the NYMEX WTI in order to price them. This is important and worth noting.

Cash settlement (a relatively new and brilliant invention) opens access away from our traditional, hands-on participant. A cash settlement means *there is no exchange of actual physical product* implied by the contract. Instead, there is an exchange only of money based on the cash market prices of products at the time of expiration. Because cash settlement doesn't ever involve necessary contact with obtaining or storing real oil, it has opened up the option of trading, investing, and speculating in oil to just about anyone with the necessary risk appetite and reasonable capital base. But the few and relatively remote numbers that can be culled to chart the astronomical growth in OTC oil contracts gives you a good idea of just how large the trading world of oil has become since these products were invented.

Investment banks do not provide data on the notional value of oil that they trade outside of the regulated futures environment. What we have seen reported are the daily average commissions on OTC contracts being cleared through the ICE screens. Remember, the contracts that are cleared here are the most common type, and are only sent through the common clearing mechanism of a regulated exchange because their access to credit for bilaterally cleared contracts is in doubt compared to the larger banks. Those that clear ICE are therefore the slush of the OTC world—the less-well-capitalized funds, traders, and banks. We know that no one would elect to clear at the ICE if able to keep the clearing fee themselves, and therefore we know that the amount of business transacted at the ICE is a tiny, almost insignificant fraction of the percentage and nominal value of oil being traded over the counter presently.

Still, that overflow of business has seen astronomical growth in the last 6 years: average daily commissions for ICE clearing on OTC contracts has grown from about $136,000 a day in 2003 to more than $1.11 million in 2008—an increase of more than eight times in five years. Can we guess at the real level of OTC trading in oil that's going on based on these thin numbers?

The Bank for International Settlement endeavors to track the growth of derivatives of all kinds, most notably for interest rate swaps, but it also collects information for the commodity space. Oil and oil products are not charted by themselves, but they are included in the nonmetals category, most certainly as its prime component, because oil is 20 times larger in notional value than the metals. An enormous growth in OTC swaps and options is seen in these figures, reaching an apex not surprisingly in 2008 of more than $12 trillion—not a shabby figure, considering that the total notional value of *all* swaps (outside of interest rate instruments but including credit-default swaps) was about 10 times that in 2008.

None of these OTC contracts exists in a vacuum (although the inventors and traders of them inside the investment banks wish they would). For every contract (OTC and otherwise) that passes through a desk at a bank, there's an advantage to be gained, either with a commission, fee, or just the knowledge of controlling the flow. Trading desks inside Morgan Stanley, JP Morgan, and Goldman Sachs would like nothing better than to initiate, clear, and retire every commodity contract themselves, if they could.

Investment Banks Want Control of the Oil Market

In fact, there has been a tacit war between the investment banks and the regulated futures exchanges since the investment bank-inspired OTC markets in oil began gaining traction at the turn of the twenty-first century.

The love/hate relationship certainly comes from both sides: Nothing disturbs the investment banking industry more than taking a possible piece of their profit model on derivative sales and trading and delivering a piece of that for exchange fees. And yet, they would be the first to grudgingly admit that they rely on transparently traded benchmarks like WTI and Brent crude in order to price their outside market and OTC products; the running tape of the NYMEX and ICE is on every oil trader's desk, regardless of what outside market they deal with. Without a benchmark with which to get at least an idea of their basis risk in specialized derivatives, they'd be flying (and trading) entirely blindly—with little clue on how to price the risk of the other oil markets they're covering.

From the exchange side, the war is as deeply intense: Although commodity centers like the CME know that the investment banks would like nothing better than to control the marketplace where benchmark oil products are priced, they are still publicly obsequious to those banks, which provide their greatest source of volume growth. They need them as fiercely, even though the banks mean them nothing but harm.

The ICE's roots and the cozy nature of their founding bank investors have always garnered suspicion from floor traders. To them, it is an incredible conflict of interest to have had a regulated exchange of OTC and futures products created under majority control by the investment banks. During its history, the CME has consistently butted heads with the ICE, both in its own growth and in its history of acquisitions. This is not just friendly competition, as these two exchanges specialize in different areas of the commodity sphere. Advocacy of the investment banks and other off-floor and large screen-based participants is represented better by the upstart ICE, while the longer established and more transparent CME is better represented by the more independent and smaller manager and trader. As both of these exchanges have fought for space in the expanding domestic commodity markets, they have often been at extreme odds with each other.

Goldman Sachs' Attempt to Buy the NYMEX

In 1998, the NYMEX also seemed an opportunity for conquest and only barely missed being bought out by Goldman Sachs directly. Gary Cohn, President of Sales and COO of Goldman Sachs (currently listed as the 56th largest global company on the *Forbes 2000* list), was then a member of the executive committee of the NYMEX, running the Goldman Sachs oil operation. Proving what incredible foresight he had for the future of oil trading, he brought a plan to secure a controlling interest in the exchange's clearing mechanism to the NYMEX board. He was very convincing at a time when oil trade's growth was hardly assured, and he retained support for the plan from then-Chairman Dan Rappaport. However, NYMEX members (being the independent traders that they are) rejected the idea without much consideration, despite the advocacy of their chairman. It was not an unusual reaction from exchange members, no matter how compelling the plan.

Of course, that independent instinct proved to be an incredibly smart one, because less than 10 years later, those members realized 20 times that amount for their seats (as I'll describe in Chapter 5). But since that moment when Goldman Sachs attempted to buy out NYMEX, members and traders continue to have tremendous suspicion of that house and many other large investment banks. As an ex-member and a potential victim, my biases are still largely intact. Goldman Sachs is, in fact, the devil to be feared—looking to control the planet, take every advantage, and keep all opportunity for itself.

The Creation of Energy-Based Financial Instruments

Oil followed the same pattern inside the plan of Goldman and other banks as with other expanding capital markets. Financial instruments were created and sold to add to the bottom line. Using the same models they had successfully used with interest rates and currencies, it was likely and obvious that oil would see the same kind of derivative penetration from the investment banks. Enron was the trailblazer, of course, showing the world how to have tentacles in every aspect of the energy market, then doing the investment banks (and the NYMEX as well) a tremendous favor by blowing itself up unnecessarily over accounting issues. (For a recap on the incredible rise and spectacular fall of Enron, see the sidebar.)

Enron-online (the Houston company's proprietary electronic platform for energy derivatives, including futures) was becoming a strong competitor to floor-traded oil futures long before CME's Globex system gained traction. Without Enron's timely demise, NYMEX market share would probably not have lasted until the November 2006 IPO. Certainly, it would have been massively weaker. In incident after incident, it seemed the markets at NYMEX continued to walk on water, timing their entry with luck, and watching competitors shoot themselves obligingly in the foot.

The Ultimate Model for Energy
Market Profiteering: Enron

It's worthwhile to briefly mention Enron, since the company will go down in history for some of the most blatant and wide-scale financial fraud ever committed by a major American corporation. Enron was also the major impetus for the Sarbanes-Oxley restrictions on corporate financial reporting: It will forever be known as the company that did the most miserably. Ken Lay, Jeff Skilling, and Andy Fastow were portrayed as the gang that couldn't shoot straight.

As I and the rest of my colleagues on the NYMEX witnessed the fantastic rise of Enron in the energy markets, we could only be frankly amazed—and frightened—by how much the company had gotten right.

In natural gas, Enron single-handedly turned a sleepy and physically scheduled and traded market into a totally financially driven, derivative marketplace based on sales to commercial customers. This change foresaw the future of commodities everywhere. Admittedly, Enron accomplished this by bullying—and with the incompetent, confused passivity of the Federal Energy Regulatory Commission (FERC). Still, Enron left an entire natural gas industry in its wake, gasping to catch up.

Enron added physical assets when it needed them to exert influence in markets, using an entirely different metric for their value. The growth potential or resources any asset could give you wasn't important; instead, that asset's value was proved only by its potential to help dominate and clean up on the trading floor. It was a brilliant plan to maximize profits, and you couldn't help but be impressed.

Once in power, Enron pushed through and was at the forefront of a totally manipulated deregulated power market in the West, particularly in California. Whether the company inspired the rolling blackouts in the Golden State in 2001 or simply took advantage of some very timely outages and tough weather, Enron's

(Continued)

**The Ultimate Model for Energy
Market Profiteering: Enron (*Continued*)**

traders were certainly smart enough to squeeze the most profit out of the trading situation as they could, at the expense of California consumers. They had created the market, put themselves at the very center of it, and were best situated to make the most money from any volatility that came along. Traders understand this, and we were envious of them and hated them.

Enron-online (E-online) was also the first honest stab at an electronic marketplace to replace the on-floor and telephone swapping of derivative contracts. It was a miserable platform, yet still became an immediate and enormous success. As a trader and seat owner at the premier energy derivative exchange in the country in late 1999 when E-Online debuted, I was personally petrified, and I know I wasn't alone. NYMEX seat owners tended to be myopic, but many of us could see where the e-online revolution was going, and going fast—toward electronic trading.

That Enron was so far ahead of everyone else in seeing this and having a viable and accessible platform made for an even more intense worry: that the industry and the market wouldn't wait for NYMEX or anyone else to catch up on the electronics; e-online was going to become the benchmark for derivative electronic trading and perhaps not so slowly start stealing our markets and our livelihoods from us. NYMEX rushed an incredibly inferior platform of their own to market—E-Nymex—but no one in the industry liked it (as I'll describe further in Chapter 5), and most seemed ready to convert their loyalties of many years over to the startup exchange in Houston and abandon us in New York.

And then, like a prayer being answered, Enron shot itself.

First, it extended itself into weirder and weirder markets, going full into the trading of bandwidth and then into an even more ephemeral idea of trading weather futures.

Then, analysts finally found some of the financial irregularities that the astronomic and steady growth of Enron (and Enron stock) should have made obvious and the crazy special investment vehicles that the company was using to hide all losses.

The Ultimate Model for Energy
Market Profiteering: Enron (*Continued*)

Also, California finally fought back in the power markets by capping costs by power marketers. I spent three years at NYMEX trying to bring this credit-ravaged national power market back to life by bringing power trading onto our regulated and cleared exchange from 2002 to 2004, but the players of the Enron-inspired power disaster and others in the Midwest had become gun-shy and reluctant. I had very limited success, although I helped to at least start the rebuilding of a fair and deregulated power market again.

We watched as Enron stock began to drop and then plummet. We cheered and made Enron jokes on the floor, wishing them all dead. Their traders were the most arrogant and the least liked. In less than three months in 2001, their stock traded from above 80 to the single digits, and most of their serious threats to our energy market dominance evaporated almost overnight, as shown in Figure 4.1.

We were saved.

But not because of anything we had done. Enron had seen the future, and except for some incredible hubris, Enron had seen it correctly.

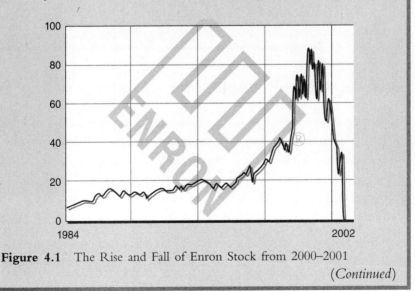

Figure 4.1 The Rise and Fall of Enron Stock from 2000–2001

(*Continued*)

**The Ultimate Model for Energy
Market Profiteering: Enron (*Continued*)**

The company is gone now, but it should be remembered not for its mistakes but for the model it set up to make big money in commodities:

Establish huge, seemingly free, and easily accessible markets that allow you unique freedom to the nexus—either by owning the platform or having faster and more complete access, or both.

Strive to make money not by making or selling energy, but by *trading* energy. Do the former only when it benefits the latter.

Do whatever you can to inspire those markets to move—violently. *Volatility is the key to superb profits.*

That Enron model served to educate other traders, particularly those at the investment banks, in how best to leverage their OTC energy access to make superior profits with less and less risk. It was only after that innovative Houston company showed the way that the big banks really started to generate fantastic revenues from oil by connecting the marketing and trading of energy derivatives. This is the real legacy of the Enron story: it's a blueprint for sweet trading yields and, for oil, financially derived prices.

How Investment Banks Make Money Trading Oil

So how do they do it? How do those great big banks like Goldman Sachs make so much money, a couple of billion per bank a year, in oil trading alone? To find out, let's follow one typical oil trade moving through the desks and try to see how they make their money.

Trading Oil at Morgan Stanley

No one has been more successful at taking advantage of the many different facets of oil trade as the U.S. investment bank Morgan

Stanley (MS). Indeed, it has been one of the very few financial oil players to penetrate the physical side of oil storage, which I write about in Chapter 6. It may look like I'm heaping it on to MS, even as the list of profitable banks and funds trading oil are legion, both here in the United States and elsewhere.

But I choose MS as this poster child for a specific reason: it is the best.

Inside the oil group at Morgan Stanley, separate desks take care of very clear divisions. There'll be one or more for retail and commercial brokerage of exchange-traded oil contracts. Several will be committed to exchange-cleared OTC products. Others will be committed to grades or specific products that have established participants, like jet fuel or diesel or Mars crude. There'll likely be a desk committed to the modeling of customized derivative products. And across all of these desks there'll be a group of traders, running the proprietary portfolios for the firm.

Let's start with a legitimate commercial client looking for a hedge: A trucking company trying to lock in diesel costs for its trucks for the next 12 months. The firm can fashion a perfectly specialized product for this client, including exact scheduling and location – and do it without charging any commission. The only fee will derive from the price that is offered and the profits the firm believes it can make from taking on the risk of the opposite side of this hedge and trading out of it. That position will now probably be converted into something that can be traded—a 12-month strip. (A strip is an average price of monthly prices over a quoted period.) Diesel strips will likely end up coming to the heating oil desk (because diesel is a distillate refined product, like heating oil, and the two trade very similarly). The heating oil strip, however, is very common, readily quoted, and active. Once our trader gets this position, the choices he has increase. First, he'll likely break down the trade into the 12 respective contracts that the strip represents. Then, he can hedge off any piece he thinks he can't easily profit from. He can buy a correlated month or two in the futures markets that will immediately offset that month's risk, or look to buy non-correlated months that he might think are undervalued and create spreads for portions of the 12-month trade. He can buy crude oil to create a crude/distillate crack trade. He can choose to offset his basis risk between the original diesel fuel and the heating oil contracts he has already bought; or choose to not offset it, if he considers the basis trade to be off-value. He could, of course, just stay short for a while and see how things go. But the point is, from this one order, looking to legitimately hedge one end-user's risk to diesel prices, 12 smaller orders are created, with perhaps 25 or 30 more trades before the position becomes even temporarily established in the trader's book. Every one of these smaller trades can spawn another or several offsetting or speculative trades as well—depending on who's on the other side.

The trader's art (as with all trading) is in keeping those pieces of highest perceived value, incompletely offsetting risk, and waiting for a market move when a more advantageous moment arrives to lock in a bigger profit.

The order flow from clients coming through the oil desks gives investment bank traders a huge edge in predicting short-term motion in oil prices, much like I could see more buying than selling enter the pit and convince me which side of the market was more likely to be profitable that moment or that day. One broker I know who works a specialized order desk in oil at Morgan Stanley grouses to me yearly about his bonus. "Do you know how much money I've made for my traders? Look what they give me!" he always says. I believe him. Every order passing through the desks is a risk, but also an opportunity to be captured. It's a great business.

And the numbers prove just how great. Oil traders at the big banks have been hugely successful at what they do, and although banks are close-lipped about specific oil trading profits, financial reports give a decent indication of how well they have done and how quickly their profits from trading have been growing. Morgan Stanley posts revenue from all commodity trading, but *The Wall Street Journal* estimates that fully 80% of commodity profits stem from oil. In the years from 2001 to 2008, Morgan Stanley reported these figures:

- from 2002 to 2008, the firm's commodity trading business climbed an aggregate 680%.
- only in 2007 did the figure decline year over year (I imagine from a very bad oil bet).
- but in 2008, Morgan Stanley righted the ship and earned close to $5 billion—an increase of 162% over the previous year, in a

market that reached an apex in July and fell precipitously from there—so obviously, Morgan Stanley's total commodity trading profits weren't entirely tethered to oil going *up*.

- Indeed, although year-end reports for 2009 are not yet available, first half profits have been declared at the trading division to be even "higher than a year ago," pointing to their best year ever.

Trading Oil at Goldman Sachs

Goldman Sachs is as secretive about its trading profits as it can possibly get away with, while still complying with reporting standards. Brad Hintz, the analyst at Sanford Bernstein, has done the most work on this, citing an average of 7% of total revenue deriving from oil commodity trade; the following estimates are Hintz's. When Goldman has chosen to cite trading revenue, we can use those to get some rough idea of how well the company has done in oil.

- In 2004 and 2005, Goldman made somewhere between $1.35 billion and $1.5 billion a year trading.
- In 2007, the estimate stood at $2.63 billion.
- In the magic year of 2008, Goldman refused to comment on oil trading profits, calling it instead "particularly strong."
- And in the first half of 2009, profits had topped $3.4 billion—again, *that's only for the first half of the year.*

Trading Oil at Phibro/Citigroup

Not all of these great traders have managed to stay under the radar, showing how nothing is too much when it comes to compensating talented traders who make a lot of money for the bank. Andrew Hall, a proprietary oil trader from Phibro, owned by Citigroup recently held out to be paid his previously negotiated bonus of more than $100 million. Hall is not your typical oil trader: His bets on long-dated options and physical trade of oil go beyond what most traders at most banks are normally capable of. Still, the standard 10% of profits bonus that great oil traders command at the investment banks shows just how much money even a single trader with great foresight or terrific luck can earn in a single year.

In fact, Citi's recent sale of Phibro to Occidental Petroleum (for a measly $250 million) was inspired by the public embarrassment of this one trader's outsized salary, in a year when Citigroup needed $45 billion of bailout money from taxpayers. Occidental has indicated that they believe Mr. Hall is worthy of these bonuses, and the company hopes he will continue to make big money for its new trading arm.

Phillip brothers—Phibro—was the first great proprietary group to enter the oil markets in the 1990s. Watching them from their beginnings, I and my compatriot independent traders shuddered on the floor as their enormous orders (the size of which would make the major oil companies blanch) would be fired into the rings. Their seemingly endless appetite for risk (and their uncanny ability to be right) proved just how large the potential profits from oil trading could be. That this great icon of oil trade could be sold for relatively so little money speaks of the embarrassment and shame that the industry must feel when the true size of their yearly take was publicly displayed, as in the case of Andrew Hall. But they are hardly alone.

It was Phibro first, but they were closely followed by Morgan Stanley and Goldman Sachs and the other major capital accumulators. Big money was being made, and everyone looked for a proprietary way to grow the market and take a piece. As the investment banks and proprietary traders dominated the markets, they left the old-time physical players in their wake. But no one wanted to be left out of this new profit waterfall, particularly those who had dominated trade before the invasion of the huge proprietary traders and OTC financial instruments—that is, the oil companies. Personally, I had three job interviews in the 1990s that showed me how fiercely they were fighting to keep control of markets they once owned and how outclassed they ultimately would prove to be, which I describe in the following sidebar.

Conclusion

Obviously, profits for the investment banks in oil trade are secretive for good reason: they're *outrageous*. Again, unlike equities, commodities cannot benefit everyone equally: for every winner there must inevitably be a loser—it is a zero-sum game. Inevitably, the losers in this game will be the industry participants who have bought into the need for risk management in energy from their friendly financial institutions. But more often, any increases in prices or costs associated with programs to control risk will be passed along to the real end users: the consuming public. Make no mistake, the lion's share of the bonus pools for the great oil traders in the big banks and commodity hedge funds is being paid by *you*, every time you fill your vehicle with gas.

Although trading profits are ultimately borne by consumers, they are hypercharged by an ever-increasing desire from investors to have a stake in the price of oil. Part III describes how access to the price of the crude barrel became widespread and, unfortunately for our economy, universally accepted.

"Oil?! You Can't Make Any Money in Oil!"

In the early 1990s, I had become really disenchanted with the futures world. Foolishly, I felt that my brain was entirely outsized for the tasks that I was performing on a daily basis—that is, to buy, sell, and capture pennies on spread calculations that a fourth grader could do—every day, day after day.

People find it hard to believe now, but between 1987 and 1995, the price of oil basically bounced around between $17 and $20 a barrel. Coincidentally, this was during the first eight years of my marriage. I had a new wife and two young children trying to make a go of it in Manhattan, where trying to make a living trading oil was tough, tough sledding.

I remember going to a family function during those flat market days early in my marriage, to an event hosted by one of my wife's relatives, who was a very successful attorney and real estate speculator—a real dealmaker. He had his own firm, a big apartment on Fifth Avenue, all the trappings I aspired to and imagined I was going to find when I began my career on the trading floor.

"What are you doing these days? Are you still in oil?" he asked me. I'm still not sure if he was trying to rub something in my face or not. More probably, I didn't even register on his radar, and he

(Continued)

"Oil?! You Can't Make Any Money in Oil!" (*Continued*)

was just checking his memory of me. I nodded my head yes. He smiled broadly at me and clapped me on the shoulder.

"Oil!?!" He laughed. *"You can't make any fucking money in oil!"* He was as sharp a guy as I've ever seen and was correctly summing up the last two or three years of my trading history pretty succinctly—and it hurt.

Of course, ultimately, he was wrong about the opportunities to be had trading oil, but at that moment in the early 1990s, boy, was he ever right. You couldn't make much fucking money in oil at all. I considered a career change.

In those days, the commodity/futures/derivative world wasn't moving very fast. There were some start-ups, some places that were looking to position themselves for the wave yet to come, and there were others still in the dark ages. I didn't stand on ceremony. I took every contact I had, worked the phones, and sent out a ton of letters and tried to find a fresh opportunity wherever it might be hiding. Not too much came out of the woodwork to greet my efforts. My personal reputation was fine, but the general reputation of floor traders, particularly floor traders looking to escape the floor, wasn't very good at all. We were (I think sometimes not unreasonably) labeled as baboons, cheeseburger-for-breakfast-eating, foul-mouthed, uneducated bums who would normally be turned out of taxi-driving school if we didn't have a trading floor to scream at each other on.

Because of this, any high-falutin' job I might want to pursue in Manhattan at any of the major investment banks and their burgeoning commodity divisions was definitely out. No Goldman Sachs or Morgan Stanley would touch a floor trader with a 10-foot pole for as much as fetching coffee. All the large investment banks had their own floor operations at the NYMEX and knew all of us far too well, I guess. Of course, this is where I really aspired to be: inside the white-shoe firms, where commodity trading wasn't spat on as the weaker sister to equities. I yearned for recognition inside the hallowed halls of Wall Street's titans, but my

"Oil?! You Can't Make Any Money in Oil!" (Continued)

resume gave me away to them. I quickly changed my tactics to look elsewhere for alternative employment.

I had written my resume and curriculum vitae in such a way to try and position myself as a risk manager—a laughable attempt to doll up what I was capable of doing coming from the floor and being mostly a scalping spread trader. Of course, in those days, the idea of risk management was really getting the airplay on Wall Street and elsewhere—for all the nonsense that such a position provided. Whether I was capable of structuring a viable (if unnecessary and costly) risk portfolio for anyone exposed to oil price movement is one item to think about (I *was* clearly capable of this), but moreover, I wonder now in retrospect why in hell I would aspire to *be* a risk officer in any capacity whatsoever. What would be the joy of being an ersatz actuary of price risk? I'm sure, if given that opportunity, I might have spent many years in a small dusty office, running options models and writing reports for corporate officers to throw in the garbage.

One early response to my letter writing came from a Natural Gas transport firm in Omaha, Nebraska. As I did some internet research on the firm and tried to understand what Warren Buffett found so damn wonderful about the place, I approached my wife with the idea of taking an interview there.

"Where?" She questioned.

"Omaha." I responded.

"Nebraska??" I nodded.

"Well, have a good time there," she replied only half-jokingly. "Just remember to send the checks to me and the kids in a timely manner."

I didn't bother taking the interview.

Of the many contacts I made during this time, only three of them came to serious interviews, and the story of each is interesting because they describe beautifully just how the oil markets were changing—how an old-school oil company was trying to compete

(Continued)

"Oil?! You Can't Make Any Money in Oil!" (*Continued*)

in the new-school Wall Street–influenced oil markets and failing, how a more modernly run oil company was making the transition successfully, and how the large and powerful new OTC markets in oil were accelerating these changes.

My Interview at Coastal, a True Texas Oil Company

I was never really sure whether I was serious about ending my career as a floor trader, but I sure thought about it a lot. But in the back of my mind, I always thought that the next month or the next year would bring that killer market in oil, the one that would get me clean. When I went to interview with Coastal in the summer of 1994, that market was at least seven years away. So if there were ever a good time to escape, I had found it. That was my one legitimate opportunity to get out of floor trading, and I was absolutely ready for it.

At that time, Coastal oil was an immensely successful independent oil company: it was engaged in all aspects of the oil business, both in natural gas (where it had started) but also in crude and crude products—exploration, transport, and refining, plus quite an extensive network of retail gasoline stations across the United States. It was a very impressive firm to have the opportunity to interview with, and when I was offered a chance to go to Houston and talk to the principals of the company, I wondered why they had any interest in a Jewish floor trader from New York. I was, after all, as far away from their corporate image and their history as anyone probably could be.

Coastal was from the old school of oil companies: Founded by Oscar Wyatt in 1955, Coastal had always gone in the aggressive direction that Wyatt wanted. As a former bomber pilot in World War II, Wyatt started Coastal with a small network of natural gas pipelines, but through aggressive and sometimes ruthless business practices, he grew the company quickly. In 1962, Wyatt purchased the assets of the Sinclair oil company, expanding from natural gas to become a fully consolidated oil player.

"Oil?! You Can't Make Any Money in Oil!" (*Continued*)

Some of the events in the history of Coastal marked Wyatt as a shrewd and vicious player and marked the company as a pack of lethal corporate wolves. For example, Wyatt disliked the prices he was receiving for fixed natural gas contracts in the 1970s as prices were rapidly increasing (remember those long lines at gas stations then?). In response, Wyatt shut off supplies that his subsidiary was contractually obligated to provide to San Antonio and Austin during the winter. While inciting the obvious rancor and lawsuits of the people of those cities, he also managed to renegotiate those contracts in his favor.

During the deregulation era of natural gas in the 1980s, Wyatt became a fierce corporate raider of distressed gas companies: he acquired Colorado Interstate gas, Belcher oil company, and American natural resources, to name just a few he targeted. Very few of these deals were greeted happily by oil insiders, although the stocks of the companies Coastal took over were some of the hottest on the street during those days.

Other issues emerged showing the independence and fearlessness of Wyatt and Coastal. In 1980, Wyatt pleaded guilty to crude price-fixing schemes. Despite State department bans on foreign trade, Wyatt inked oil deals with Libya and its rogue leader Muhammar Khaddafi in 1987. In 1998, Coastal was a principal participant in the suspicious oil-for-food deal with Saddam Hussein in Iraq (a case that still haunts the company in Federal Courts). Even in my cursory overview of the company as I prepared to fly down to Houston, I knew that the team that Oscar Wyatt had brought together were some mean sons-of-bitches who knew the oil game as well as anyone and better than most and let few competitors stand in the way of their success. I was petrified.

But I wasn't disappointed. The group uniformly reinforced almost every stereotype I had. In the day I spent interviewing with the four top officers of the company, I got a real taste for old Texas oil and their world and how vastly it differed from oil in mine.

(*Continued*)

"Oil?! You Can't Make Any Money in Oil!" (*Continued*)

I arrived at the Coastal offices and my first interview of any consequence was in the offices of Sam Willson, the VP in charge of Sales and Marketing (a euphemism for the trading division). Willson was one of the directors of the Libyan oil deal that had angered BP and other major oil companies, and he had been one of the defendants in a subsequent lawsuit brought against Coastal and its refining subsidiary Valero. That lawsuit was brought by none other than the Hunt brothers (of Hunt's ketchup, the same Hunt brothers who cornered the silver market in 1979), who claimed to have exclusive rights to Libyan oil based on a concession granted them by the Libyan government in 1957. In other words, the Hunts and the rest of old Texas oil didn't object to under-the-radar deals with rogue states in the Middle East; they just wanted their cut. Talk about your Texas oil soap opera, Sam Willson had lived it. Willson was as sharp as they came, pleasant on the outside and friendly. But I knew him as the architect of the fast-growing trading division at Coastal, a fearless and tireless worker who loved the business and his people. And everyone loved Sam Willson.

We talked for a while about my upbringing and education and time on the floor, and then he got down to the nitty-gritty: They were looking for some help in what he called more long-term strategies, which to me didn't mean anything at first but became clearer as the day of interviews went along. I was slow to understand what I was doing there and started pulling out charts with various technical indicators on them, trying to show my understanding of market dynamics. I must have looked the total fool.

Willson brought in his trading team, including his front shelf top trader, a good ol' boy in his 30s, who looked at me with disdain and questioned whether I had any idea of what it was like to be responsible for a book of many million barrels of oil every single day. He was right: I didn't have any idea, but I fought back his stares with smiles and an I'm-from-the-New-York-pits look that I thought convinced everyone in the room that I had some

"Oil?! You Can't Make Any Money in Oil!" (*Continued*)

experiences that *they* had very little insight into. Everyone outside of the principal officers looked at me with a what-the-hell-are-you-doing-here? look that I resented, but things were becoming clearer. That they even had time to bring me down and listen to me meant they were in dire need of help.

Next I was sent to meet Dave Arledge, who was then president of the company. For a brief moment in Arledge's office, I was even introduced to the man himself, Oscar Wyatt, but he quickly departed. Dave was clearly in the process of taking on many of Wyatt's responsibilities in the company (and in 1995, Arledge assumed the CEO role officially). Again, we discussed my background and history and again, Arledge referred to long-term strategies where a new voice was needed in Houston. I was just as puzzled by this reference as I was when Willson had said it, but one thing was for sure: The mere fact that I was meeting the founder and president of this huge company meant that there had been serious discussion about whatever role I was interviewing to fill.

Finally, I met Karl King, another vice-president, who clearly controlled much of the physical assets and their operation. I believe Mr. King had been a survivor from one of Oscar Wyatt's acquisitions and had stayed on after being bought out and folded into the mother firm. Even being 25 years older than I was, he was a daunting sight behind his desk. He was huge; his hands were still calloused, I imagined, from years of running cable through his own rigs; and he spoke slowly with a scowl and a typical West Texas drawl. I was afraid that at any moment he might spring from behind his desk and remove my arm from its socket just for fun. He looked easily capable of doing it.

During our meeting, King almost yawned: He was so clearly uninterested in my discussions of options trade and hedging strategies, even if he had no real clue. He continued to refer to options as insurance, an oversimplification of the strategies I had brought

(*Continued*)

"Oil?! You Can't Make Any Money in Oil!" (*Continued*)

to display. It was clear Mr. King was an old-school wildcatter from the 1950s, who entirely mistrusted anything coming out of Noo Yawk, as it applied to the oil business.

I finally gathered up a little courage and asked Mr. King a pointed question:

"Mr. King, I know you have a lot of crude and natural gas supply and refined products you need to account for. And I understand that you use the markets to help you manage those risks."

"Yah, we do.......that's right," he said.

"But one thing I don't understand, if I can ask—when is what you do in the market a HEDGE, and when is it a TRADE?"

His answer startled and educated me:

"Yah see, Dan...........when we sell 'em and they go up, that's a HEDGE. But when we sell 'em and they go down, that's a TRADE!"

Never has commercial trading in the guise of risk management been summed up more clearly.

But with that sentence, I had finally caught on to why I was there, what Coastal was looking for: The company just hadn't been able to keep pace with the changes in the oil markets, and it was being run over by the new financial products coming into the oil game. I had seen this time and again in small ways, but here was a huge behemoth of an oil company that had fallen into the trap that the entire oil industry was following.

These guys, all of them, had literally controlled the oil markets—cash, futures, forward, and retail trade. They had dominated and moved the markets at their beck and call. Because of this incredible advantage that they had stemming from owning assets and producing and marketing tangible products, they had continued to increase the trading parts of their operations. It took a decade, but trading started to dominate and in some ways overshadow their core businesses, particularly at Coastal. Their bottom line had depended more and more every year on the outcome from the trading desk, and the trading desk wasn't any longer just

"Oil?! You Can't Make Any Money in Oil!" (*Continued*)

hedging the supply and production that Coastal had. No, they were trading far more than just the assets that needed hedging.

Mr. King was telling me something, something that probably really burned him up. As an old-time oil man, King was suspicious about oil trading and resented that it had become such a big part of his company's strategy. In his mind, they were in business to find and process and sell oil, not trade it.

So he wasn't kidding me, he was being truthful and also sarcastic—those guys up there, those trading guys, they had the company's life in their hands, and it had nothing to do with the oil business as far as he was concerned: It was a hedge, or it was a trade—they decided as it suited them and on the basis of whether the position was a winner or a loser.

Despite suspicions of officers like King, for the last 15 years, the trading business was a terrific moneymaker for Coastal, and the early 1990s had been the best of those years. Sure, all the big consolidated oil companies had them, but Coastal was one of the few smaller independents that had purchased its own seats at the NYMEX. Coastal was deep into trading and was doing very well with it. After all, the only competition that Coastal had ever seen in its marketing and trading businesses had been with Chevron and Sun and Conoco/Phillips. On the floor where I worked, the story was the same during the 1980s and early 1990s: The paper being executed from BP and Hess was the most important paper and the most sought after by the brokers. But now the competition was increasingly coming from Goldman Sachs and Morgan Stanley, and that competition was fierce.

Now that things were changing in the market and the boys from Texas were losing some of their edge, the reliance that Coastal had on trading was really starting to bite back. Coastal's trading divisions were making far less. They were even starting to *lose* money. In 1992, sales and marketing racked up a $192 million loss. Three or four years after my interview there, Coastal became

(*Continued*)

"Oil?! You Can't Make Any Money in Oil!" (*Continued*)

a big story on the NYMEX floor as we heard that they had blown up in the natural gas pit. The exact amount of their losses wasn't ever known, but after that episode, Coastal shut down its New York floor operation.

It was a downhill run from there for Coastal—the company never seemed to be able to return to the core businesses that had made it successful. Finally, in 2003, Wyatt went back to his old formula and tried a hostile takeover for natural gas giant El Paso. Unfortunately, El Paso was on the very wrong side of the balance sheet at the time and represented an awful investment for Wyatt and Coastal. Coastal was ultimately folded into El Paso, where some of the same overtrading problems had seen their stock go from over $70 a share in 2001 to close to $3 in early 2003. (Similar stories were seen at other natural gas companies like Williams, which went from a $50 stock to a $2 stock.)

And Wyatt? He stayed true to form throughout the loss of his company and the loss of hundreds of millions of his own dollars on El Paso shares. In 2005, at 81 years old, Wyatt resisted arrest from eight Federal agents who knocked on his door to get him to court to answer for oil-for-food charges. He needed to be restrained against a wall and handcuffed. I can imagine that old wildcatter taking on eight guys each 50 years his junior. Sentenced in late 2007 to 18 to 24 months in jail, it's not clear how much time Wyatt (at his advanced age) served, but in early 2008, he was remanded to a halfway house and went back to his home because of good behavior. To this day, Wyatt fights the charges and tries to clear his name and maintains his own web site with updates about his perceived mistreatment in the oil-for-food case. What a fighter.

And me? I was glad, in retrospect, that I didn't get offered that job. I would have taken it and probably not lasted long: It was clear Coastal was looking for an antidote to the new competition at Goldman and Morgan. I would have failed utterly to find a new strategy to beat them and their increasing advantage. I thought I

"Oil?! You Can't Make Any Money in Oil!" (*Continued*)

saw the trend coming, and I would probably have advised Coastal to slow down the trade of the markets and get back to its core business. That wouldn't have satisfied anyone. In that moment, all the oil companies, but particularly Coastal, were in disbelief at losing control over the space that they had dominated for so long. "How could someone from Wall Street understand oil the way we do? We *are* oil." They just couldn't imagine it. And they didn't believe it until it was proven to them in the only way that mattered—on the bottom line.

Five subsequent years of losses in trading after I interviewed there convinced them in a way that I never could and ran them out of the trading business. For Coastal, it ran them entirely out of business. Other firms like Williams and El Paso barely survived.

And I went back to the trading floor.

Interviewing at Northville: Sell Oil? I'd Rather Trade It

I interviewed with Northville Gas in the late 1990s. Northville is a Long Island firm founded by a pair of brothers, Ray and Harold Bernstein, who had put together a formidable web of storage facilities and retail gas stations throughout Long Island and in other locations in New York, New Jersey, and Connecticut. Harold also happened to be a member of the Glen Oaks Country Club where my father-in-law was a member, and they had become decent friends. I never would have had any chance of an interview there without that connection.

Still, by the time I got into the offices of Northville, the old man had given up the reins to the family business to his son Jay—a real sharpie. The interview turned out to be mostly boring: Jay was just doing a courtesy at the request of his aging father, and he couldn't have been less interested in a floor trader of gasoline as an addition to his team. But I did learn a few things about his company that were hugely interesting.

It was clear that the trading bug had hit Jay hard, a lot harder than the old man had ever considered it would become part of

(Continued)

"Oil?! You Can't Make Any Money in Oil!" (*Continued*)

his company. Northville's interests and insight into the gasoline cash markets were huge, particularly in the New York–delivered cash markets that the NYMEX benchmark served. While the energy futures markets had exploded in the late 1980s and into the 1990s, Jay had figured out how that insight could translate into trading profits. In those days, the cash market still controlled, to a very large degree, the movement in futures prices. More buyers or sellers of physical gas would inevitably send marketers into the futures markets directly connected to New York gasoline delivery to hedge price risk. Prices in those days had to converge from the futures to the physical market, and cash deals that Bernstein at Northville was seeing negotiated, both with him and around him, were telling him of oncoming trends that were yet to be reflected in the futures pits.

Of course, the money that could be made trading gas with this kind of an edge reflected a terrific return on capital, with far less effort than the traditional marketing, transport, and retail sales business ever could. The temptation must have been overwhelming, and Jay was clearly succumbing to it.

In other words, Northville was quickly changing from an oil company to a trading company.

In front of Jay Bernstein, I pulled out my charts and discussed my experience and insight into the gasoline market from my vantage point of the pits. In retrospect, it must have been hard for Jay to keep a straight face through this performance. Here I was pulling out astrological talismans to help divine the coming trend in prices while he had direct access to inside proprietary information from a closed clubhouse marketplace where he was one of the few invited participants. He was probably too bored to laugh at me. To give me a job there would be nothing but a favor. In regard to the business he was doing, I had very little to add.

I walked out that day disappointed, because I knew that Northville would be making a lot of money over the next few years, and I followed their trajectory as best I could. Over the next

"Oil?! You Can't Make Any Money in Oil!" (*Continued*)

few years, Northville either sold or retired all of its retail gasoline stations, until I couldn't find a single one of those blue-and-white signs on Long Island anymore. Did the retail gasoline business become too difficult to manage? Did the profit margins on it shrink? Those stations had been the backbone of the operation that the old man had created through the 1960s and 1970s.

A few years after I interviewed there, Northville also gave up the sponsorship of its annual Northville Classic golf tournament, a senior tour event held at the tony Meadowbrook Country Club, which had been Jay's pet project. Northville did retain its tank farms and Panama refinery, but it was clear that Northville's resources were being overwhelmingly committed to trading the markets.

As the markets further changed and the cash markets no longer impacted the futures markets directly, I'm sure that Northville's trading profits suffered. I wondered whether the company ever regretted disbursing its retail operations when the trading waterfall stopped flowing. I cannot name an independent retail gasoline operation that survives either locally or nationally anymore, so I doubt that Northville's stations would have survived either, even if the company had chosen to keep them. Northville has had continued success, so I can't argue with its business decisions.

But for me, that meeting was the closest and most real example I got of oil companies that were tempted by the siren song of trading to change their business plan and change the nature of the oil markets with it.

Interviewing at the OTC Brokerage House that Couldn't Care Less about the Price of Oil

One day during my job search in the 1990s, I received a phone call from an operation in New Jersey looking to talk to me. This was great news. They were local enough that my wife could hardly complain—the worst case would require a moving van to

(*Continued*)

"Oil?! You Can't Make Any Money in Oil!" (*Continued*)

go across the Hudson River. I scheduled an appointment and interview.

I arrived at a nondescript office plaza in a tony section of Northern New Jersey and entered a five-story office building. The firm I was interviewing with occupied the entire fifth floor. As I entered, there was no mistaking that this was a successful operation: there were leather wing chairs everywhere, a number of television monitors on the walls all tuned to the financial news networks, and a couple of offices set apart from the main trading floor. This trading floor wasn't at all like the one I was used to: Instead, it was broken up into several cubicles, but with at least one common open section so that each trader had easy access to the central space. Each cubicle was populated with the latest Bloomberg terminal (the finest electronic information source for markets in its day), a multi-line telephone system, and a personal fax machine. I sat down with the principal of the firm, intending to interview on some sort of risk control position. I was entirely wrong as to the nature of the interview.

We spent about 20 minutes talking about my experience on the floor and particularly my contacts off of it. We went through some personal aspects, and I asked some generalized questions about the office I was in and the partnerships and structure of the firm, but I was careful not to expose my ignorance as I still had absolutely no idea what kind of business their firm was engaged with. At that point, the president invited a trader and another partner into the room, and we went through some of the same questions. The trader started to discuss with me the nature of his day, and it became slowly clearer to me what business they were engaged in. They were one of the few, but quickly growing, ranks of OTC brokerages starting to spring up on the backs of more viable commodity markets that had been growing through the late 1980s and into the early 1990s.

OTC products refer to any kind of contract that isn't covered by a standardized product on the regulated exchanges. In oil, the

"Oil?! You Can't Make Any Money in Oil!" (*Continued*)

amount of notional value in the OTC markets was quickly swamping the amount of trade in the regulated markets that I was familiar with. And to a large degree, the growth of OTC contracts made a great amount of sense. These kinds of derivatives had emerged from the credit and currency markets, largely to take advantage of (or more probably avoid) some unique national tax obligations in your home country. As with all things financially created out of the ether in the genius of the modern financial world, these vehicles started life with a positive effect in mind; it was only later that they gained Frankenstein life and variations that sunk our collective economy through 2007 to 2009. The early currency swap derivative products accomplished great things. In essence, if you were trading goods across the globe, many of these products served to generate positive tax results and therefore stronger earnings results while simultaneously avoiding many national obligations. (The morality of avoiding tax liabilities while opening up international trade is for another book and another author.) Early swaps, the first kind of OTC products, found many ready and enthusiastic customers. And the enthusiasm of customers willing to pay a premium for the simplest of these instruments inspired every investment bank to start new divisions to create, market, and, of course, sell these products to waiting customers. A whole new world of financial engineering emerged to offer fresh products to a brand new type of commercial investor.

The craft of structuring these products remained inside the currency and fixed-income markets for years before suffusing into the commodity markets and into oil where I was sitting. But when these products found their way into the commodity and the oil world, they emerged with a vengeance. I was well aware of the existence of these products and the kind of customer they were designed to entice, but this was my first direct contact with that quiet, dark world. Actually, I should be much fairer about it: I had entirely discounted the effect of the OTC market when it first

(Continued)

"Oil?! You Can't Make Any Money in Oil!" (*Continued*)

emerged in commodities. And in oil, by the time I interviewed with that brokerage in New Jersey, interest and volume in OTC products was ramping up at a staggering pace.

In many cases, as with the simple currency swaps from which they were descended, these customized oil derivative products made a lot of sense, at least at the outset of their introduction, and this is why: At the NYMEX, we traded three contracts in the energy market—West Texas Intermediate Crude (WTI), New York Harbor Heating Oil, and New York Harbor Leaded Gasoline (yes, still leaded in those days). The names should immediately tip you off to the necessity of a secondary derivative market in oil.

While the NYMEX unquestionably traded the benchmark pricing mechanism for crude, the absolute price that was represented on the board reflected a very small actual market in reality: WTI prices quoted on the NYMEX refer only to a pretty rare grade of sweet crude named for a small patch of ground in West Texas where it was most readily available, and to a specific delivery point for those barrels of WTI crude oil in Cushing, Oklahoma. In no way could the pricing on this one product be the ultimate benchmark for price on the hundreds of other grades transported and used to the hundreds of other end points for delivery for the complex domestic crude oil marketplace. Clearly, this one product could not possibly be sufficient to take care of the hedging needs of every participant involved in the oil markets in the United States, much less worldwide.

There are, in fact, more than 3,000 grades of crude listed in most databases on the stuff and of those, few of them are of the sweet variety that we traded in New York. These other grades traded, or were more commonly just bought and sold on the cash markets closest to their specific delivery point, just as WTI was delivered and sold at Cushing. To understand the price relationship between different grades of oil delivered from various ports to even more diverse end users requires an understanding of basis. But the

"Oil?! You Can't Make Any Money in Oil!" (*Continued*)

relationship in price between grades at their delivery points was, for a large portion of the history of oil sales, a fairly constant number.

To give a rough example, West Texas Crude delivered in Cushing, the recognized NYMEX benchmark was about $5 more expensive than, let's say, Gulf Coast-delivered Mars crude. If this were a difference in price you could always depend on, you could limit yourself to trading WTI futures prices and discount your costs forever by $5 and have a perfectly logical and reliable hedge. However, while the price risk exposure of oil in general moving up and down was the greatest risk to have to bear, the risk you took on between a benchmark like WTI and whatever other kind of oil you really depended on (called a basis risk) wasn't at all insubstantial.

This is a simple example, but it describes the need for a third party (most often an investment bank or quick dealing oil group) to come in and help you manage your basis risk. There were other risks to be managed, of course, if you were the CEO of a company dumb enough to have hired your own new-fangled risk manager who was pushing these products on you—the type of risk manager, of course, that I was looking to become and thought I was interviewing for at this office in New Jersey.

It quickly became clear to me that this very successful outfit in New Jersey was not in the slightest interested in basis risk—it didn't even care about the price of oil. Its sole purpose and means of income was in matching participants in this fast growing market of OTC products. Some of these products were standardized, like the WTI/Mars basis swap I described—and there were a lot of players interested in these products. Others were far less standardized and required a custom product to fill a specific need a client might have. It didn't matter. This group I was interviewing for a position with didn't have any desire to assume any risk, or write any contract. It merely wanted to charge a matching commission for putting together trades.

(Continued)

"Oil?! You Can't Make Any Money in Oil!" (*Continued*)

Even more surprisingly, it became clear that they cared even less about how well I understood the products that they were matching. In my conversations, no one bothered to quiz me about the nature of OTC swaps or what I understood about basis risk. Only two factors seemed to matter to them: How deep were my contacts off of the floor, specifically to the investment banks and even more important, how strong were my sales techniques. It was clear that no real trading was going on here. Instead, brokers were hard dialing: calling their contacts in the investment banks, other brokerages, oil and transport companies, and retail customers every single day and searching for trades to match. Sometimes, matching required some serious convincing of clients that prices were about to move and the protection you were buying was a fleeting opportunity that would sink you tomorrow if you missed the boat. Convince a client, call the opposite side upstairs at the banks, push faxes from both parties into the brokerage, and send out the bill. Of all of these steps, convincing a client of the dire necessity to lock down his risk was the most important part of the process.

That I had had absolutely zero exposure to this type of work didn't seem to bother the principles of the firm one iota: In fact, even after I demonstrated that my contacts to the risk takers upstairs at Morgan Stanley and Goldman Sachs were weak, they still had great enthusiasm for me because I demonstrated that I could readily talk the talk—in other words, I could convincingly use the jargon to sell products that clients (mostly end users) didn't really need or want.

Also, it was a small risk for them to take, particularly on me, because their business was almost entirely commission-driven. They paid for your desk and phone system and gave a subsistence wage to keep you alive for the first few weeks. After that, it was all up to you and how hard you could work the phones. The system was simple: sell more, make more.

I walked out of the interview knowing I couldn't take the job but also knowing that someone would subsequently make a pile

"Oil?! You Can't Make Any Money in Oil!" (*Continued*)

of money at it. It was a business that was rapidly expanding, and these guys were hiring at the right time. Indeed, PVM Associates, where I interviewed that day, has become the world's leading OTC broker of oil. But I was a trader, not a salesman. So I again went back to the trading floor.

Looking back on these job interviews, it seems I caught them at inflection points in the oil market: Every interview I took signified an important event in the changing of those markets, and the companies I interviewed with were searching for answers in coping with those changes.

Chapter 5

Increased Access to Trading Oil

The Trading Floor Goes Online

I t was of course inevitable that electronic networks would replace the trading floor where I traded oil for so long. It might have been inevitable, but for the sake of our economy, it has also been regrettable. The crazy swings and unfathomable prices we've seen for oil since 2003 have been all about *access*—fantastic increases in the total number of participants and amounts of money able to get at and bet on oil. Electronic access to futures markets, which replaced floor execution, leveled the playing fields for individuals who wanted to trade commodities. *You* can now access futures markets today in just the same way as I can, and except for the experiences I've had as an oil trader, you are equally equipped to trade them as I.

But just because you're as well equipped as I am doesn't mean you should download some software, open an account, and start trading oil. No, leveling the playing field has perhaps closed the trading gap between us, but it has undoubtedly also widened the gap between me and the traders at the derivative desks at the banks as well as the traders monitoring the algorithmic black box programs at dedicated energy hedge funds, snapping off hundreds of trades every second. You'll get no debate from any individual trader who's old enough to have dealt in both venues: The floor provided opportunity and edge, while the screens have given almost all the opportunity and certainly every bit of an individual trader's edge away to others. *I hate the screens.*

On the first full year that I traded off of the floor and attempted to make a living exclusively from screen trading, I mapped my time and results pretty closely. The results were discouraging: I spent almost 50% more time monitoring my positions while trading about 12% of the volume I had regularly traded while on the floor full time. My bottom-line results were pretty dismal for the extra effort. I made only about 15% of the money I had averaged while on the floor in my last five years there. So I spent more time, did less volume, and made a lot less money. For me (a typical floor trader moving to the electronic world), the progress of our markets going overwhelmingly electronic wasn't helping me in my trading one bit, and I assume will treat you even more poorly. If there's one thing to gain from this story for yourself, it's *don't trade oil;* in a new electronic world, you are more likely than ever to be fodder for smarter traders with faster machines and better information.

Traders Lose ... But the Exchanges Gain

But electronic access has made the exchanges gleeful. Volume for the exchanges that were fully electronic and offered access to anyone with a futures account and an internet connection grew at rates that were difficult to imagine. Each year, the Futures Industry Association (FIA) maps volumes for domestic and international derivatives exchanges and reported its findings in its celebratory year-end report: check out Figure 5.1.

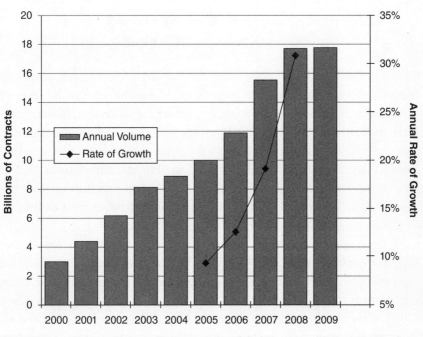

Figure 5.1 Shooting Upward: Growth in Global Futures and Options Trading, 2000–2009
SOURCE: Futures Industry Association (FIA)

Where was all of this new volume coming from? Every traditional participant I knew of who needed access to oil futures for true hedging of positions or risk management of large exposure to oil prices had been engaged in the markets for years prior to this. It was clear that easy access to oil price trading was creating a new, less traditional participant in the oil market, a participant encouraged to bet on future prices by a mechanism that was becoming as easy to tap as other, more traditional capital markets like stocks and bonds had been. As Figure 5-1 shows, the total volume of contracts traded on all exchanges increased fivefold in the four years between 2004 and 2007. Even in 2008, with bubbles exploding in all of the major markets, commodity and derivative trade still managed to register an increase, although at a more modest 13.7%. Only one factor can account for such rapid-fire expansion and incredible rates of growth: *electronic access.*

Electronic Access Was Spawned by the Intercontinental Exchange

The most astounding example of the power of electronic access in the oil markets capable of tapping this new participant can be seen in the incredible growth and continuing influence of the Intercontinental Exchange, aka the ICE. In 2000, Jeffrey Sprecher, a chemical engineer and race car enthusiast, recognized the underexploited power of electronic platforms and devised a bold plan. He assembled some of the largest energy trade participants in the world, including Morgan Stanley and Goldman Sachs, and he convinced them of the possibilities of a fully electronic marketplace in oil derivatives.

These investment banks became the founding shareholders of the ICE. Before that time, most of the trading in over-the-counter (OTC) oil products was accomplished using hardwire telephone and telex transactions (akin to the mechanisms I saw at the PVM associates office I interviewed with in New Jersey, which I described in Chapter 4). But through the new technology, putting quotes through internet servers and allowing matching online increased speed and efficiency immensely—and volume began to skyrocket.

But Sprecher did not want to limit himself to the OTC markets. In 2001, he purchased the International Petroleum exchange (IPE), a London-based energy exchange specializing in Brent crude futures (a sweet crude grade common in Europe) and gas-oil, a distillate-like product (closely related to the NYMEX traded #2 heating oil). The IPE was a floor-based exchange, like the New York Mercantile Exchange (NYMEX), but the IPE's participants (before they were bought by ICE) were localized, and their volumes never threatened to be a serious competitor to the NYMEX.

When Sprecher took over, all that changed. Although he had promised to protect the floor-based operations and the floor traders there in order to secure the merger, his long-term plan began to emerge: The ICE would be bringing its electronic platforms to trading of exchange-cleared oil contracts, while the IPE would contribute its established clearing operation: LCE-Clearnet.

It wasn't an instant success. Oil traders are creatures of habit, and most had long and good relationships with the brokers who looked after and executed for their accounts. But slowly and surely, habits began to die. Participants who were, in general, suspicious of the floor welcomed the transparency that the screens began to give. On the screen, you never had opportunity to complain about a bad fill or a miscommunication or an outright human error. Costs got cheaper.

Interest in commodities, and particularly oil, was growing. There wasn't anyone who was newly entering the energy space, whether a hedge fund manager, individual trader, or commercial risk manager who saw an advantage to the floor-based mechanisms and opted in almost all cases to trade online if that option was available. Volume numbers for the ICE measured the pace of their success.

- In 2001, when the ICE first began offering Brent and gas-oil trading online, total volume for futures and options exceeded 24 million contracts.
- By 2005, when the ICE finally completed its transformation of the IPE and closed the floor entirely, becoming an exclusively electronic exchange, volume exceeded 41 million contracts—an increase of more than 70%.

Electronic trading in OTC contracts (which had been the ICE's previous strength) increased similarly.

By way of comparison, take a look at the numbers for NYMEX, which was still the dominant exchange in energy trade.

- In 2001, the NYMEX amassed a total volume of 72 million contracts (compared to ICE's 24 million).
- By 2005, that volume increased to 112 million—a very healthy 54% increase (again, compared to ICE's 70% increase).

Still, it was clear that electronic trading was gaining its proponents. And it was getting more and more difficult to continue to make a case for growth of floor-based trading–online seemed to hold the future.

In 2006, the ICE and Jeff Sprecher took its most direct shot at the NYMEX and its preeminent role in energy trading: It listed an almost exact-lookalike West Texas Intermediate (WTI) contract in February, to be traded exclusively electronically and cleared overseas at London Clearing House (LCH). In New York, traders on the floor met this announcement with skepticism. During the long history of commodity contract listings, many exchanges had tried to wrest control of key contracts from others. It had been tried with New York financial futures competing with benchmarks in Chicago and with Chicago Gold contracts competing with Comex benchmarks in New York. In all cases, finding a foothold in an already established commodity and moving customers away to a new exchange had proven almost impossible. So no one believed that the ICE experiment in WTI would be any different.

But they were wrong.

In the first year, ICE WTI registered more than 28 million traded contracts. In 2007, ICE almost doubled the figure, trading more than 51 million WTI contracts. NYMEX volumes during these years did not decrease, and it is still unclear whether ICE managed to take market share away from the NYMEX or merely created a fresh market of its own.

What became immediately clear, however, was that a community of online traders and managers was forming that would not ever consider trading using an archaic floor-based system. ICE WTI became, and still is, the only contract of a lookalike in commodities on record to have succeeded in tandem with another, already established benchmark. In 2008, NYMEX WTI traded 134 million contracts, whereas the ICE WTI traded a very significant 51 million itself.

NYMEX didn't entirely take this onslaught lying down. It fumbled during these years with an electronic platform of its own, which it called E-Nymex, but most traders didn't like it. It hardly mattered, because NYMEX was still committed to its floor traders and could not easily allow the same fate to its floor community as had happened to the floor traders at the IPE under the Sprecher plan. During those years on the floor in New York, the common question among traders was how much longer the party would last: Although it was clear that floor trading would lose its preeminence in the end, most traders overestimated the longevity of their trading futures.

Personally, I didn't think being an individual trading local on the floor had much more time to it by the end of 2005, but many others still imagined five or more years lay ahead. Despite the experience of other exchanges that had begun full conversion to electronic trade, many at NYMEX thought oil was different, with a clientele that somehow would continue to prefer the floor for its execution.

The NYMEX leadership followed the wishful thinking of its members in policy. In 2004, NYMEX actually mounted an offensive of its own and tried to invade ICE territory by listing a floor-based Brent Crude contract after the closing of the IPE London floor, imagining that there was a group of participants who still preferred going to a floor to execute their trades. It was a smashing failure.

As NYMEX supported its floor system, ICE and Sprecher did all it could to strategically delay New York's entry into the online marketplace. Every month that went by saw ICE gain stronger volume and participant support, while the NYMEX continued to cling to a mechanism rapidly becoming obsolete, at least for futures, if not for options on those futures.

How Online Access Increased the Volume of Oil Trading

It was not until the inevitability of online trade could no longer be denied that the NYMEX finally engaged with the Chicago Mercantile Exchange (CME) to list its products electronically on the CME's state-of-the-art Globex platform in June 2006, giving participants a real choice of the floor or the screen. The CME had been significantly less myopic than the NYMEX with regard to technology: The CME had invested years and millions of dollars in developing (and continuing to update) a proprietary online matching system, which was the envy of the commodity world. The CME had offered the option of online trade in many of its own products, allowing trade to migrate to the screen if participants expressed a preference for it, and protecting the floor products in other cases. Commodity desks were familiar and comfortable with Globex, and most had used it confidently for other CME products. Managers and traders welcomed the familiarity of the platform and embraced the switch when energy products from the NYMEX were migrated to it. With Globex, the hemorrhaging of energy market share to the ICE was stopped, although ICE's foothold in exchange-traded and cleared energy products could no longer be prevented.

The quick ICE penetration into the energy markets proved just how powerful technology and the internet could be in changing the nature of commodity trade. The mechanisms for trading oil became easier for everyone. In the old days, if you wanted to trade oil and you weren't on the floor like I was, you needed to open a specialty commodities account with clearing privileges in the major exchanges. In addition, many of those clearing accounts didn't have direct brokerage access, so you also needed to create a relationship with an oil broker, who acted as a go-between to the floor or had memberships and had dedicated people for order execution. Finding good relationships that you could trust could be very difficult, and complicated paperwork and disclosure documents met the initiation of a dedicated commodity account. Commodities were a dark world. Well-known stock brokers to the retail public didn't bother with commodities—the interest just wasn't there. Familiar and comfortable retail stock names, like Smith Barney and Merrill Lynch, didn't exist on the commodity sell side. Instead, potential customers who wanted to trade commodities were forced into new relationships with less familiar names like Sempra and Heinhold.

The Party's Starting and Everyone's Invited

But widespread electronic access to oil and other commodities changed the game. Software platforms to access electronic markets began to be developed, and the number of good ones increased. Major retail brokerages began making alliances with smaller commodity brokers to offer commodity trading to anyone—you need not leave your favorite broker in order to execute futures orders, most often using the same account as you used for stocks. Matrix trading screens that appear almost exactly for commodities as they are presented for stock quotes went a long way to making stock managers and stock day traders more comfortable with trading oil.

In the early days of online trade, most of us relied on one platform from TT Technologies, still a benchmark for interfacing with Globex matching engines and trading the screens. But competition emerged. Currently, anyone can access futures markets using the same online platforms offered by many of the largest online stock brokers, including E-trade, Tradestation, and Interactive Brokers.

Access to commodity trading became as easy as access to stock trading. For a marketplace that was quietly trading among its own, even a small increase of participants from the gigantic world of equities made for astounding growth. Nobody questioned this kind of growth, of course.

For commodity exchanges, it was the ultimate dream. They moved from small localized businesses to become powerful sisters to the much larger and more visible equity exchanges like the New York Stock Exchange (NYSE) and the American Stock Exchange (AMEX).

It got even better. Compared to those behemoths (the NYSE and AMEX), commodity exchanges had an overwhelming advantage over the stock exchanges they chased, because customized derivative contracts weren't easily threatened by competition. As the advent of internet-based trading began to take hold at all of the major exchanges, the equity exchanges faced much more difficult threats to their survival. With equities, a share of Citibank stock (for example) is the same, whether it's exchanged in London or New York or Tokyo. Therefore, the advent of electronic access forced big stock exchanges to battle upstart exchanges and Electronic Communications Networks (ECNs) for trading business constantly.

In contrast, commodity futures, created with obtuse specifications and delivery directives, were much more difficult to recreate. NYMEX oil (the recognized benchmark) was a 1,000-barrel West Texas intermediate grade delivered after the 25th day of the month in Cushing, Oklahoma. Something that specific proved impossible to recreate at another competitive exchange.

So when electronic access exploded, the increase in access to oil trade (at least to exchange-traded contracts) benefited the NYMEX and ICE exclusively. For the stock exchanges, the result was different. Surely, increased electronic competition in stocks helped permanently cripple the former archetype AMEX exchange during this time.

For shareholders of commodity exchanges, increased access and unprecedented growth meant unbelievable share appreciation. The Chicago Mercantile Exchange moved from a member exchange to become a public company in December 2002, listed on the New York Stock Exchange. Its initial public offering (IPO) debuted at $35 a share—and 25% to 35% volume growth for the next several years hoisted the stock price to incredible levels. In December 2007, CME reached its peak, at more than $700 a share, *an increase of 2,000% in only five years.*

Similarly, when the NYMEX finally IPOd, in November 2006, its IPO price was $48 per share (believed to be a very rational price), but on its first day, it traded in the range of $120 to close to $150 a share. In its relatively short life before merging with the CME, NYMEX shares often sported price-earnings (P/E) ratios over 60—normally the stuff of only the most speculative growth start-ups.

Access and growth in commodities, particularly oil, had the most spectacular effect on floor traders like me—especially if, like me, you were a floor trader who *owned* (rather than leased) a seat and therefore had an interest in the exchange. We watched with incredible envy and (at least for me) a great bit of disbelief, as the astronomical growth played out with already public commodity exchanges like the CME and the ICE. We knew our turn would inevitably come, but we could have never imagined how perfect our timing of becoming public ourselves would turn out to be.

Of course, that timing was entirely lucky, spurred mostly by incompetence and almost incestuous infighting among member groups that alternately delayed and threatened to derail the IPO process. Every mistaken turn that the NYMEX took, it now seems in retrospect, helped to place the public offering of our exchange at the most opportune time for us. For insight into how that affected seat owners and me personally, read the following sidebar; on the other hand, if you're eager to understand why oil traders don't care about the price of oil (and why *you* shouldn't either, as an investor) you can skip to the conclusion of this chapter, which leads into Part II.

Electronic Access to the Oil Markets Actually Made Me a Fortune (The Real Money in Trading Oil Came from Selling My Seat on the Exchange)

Becoming public marked the beginning of the end for many of us as floor traders. As the markets went exclusively electronic, I and the rest of my friends on the floor quickly lost our trading advantages. It became very clear that trading oil as an individual—a career I had held since 1982—was disappearing quickly, never to return. It bothered me, because I saw ever-increasing price ranges and enormous volumes in crude oil, which had always signified fabulous trading for me in the past. But I had the luxury not to have to fight this frustration of phantom opportunity too hard, because I owned my seat on the exchange and because NYMEX was going public. In fact, I began to worry quite a bit more about my stock than my daily positions on the floor, as the migration of volume from the floor to the screen really began in earnest in 2007.

Of the 816 seats outstanding at the exchange, more than 500 were held either by members actively trading on their seats and earning their livelihood from it or another huge class of equity owners who leased their seats on a monthly basis to other active traders and brokers. Both classes had one obvious and overwhelming request of the exchange and its administration—the maximum possible profit.

We had a very basic but uncannily true measure for the value of the memberships: For many years, the seat was approximately equal to the average trading income of the median local on the floor. For almost the first two decades on the floor, the seats themselves were hardly a commodity in short supply or even sought after by most of the traders engaged with oil. Few considered them an asset worth having and keeping just for the investment value.

To tell the truth, neither did I.

There had always been two classes of traders on the floor: those who *owned* seats and those who rented them. I was a renter first,

(*Continued*)

Electronic Access to the Oil Markets Actually Made Me a Fortune (The Real Money in Trading Oil Came from Selling My Seat on the Exchange) (*Continued*)

then an owner. I entered the floor in 1982 on a leased seat from a wonderful old woman named Ethel Jacobson whose husband had been one of the very earliest men on the exchange. Seats in those days leased for $400 a month and sold for less than $50,000, an 8.5% return for leased seats that was a consistent benchmark. When I chose to buy a seat instead of continuing to lease, it was a decision borne more out of convenience than great financial acumen: I had had a particularly good year, and I was rather annoyed at having to mail out a rent check at the end of every month.

Owning a Seat on the NYMEX Wasn't Always Desirable
Decades ago, other exchanges (particularly those in Chicago) seemed to be far more developed and profitable for traders. Many of us wondered if oil would continue to be a worthy commodity to invest our skills in, or if it might die away. I was probably stuck in New York, but many of the traders figured they'd go where the money was—whether it was in oil or gold or grains or financial futures. I knew a few guys who held a mixture of leased and owned seats on a number of exchanges, including some in Chicago. They'd be on the plane, perhaps spending a few weeks or a month or more out there if one pit got especially active. Most of these guys didn't have wives, and I did.

But the point was financial: If oil were to get hot at some point, yes, the seats were sure to appreciate. But if they appreciated, so would the opportunity to make money trading oil in the pit. If you were a swashbuckling trader just chasing the action, why would you anchor yourself to one place where you weren't sure of the future prospect? You wouldn't. Many traders I knew just did the math: *"If I can make a million dollars a year trading oil or anything else, what problem do I have paying $25,000 a month to lease a seat? I don't."* This was precisely the rationale that allowed many of the traders, many of whom had more years invested in the

**Electronic Access to the Oil Markets Actually Made
Me a Fortune (The Real Money in Trading Oil
Came from Selling My Seat on the Exchange) (*Continued*)**

NYMEX and were the most senior among us, to be on the other side of the fence, as lessees when the big payout of the IPO finally came. But the calculus between the price of the seat and the rent that you could charge on that seat remained essentially the same from when I arrived in 1982 until about 2003 or so, when it occurred to some people that maybe the value of the membership was elsewhere besides just what you could make off it trading.

Buying a Seat on the NYMEX Proved to Be the Best Trading Decision I Ever Made

My own story of moving from a renter to a seat owner began in 1986, after four years on the floor, and again, I had my college roommate, Mark Burnett, to thank. We were both struggling with new careers on the floor, which made it difficult to come up with extra money to buy seats on our own. But what was important for both of us was our natural instinct to be *owners* in the businesses we were committed to. So together, we managed to scrape up the $27,000 each to split the ownership of a seat, which cost $54,000. Believe me, it was a difficult amount of money to come up with in 1986, but it proved to be the best investment decision of my life by far.

Less than three years later, a member both Mark and I knew decided to leave and sell his seat. By splitting the costs again both Mark and I became full seat owners. That half of a seat set me back $101,000, a total sale price of $202,000. I was a full owner, one of only 816 in the world in 1986—and I was luckier than hell to have gotten it done then. Seats didn't ever see such reasonable costs again.

It turned out to be a fabulous investment. In 1990, I acted as a broker for a friend who had come into a nice inheritance and was looking for investment ideas. His total capital available was slightly under a million dollars, as I remember.

(*Continued*)

Electronic Access to the Oil Markets Actually Made Me a Fortune (The Real Money in Trading Oil Came from Selling My Seat on the Exchange) (*Continued*)

At my recommendation, he handed over to me $195,000 to purchase a membership on the NYMEX, which I managed and rented for him. In the 16 years he owned that membership, he received four times his initial investment back in rent alone, and then, not wanting to make a mistake by "being a pig" (in his words), he sold the seat in 2006—for $5 million. Even with his return of 30 times his initial investment, he could have done better. But he never did anything but thank me for this rather lucky insight and windfall that he shared along with me.

Nevertheless, seats on the NYMEX weren't *obviously* great investments in the 1990s. That's a reason why so many who derived their livelihoods from the floor of the exchange hesitated to buy memberships of their own, preferring to rent seats, year after year. Here's a breakdown of seat price highs and lows for the years from 1994 until 2005:

YEAR	1994-1995	1996-1997	1998-1999	2000	2001	2002	2003	2004	2005
LOW	$361,000	$410,000	$430,000	$550,000	$685,000	$825,000	$1.15M	$1.65M	$1.83M
HIGH	$575,000	$675,000	$705,000	$825,000	$825,000	$1.3M	$1.625M	$2M	$3.775M

From the time I put $195,000 into a seat to invest my friend in 1990 (which, by the way, was the last seat from the failed Drexel Burnham Lambert bank holdings, brought down from the Michael Milken junk bond days), seats appreciated less fast than the stock market, and the risk of investing in them seemed much worse. Many derivative exchanges had come and gone during the 1990s. For example, the New York Futures Exchange (NYFE) comes to mind: It ultimately couldn't compete with Standard & Poor (S&P) alternatives in Chicago, and it shuttered its doors. So although it seems obvious now, no one was willing to confidently predict the ultimate fate of the NYMEX, with its singular reliance on new energy products.

**Electronic Access to the Oil Markets Actually Made
Me a Fortune (The Real Money in Trading Oil
Came from Selling My Seat on the Exchange) (*Continued*)**

By 2000, however, all doubt was removed. Unfortunately for many floor traders who had been waiting to be assured of the ultimate fate of the exchange, they were too late. By the time it was clear that the future of the exchange was steady and bankable, the price of seats moved quickly out of their reach. If I heard it once on the floor, I heard it a thousand times from floor traders who had wanted and intended to stop renting and buy a seat of their own: *"every time I got enough money saved and was just about ready to pull the trigger, the seat would go up another two or three hundred thousand."* I heard this chorus constantly from 2002 until the exchange went public in November 2006.

Still, trajectories continued higher through the spring and summer of 2006, while those of us who were seat owners on the floor spent much of our days speculating on the upcoming IPO, while still trying to trade a market that had hardly cooled. Full seats traded up throughout 2006, giving my friend his $5 million target fully four months before the IPO and trading, at best guess, north of $6 million a week or two before the bell sounded on the new NYSE stock issue for the New York Mercantile Exchange (NMX). As I've already noted, the first share of NMX changed hands for $120, making the share portion of the old seat worth $10.8 million, while the membership portion still traded, at least for a while, at more than $800,000 itself.

These were obviously life-altering numbers, particularly for me. Even at a very lofty yearly income, the math for me was pretty simple: 30 years of terrific trading years accumulated all at once, without paying a dime in taxes up front or needing to spend a dime in the interim to feed or clothe myself or my family. In other words, I and 815 of my colleagues had just hit lotto. Not local lotto, either: this was Powerball, five-state lotto. Four years later

(Continued)

Electronic Access to the Oil Markets Actually Made Me a Fortune (The Real Money in Trading Oil Came from Selling My Seat on the Exchange) (*Continued*)

as I write this, I am still getting used to this entirely ridiculous and incredible stroke of good fortune.

The IPO windfall also changed the floor forever, helping to accelerate the end of our previous careers and creating two classes of traders where before there had only been one. The exchange was now headed toward an electronic future: that was assured now, and while the seat owners were clearly taken care of if their livelihood would someday in the future disappear, the lessees were just as clearly up a river without a paddle. And they resented it. And they resented *us*.

I couldn't blame them, but although I had sympathy, I shared many of the reactions that other seat owners had to this newfound animosity. We had *invested* in the exchange, while they had chosen not to, although the opportunity to invest had been equal, except perhaps for those last 12 months before the IPO.

Not all, but many of the brokers began to horde the orders that were coming in to them. Many of the lessees were brokers, and they used the only tool at their disposal to exact what they considered justice: the paper flow. Those locals who were lifetime lessees began to reexamine their moral compasses. If ever there was a closing window to making money as an oil trader, it was surely now that the exchange had gone public and was ready to fully embrace an electronic future. They didn't know how long they had on a viable, profitable floor trading crude, but they knew now it was limited.

Arrangements began to be a lot more obvious between seat-leasing brokers and seat-leasing locals. In the 8 months after the November IPO coming onto the floor, before I started to ration my time away toward the screens, I was able to participate less and less in the pit. I got more nasty looks, saw more and more unreported prices go up on the boards, and was asked more than once "What are *you* still doing down here, DANO?" with a scowl

**Electronic Access to the Oil Markets Actually Made
Me a Fortune (The Real Money in Trading Oil
Came from Selling My Seat on the Exchange)** (*Continued*)

by particularly angry and jealous paper brokers. I finally gave up
on the floor in July of 2007, retiring to the screen, happy to have
left a place that used to give me such excitement and interest every
day but now was only a source of real and perceived snubbing
and angry fights.

I was a little early, maybe, to give up on the floor–but only a
little. Most seat owners who had been locals followed me out the
door by the end of 2007, despite a market that was careening ever
higher, touching a high of $147 a barrel by July 2008. By then,
however, the floor was a mere memory of what it once had been,
most of the trade having migrated to the screen, and the tiny rem-
nants of floor paper being fought over by the remaining lessees who
really had no alternative but to stay until they were forced to leave,
by an ICE-like retiring of the floor. As of 2010 the floor remained
a shadow of the vibrant opportunity for floor locals it was before I
departed, but it's still a viable source of (a lot smaller) income for
hundreds of floor traders, particularly in the options ring.

Conclusion

All of this—the incredible arc of NYMEX success and floor-trading
failure—can be accounted for by the immense increase in access to
oil markets that began in earnest at the start of the new millennium.
But in terms of the creation of the endless bid and the unnecessary
five-fold increase in crude prices that we've seen since the beginning
of the millennium, increased access—although important—doesn't
stand alone. We need to look much more closely at the mechanisms
of trading oil to get a real understanding of what's happening. Even
more generally, we need to look at *trading* itself: how it's done and
why it's done. Then we can turn back to oil and see how unlimited
access and unfettered trading destroys reliable pricing of oil. Part II
attempts to explain it all.

Part II

THE DESTRUCTION OF RELIABLE FUNDAMENTAL PRICING OF OIL

Chapter 6

Why Oil Traders Don't Care about the Price of Oil—Or the Value of the Dollar

I f trading oil has become more important in establishing price than the supply and demand of real physical oil, then it will be worthwhile to at least cursorily understand how trading works. If we can appreciate the mechanisms of trade and the motivations of traders, we'll also have a much better chance of figuring out where oil prices are headed in the future. Assetization of oil has brought a bunch of brand new players into the oil markets, and traders have done their best to exploit this new group for profit. How do they do this so successfully? A lifetime trader of oil is about to tell you all the secrets.

Most people have a very wrong view of what successful trading is and how traders make money. Most people view successful traders as some kind of supermen. Most people imagine these geniuses have greater insights into the workings and the nature of human behavior, consumer trends, the quality of one business model over another, cultural movements, and whatever else can be gleaned from the heavens. And they think these geniuses use all that information to correctly price an asset and either buy it when it's cheap or sell it when it's overpriced. There may well be a few of these Svengalis who exist on this planet.

Perhaps George Soros is one, the multi, multi-billionaire currency trader who correctly shorted the British Pound in 1992 and who recently tallied a further fortune by famously shorting the U.S. dollar against the Euro during the early 2000s. His Quantum hedge fund returned an average 30% yearly profit while he was at the helm. Or maybe people think of Julian Robertson, whose Tiger fund averaged a 32% yearly return during the 1980s and 1990s. Or maybe they imagine Carl Icahn, who finds cheap valuations on companies with poor and weak management. He typically amasses huge stakes in these companies, then threatens or takes on a proxy fight for control (a la Gordon Gekko of the movie *Wall Street*), and then he turns the company around and sells his stake for a big profit. These are the traders I believe people imagine when they visualize the breed: smart, in-the-know moguls with huge capital bankrolls to throw at a single conviction trade, whether it's the dollar or RJR Nabisco or Viacom.

These guys do exist, and there are plenty more who can look at an asset, figure out that the agreed on assessment of the general investing public (or even inside players!) is wrong, and then bet on their own idea of value being proven right in the long run. But for the vast, vast majority of traders plying their talents on a daily basis, trading doesn't work at all like this; moreover, no trader would ever claim that it does. Most traders don't for a moment imagine themselves as particularly insightful, or very good at predicting trends. I know I never did.

No matter how specific the assets that they engage in every day, whether that be municipal bonds, a single stock on the Nasdaq, student loan securitizations, or oil, rarely do the traders ever have a prediction or even a strong opinion on where those assets will be trading next week. And if they do, they quickly learn to quiet those voices in their heads as much as they can. The best traders I ever saw were the ones who traded *without any opinion of direction on the market they were trading.* For an example of one such trader, see the sidebar.

Never Let Your Opinion about the Market Get in the Way of How You're Trading

One pal of mine on the floor, Dave, was the consummate trader: he never let his opinion get in the way of making a good trade. I spoke to him almost daily during trading hours in the crude pit, just to take a break from the gasoline that I was trading less than 20 feet away. Dave seemed to always have a market opinion, and like every trader and investor in the world, I was interested in listening to it, even if I wasn't ever going to heed it. But the way Dave gave his opinions would always make me smile. He'd be standing in the crude ring, talking to me while making markets for four or five months of contracts, breaking his speech to me to call out quotes:

"Yeah, DANO, I think the market's definitely good, I like it here a lot...............APRIL! APRIL, FOUR BID AT SIX!"

(*Translation:* Dave is quoting the April contract, yelling only the last number for clarity and speed, so if the price of crude on the board for April is $65.45 a barrel, Dave is saying he will buy the April contract for $65.44 and sell it for $65.46.)

"definitely! Definitely good. The DOEs were bullish and ....APRIL! AT SIX! AT FORTY-SIX! SOLD, SOLD, SOLD!!" "TWENTY-FIVE, YOU GOT 'EM, SOLD!"

(He's selling, 25 lots at $65.46, while at the same time, he's still telling me how sure he is that the market is on its way *up*).

"yeah, the DOEs were bullish and definitely Iraq's going to get hotter, that'll spike it for sure.....................JUNE! TWENTY–SEVEN, THIRTY!"

(*Continued*)

> ## Never Let Your Opinion about the Market
> ## Get in the Way of How You're Trading (*Continued*)
>
> (Dave's on to quoting the June contract now, while continuing his conversation with me.)
>
> "I can't see the market going down here, it just can't, no way in hell.................JUNE! AT THIRTY, SOLD!!"
>
> (He's making more sales, this time in the June contract.)
>
> That was Dave: He'd stand next to you and give you 10 reasons why the market couldn't go down and had to rally, while at the exact same time he was selling 50 contracts SHORT! Now, is that a good trader?
>
> Yes. It's the best kind: one who never let his opinion get in the way of his trading.

How Can You Make Money Without an Opinion on the Market You're Trading?

But how does that work? How does a trader make money without having an opinion? How, in fact, does a trader make the most money he can by making sure that he *doesn't* have an opinion? The answer to these questions will teach you everything you need to know about modern markets and how traders operate inside them to make outsized profits, whether in bonds, stocks, collateralized debt obligations (CDOs), or oil.

I'm drawing a very simple bar line to illustrate any trade, in any asset you'd like to imagine. Imagine the mighty widget, if you like:

The fair trade value price of our widget is represented by the black line, right in the middle of our bar of prices. This bar represents just a snapshot of any moment in time we'd like, whether during the most active market period threatening near financial destruction or during the quietest moments when prices barely move; it doesn't matter. Of course, our fair trade value will change, sometimes incrementally and microscopically, sometimes very quickly and in huge leaps as time passes. That is the way that all markets work: The traded values of assets change.

Notice I did not refer to our black line as *real* value, what an asset is actually worth. Real value does exist, I suppose. A dollar is sometimes actually worth a dollar. But for traders, a real value is only a theoretical idea, and it shouldn't often enter into his decision making. A good trader never actually bothers much to care what the asset he is trading is truly worth—*the only thing that matters is if he can sell it to someone else for more than what he paid, or buy it back at a lower price than he sold it.*

To be realistic, of course, the *real* value of an asset and the *fair trade* value of an asset don't have to move independently, not at all. You'd like to think that the two prices would be somewhat in sync. In practice, real value can often come very close to what I have called fair trade value, and sometimes it can converge perfectly, as with a bond that is maturing and will be paid off at par, or with an option that is expiring. Most of the Svengali, brilliant traders who I mentioned at the beginning of this chapter are these kinds of wheeler dealers who make swashbuckling bets on macro moves in stocks or currencies or house prices. They take strong hard looks at assets and their trading values, and they bet on those values converging toward what they predict to be the real values, as they assess them to be. That's how you become known as a genius or a guru or a wizard. It is genius to be able to often and correctly assess when the crowd is wrong and be proven smarter than everyone else.

It is impressive, but not easy: even correctly predicting an asset's real value isn't always enough to make consistent money. Sometimes, convergence from fair trading values toward even correctly divined real values can take a very long time. John Maynard Keynes was certainly right when he said:

"Any market can remain irrational longer than you can remain solvent."

Still, it is lucky for the majority of traders, including me, that betting on convergences of trading values to real values isn't the only way to get rich trading. It's certainly not the most common way. To put it simply, most traders really don't care what any asset is really worth.

I'll talk later in this chapter about fair trade value and how traders find it, but for right now, let's stay away from too deep an analysis of market theory. Let's just say that our black line is a collectively decided fair trade value of our widget, like the price on a very liquid, very widely held stock. If you can either buy our widget at the line that the price represents (or sell it), you're right on the market.

The grey portion inside of the larger white bar represents a range of what I'll call likely outcomes of price motion away from the black bar. At some period in the future (whether a minute, month, or decade), our fair value price will change, and our black bar will locate itself somewhere differently on our simple price bar, somewhere randomly in the grey section.

If we bought our widget at its fair value and have decided to be long widgets, the ranges to the right of our black line represent profitable prices to us—that is, higher prices, where we'll make money if the black bar relocates there. Ranges to the left denote conversely unprofitable outcomes.

On the other hand, if we have decided to sell our widget at fair value and be short widgets, the opposite will be true: Outcomes to the left will benefit us, to the right will lose us money. Both ranges to the right and to the left are the same: Both the grey area to the right and the grey area to the left of our black line are equal in size. This is because from any fair value price today, the chances of a profitable outcome are theoretically as likely as an unprofitable one. (Remember, we're keeping this example simple and staying away from relatively priced assets, like options.)

Sometimes you'll hear my simplified grey and white ranges of outcomes referred to using more complex probability theory and the bell curve, perfectly symmetrical on both sides from the apex. The values closer to our black line—where we start—represent more likely outcomes than the areas further away, and far more likely than the areas much further away in the white areas.

The more probable outcomes are referred to in probability theory as having fewer standard deviations, sometimes denoted using the Greek letter sigma. A standard deviation represents a mathematical division of probability away from the zero line, where we start. Areas closer to the black line are more probable than the outcomes represented far away and in where I've drawn the white areas of our bar. These white areas are what we might call highly unlikely outcomes— sometimes referred to as six or seven sigma events, again referencing probability theory.

Recently, these events have also been more commonly dubbed black swan events, in reference to the title of Nassim Nicholas Taleb's book on market probability and options trading. [The title is derived from a probability case study: It was thought that swans were necessarily white—a 100% probability. Therefore, if you saw a swan, it would be white. When a black swan was shockingly discovered (an impossible event, according to probability theory), it called into question many of the assumptions of the distributive bell curve of probable outcomes. It seems that very, very rare events, like finding black swans, are far less rare than mathematicians (and most traders) think. Indeed, we seem to encounter perfect storms and one-in-a-million shots coming through surprisingly more often than anyone seems able to predict, particularly in the capital markets, and particularly in recent days.]

For now however, let's ignore the areas we've represented as white—that is, the outlier events and black swans that happen rarely— and concentrate on the most likely outcomes, the grey range that consumes almost all of a trader's time, no matter what he is trading. It is the rare trader indeed who ever contemplates a seven sigma event in his daily dealings. (And it's even rarer when he can correctly bet on one!)

But now we can finally zero in and get to the real and simple truth of trading. Are you ready? It will all seem rather obvious after I tell you, but you'd be amazed how few people who aren't traders fully understand the importance of understanding this to finally understanding the modern markets. Here it is: if a trader manages to buy (or sell) our widget precisely at the price represented by our black line, it should be perfectly clear that his chances of making money are exactly the same as his chances of losing it. Exactly 50/50. Simple enough? Buy or sell any asset in the world for whatever is the fair trade value, as I have defined it, and you're as likely to be right as wrong. (True Svengalis, who can really predict the future, are exempted, of course.)

A 50/50 chance isn't the kind of opportunity that any trader is going to look at favorably, that's for sure.

Making Money Is Simple

But let's say our trader somehow is able to buy our widget somewhere to the *left* of the black line: let's say our widget has a fair trade value of 50 zlotys or dollars or yen, but somehow, someway, our trader is able to buy our widget for 45 zlotys. What happens then? Is our trader an instant winner?

The answer is *no*. Our trader cannot immediately retrieve the fair value of 50 zlotys that our widget is supposedly worth and pocket the 5 zloty difference, at least not immediately. If he could, he'd be buying our widgets under the market, which is illegal. No, most of our markets are undoubtedly biased, but they're not (usually) illegal. If someone really wanted to pay the fair 50 zloty value of our widget at the moment that our trader was waiting around, there'd be no reason to sell that widget to our trader for 5 zlotys less. Like I said, the markets might be biased, but they're not illegal. So, while our trader might be convinced that he has bought his widget under value, he cannot realize his good purchase just yet. No, he must continue to take risk on the asset he just bought.

But look at our new simple price bar chart for our trader who's just managed to buy widgets for 5 zlotys under the fair value price:

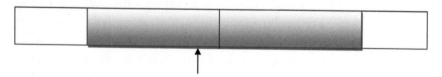

The grey area to the right of his buy price (which represents profit-making outcomes) has become significantly larger than the grey area to his left, the range of unprofitable outcomes.

Has our trader eliminated his risk? *No*. There are still plenty of places to the left of where our trader made his purchase where the fair trade value could fall later that would represent an unprofitable result. What he has done is made the *probability* of a profitable trade being the final outcome much greater than the 50/50 chance he would get by trading at the exact fair trade value price.

How much better has he made it? The answer is obvious: it is as much better as the distance he can get from the original black line of fair value to either buy below or sell above. It should also be obvious that being able to sell our widget at 55 zlotys is equally likely to generate an exactly same chance of a profitable outcome as it was to buy at 45.

Traders Are Human, Too

Maybe this is a good time to inject a little of the human factor into our trading discussion. Traders do have biases, and they are human—much as they'd often like to be entirely emotionless. There are traders the world over who are just more comfortable buying assets—they'll avoid the juiciest sale and wait exclusively for opportunities to buy assets under fair trade prices. These people are known as *perma-bulls*.

Others I have known simply love selling. While the outcomes for buying and selling are equal in probability, when selling proves to be profitable, it often delivers its profits in a quicker and more violent way. Some traders just love this excitement; therefore, they enjoy selling more than they enjoy buying. These are the *perma-bears*.

But the absolute *best* traders in the world don't care one iota which side of the trade they are on. At all times, they are equally willing to be *buyers* as they are to be *sellers*. The best traders in the world, the most profitable traders, only want to be as far away from the black line as they can get when they initiate their trades, without prejudice, whether they are buying or selling. Therefore, the best traders also don't want or need to have an opinion on where the market is headed, because an opinion can only impede execution from either side of the market. They're just looking to *increase probabilities on every trade of being right and making money, no matter which way the market chooses to go*. If you accumulate more trades where your chances of a profitable outcome are greater than your chances for an unprofitable one, guess what? You'll be a guaranteed winner in the long run.

That's trading in a nutshell, no matter what the asset: *buy under fair value or sell above it.*

Fair Traded Value Isn't the Same as Real Value

By right about now in my grand explanation of trading strategy, you're looking down at the page with a smirk, maybe even a scowl on your face. Buy under value and sell above it?? In other words, buy low, sell high? Of course! That's obvious! That's no secret at all! The secret, you're probably thinking, is again in finding out *where the real value lies.* That's what's hard to find and precisely know and that is what separates the great traders, going back to the Soroses and the Robertsons and the Icahns: they know where the black line of value is.

Not true. Like most every other trader out there, I did not care a whit about real value. For me, fair traded value was all that ever counted. Again, I never thought for a moment about the value of any contract I ever bought or sold. I wanted only to sell it for more than I paid, or buy it back for less than I had sold it for.

So, how do traders know when they are buying under fair value? How can they at least be pretty damn sure they are buying under value, and tilt the odds of a winning trade in their favor? In extremely liquid markets with lots of players trading with relatively equal access, the fair trade value is much easier to find: it's surely very close to the last traded price right in front of you on your screen. As markets get more specialized and more illiquid, it becomes more difficult to know that value for sure. One thing is for sure, however: No matter how illiquid and customized a market is, for every asset at every moment in time, a fair trade value exists.

There are lots of ways for traders to determine fair trade values, but 99 times out of 100, value is made clearer from looking at where *other* markets and more liquid benchmarks are trading. To use a simple example: Your share of Chevron stock will trade at a price at least somewhat related to the price of a share of Exxon or BP or Shell. All else being equal (and it admittedly rarely is), you'd be a smart trader to buy Chevron down 10% on a day when Exxon and BP are down an equivalent of 3%. These dislocations, as we like to call them, rarely if ever happen in liquid, widely held stock markets, because there are an army of traders who'd be willing to try and risk a dislocation of a lot less than 7%, all other information being equal. So the chances are great that if you find Chevron down 10% while the rest of the sector is only down 3%, all other information is not equal.

Comparing Apples to Apples—At Least McIntoshes to Granny Smiths

My point is simple, though. To find a fair traded value in any asset, you must correlate it with the fair traded values of other assets.

In every capital market, every asset class, every commodity or real estate investment trust (REIT) or single stock or option, everywhere there are traders, there are professionals who are trying to buy widgets for 45 zlotys when they are worth 50, and they quite often do. Sometimes, the dislocations are just micro-cents on thousands of shares of common stock, as with the institutional block trading advantage that many of the largest brokerage houses enjoy. Sometimes, the advantage is downright obscene, as with the aggressive pricing of an initial public offering (IPO), where the advantage of a cheap buy isn't only delivered to the partner funds of the lead book runners on Wall Street, but particularly to their best prime brokerage clients. (Remember the New York Mercantile Exchange [NYMEX] IPO I wrote about in Chapter 5?) But it is more difficult to make outsized profits on openly traded and transparent markets like individual stocks: you need to accumulate millions of trades if your advantage is only a few bits of a cent on them, and you need to trade them all virtually for free in order to make a living.

The best and most consistent and outsized profits will come in markets that are far less transparent and open from full view and full participation. And why is this? Why should a less-open market provide a greater opportunity for trader profit? To answer that, let's go back to our simple bar line chart at the beginning of this chapter: It's because as markets get more specialized and less transparent, our black line of fair trade value becomes far less obvious. As it becomes less obvious, insiders have an ever wider and more distinct advantage over others less in the know. And when I talk of insiders, I am talking about traders—with intense and deep knowledge of the market they are trading.

Even if it isn't obvious, our fair trading value black line is always there, it's definitely there. Whether there are some esoteric but otherwise reliable benchmarks, or whether some rocket scientist is in a back office somewhere modeling out theoretical real values and helping traders to more closely calculate fair trading values, *somebody* has an edge in finding that black line compared to someone else, and that edge gets larger the more specialized and unique the markets become. If a trader can't find an edge consistently, opportunities disappear—and so will our trader, off to find another, more promising market.

Other outside participants without these edges who still choose to engage in these specialized markets aren't necessarily wrong on their predictions and bets. In fact, some of them are quite savvy, but the probabilities of success are stacked against them in the long run. Even if these others have much deeper and incisive information on the asset itself, they will have a harder time showing a profit on their trading endeavors over time. For example, airlines that hedge fuel costs might experience a year or two of saved money using the energy markets in risk management programs, but ultimately, they must give away any of the advantages that risk-management programs deliver to them in the short run. Oil companies do well, but ultimately fare more poorly at trading oil—on a per capita basis—than financial trading giants with no direct connection to the commodity.

The most obvious example of smaller and more specialized markets delivering spectacular trading opportunities are in the fixed-income markets. Year after year, fixed-income trading divisions lead the list within the investment banks for earned revenue. This includes the trading of corporate and municipal bonds at the trading desks of the largest brokerage houses in the world. Instead of a centrally cleared market for bonds, there are individual desks inside brokerage houses that will quote each individual issue. Because each of these instruments is unique and highly specialized, each bond essentially trades in a separately created market, by a very small group of interested and well-capitalized traders and brokers. You can shop around for prices for any particular bond, whether you are a buyer or seller, but your ability to make a trade depends on a desk either having an inventory or knowing where an inventory of a specific issue is, and also whether the market is advantageous enough to deliver a decent trading opportunity to make a profit.

And although these desk traders aren't precisely sure where the black line of fair value for Buffalo Sewer 2025 7.25% municipals or Chevron 2035 6% corporate is, they have better access to the benchmarks of other similar debt instruments, and they either make a bid that they are fairly confident is a good bit to the left of where that black line lies, or they offer the bonds a nice gap from where that line falls on the right. The immense profits racked up at the big trading desks for fixed-income groups is testament to their ability to correctly assess where that line is on any specific debt obligation far more often than they get it wrong.

But nobody's perfect, and even the most sophisticated and hooked-in trader can get things wrong—sometimes spectacularly so. Consider the famed meltdown of CDOs and other securitized debt obligations (as discussed in Chapter 4): Although they lost lots of money for institutional and individual investors, they also lost lots of money for the banks that sold them, particularly Citibank and Bank of America, which had enormous portfolios of these unhedged securities on their own books. The simple truth is that this was a rare case of bond traders inside Citi and BofA being convinced that the *traded values* they had used were very, very close to the *real values* for these bonds. So they loaded up on bonds they bought for 45 zlotys that they were convinced were worth 50 or 55—but which moved very quickly and turned out to be worth far less.

What's rarely mentioned in the CDO or mortgage trade was that although Citi and others had the real value wrong, they still had the fair traded value pretty much *right*—after all, it seemed everyone had these bonds on their books, marked at a profit. Citibank and BofA could have sold some other benchmarks to hedge their positions, as Goldman Sachs made clear by being hedged and even a little short these instruments when the big collapse came. Citi's big mistake was in believing its own assessments of real value, instead of remaining a disciplined trader and only caring about the fairly traded value. Citi had trades on that looked (to Citi) to be even better than Citi could have imagined, but ultimately, Citi made the trader's cardinal sin: The bank got an opinion and stopped trading.

The Oil Markets Are Not Like the Bond Markets

Oil has become precisely like the fixed-income markets I've just outlined. For day traders like me, we found our advantage (as slim and fleeting as it was) in other benchmarks we could easily spot and recognize—such as a bid in another month, or a spread offer that promised some value; sometimes, it was enough to see the look on a broker's face, promising that the selling he was attempting in the pit was from a very large order and likely to continue for a while.

Oil traders trading elsewhere (outside the pits of the NYMEX, without a seat at the exchange) had to find other advantages, other ways of determining the black line in a superior way. Over-the-counter (OTC) markets, using crude and product futures market at the NYMEX as benchmarks, were the creation that delivered that edge to these traders off the floor. While new OTC specialized markets in oil were sold to clients as innovations answering the needs of ever-more-unique customers, each new OTC product required the creation of a new and specialized market to trade those products. Those markets attracted traders who were able to understand the dynamics of the market better than the customers to whom these products were being sold. These traders were also overwhelmingly employed by the same companies making the sales of these OTC products.

By using the benchmarks already established by cash and futures markets on the NYMEX, desks of other proprietary traders (particularly at the major investment banks) were able to deliver customized derivative oil markets to clients and install themselves as the most influential trading partners inside of them. Helping clients gain a better grasp of price risk in oil products or helping trade groups better manage their own more traditional risk in oil futures was only a small reason for creating these instruments. By far the best reason to create a new derivative and specialized oil product was to be able to trade it from the inside. The more new markets you could create, entice an audience of clients to participate in and understand, the more trades you could put on, confidently and advantageously to the right or left of the black trading lines of these markets.

You could practically assure yourself of being a consistent winner, month after month, quarter after quarter, year after year. And you didn't need to take any grand shots to do it, or rarely needed to take on any great risks, unless you got greedy (which the smartest traders just refuse to do). And, as we saw in Chapter 4, Goldman Sachs and Morgan Stanley did just that—and continue to do it in oil, every single day.

How Floor Traders Make Money Trading Oil

Trading oil (or trading any market, for that matter) is pretty much the same no matter if you're sitting on the desk of the most powerful hedge fund, or if you're a bank trading the most esoteric issue with little to no liquidity, or if you're a day trader trying to scrape out a living cutting a few cents of profit in Citibank stock. It's the same, that is, if you are at all successful.

I've outlined what it takes to make money trading. To make money, traders have to know the current trading value of an asset better than the other participants in the market. They can also gain an advantage by being better at guessing it, or modeling it using fancy spreadsheets or algorithms, or by just dealing in a market where a lot of other participants don't care quite as much about getting that number exactly right while entering a trade. In oil, you've got a combination of all three.

Floor traders like me (at least, when there were floor traders) could virtually know the fair trading value of oil at any single moment. My advantage was in the quick access I could apply to make that value, no matter how brief, count for a better-than-average chance at a profit. And sometimes, that could be very brief indeed. Hedge fund managers will count on developing models that will give them a better view of fair trade value, whether their insight comes from mathematical modeling or historical ideas or fundamental trends. Much of the money that is made from investment bank oil trading is made because the participants in their realm are often clients who see oil trading as a risk management exercise. Consequently, their interest in oil is only a side story to their businesses, and they are far less likely to care as much over the premium or discount that their programs cost them to put into place. Most of these clients have computed the costs of their risk management programs into their business models and, although they'd certainly like their trading arms to show a profit, in the end, they can always pass along whatever those costs are to their customers. To put it simply, these are the clients that just don't care about the fill quite as much. (This kind of participant isn't as rare as you might think, either.)

But whether you are a floor trader or a trader on a desk at Chevron or a trader of Brent/West Texat Intermediate (WTI) swaps at Morgan Stanley, you've got your own method of obtaining an advantage at putting your trade down advantageously to the right or the left of our critical solid black line of fair trade value. But having done that, your job has only begun. It's one thing to get the trade down at an advantageous price, quite another to convert that into a profit on the profit and loss (P&L) statement. A profit on paper is one thing, but as the old saying goes, profits only become real based on how you get *out*, not how you get *in*.

I'm going to go into a little detail on floor trading and how floor traders go about turning an advantage into a profit. From that explanation, it's an easy leap to the seemingly most complicated trades on the desks trading the most esoteric oil products in the world. Understanding how the engine of trading works will shed a brand new and critical light on the profit motivations of all the players in the oil market and how those motivations contribute to the endless bid and ultimately drive prices and volatility to the extreme levels we've seen in the last several years.

Floor traders like me can often be absolutely sure they are buying or selling better than fair trade value at certain times. The way they do this is through simple *spread trading*. Remember in Chapter 1, when I described the difference between outright trading and spread trading? If not, here's a refresher: Futures markets are traded with monthly deliveries. That means that for each month there is a separate contract, which can price independently of every other month being traded. Although these monthly contracts can price independently, they almost never do, unless there is a specific issue associated with that one month. Normally, though, each month's contract will move in a certain relation to every other month's contract. Those relationships, those differentials in prices are called *spreads*.

Spreads are a trader's lifeblood, whether he is trading stocks or bonds or oil futures. It is through spread relationships that traders find those all-important benchmarks that we use to figure out the likely spot of that elusive fair trade value line. The easiest way for me to illustrate this idea is with an example, the kind of example of spread trading that I and other floor traders used every single day of our trading lives to try and convert an advantage to a profit.

I was a gasoline trader mostly, but for this example, let's use crude oil instead, because its simple, base-10 type of pricing is easier to work with. The gasoline contract was a 42,000-gallon specification moving in increments of 5/100ths of a cent—and although gas traders get accustomed to the money conversions we need to make spread calculations quickly, it's far more complicated than the 1,000-barrel crude contract trading in 1¢ increments, each worth a simple $10 a tick.

Let's imagine I am trading crude oil, in the middle of April, and I am watching the first several months of the market. Let's also make up a simple curve of market prices, not unlike what we might see today:

Month	May	June	July	August
Last Price	$63.00	$63.50	$64.00	$64.50

I've represented the first four months and what we might see on the board for the last price traded for each of these months. The last price traded in May was $63 a barrel, June last traded at $63.50, July at $64, and August at $64.50. From this board, we might assume that the spread price for May/June was 50¢, but that is a bad assumption: Prices on the board only indicate *where the last trade was* and not *where the market actually is.* However, for our example, I'm going to remove an important piece of a trader's risk puzzle as I did in the previous section and tell you right off that 50¢ is precisely the correct fair trade value for each of these spreads.

Now, let's add some real orders—real paper we can try to trade off of and try to make some money. To start off, let's quote the spread May/June at 48 points bid and 52 points offered. Notice how I suggested a bid underneath fair trade value and an offer above it. Of course, we often find it difficult to execute trades at fair trade value, as every other participant is also looking to beat the odds of the market, just like us.

Let's consider what the math is for trading these spreads and the opportunity to make money. We could trade them directly, as spreads, and do the buying of one month and the selling of the other simultaneously if we chose. That would be the 48/52 spread quote now in the market. We could simply hit the bid for the May/June spreads and sell June contracts 48¢ over May or take the offer on the spreads and buy June 52¢ above. (As an aside, it makes a huge difference to a trader to know just *who* is bidding and offering these spread markets, because the reliability of the order is almost as important as the price being paid.) For our example, though, let's make the market airtight: Those bids and offers in the May/June spread are rock solid, and we can depend on them, at least for as long as this example will take to explain.

I'll put each spread on equally rock-solid footing as well: June/July is quoted at 48/52, as is the July/August. We could put quotes together and say that July can be sold 96¢ above the May contract and bought $1.04 above it by combining the two single-month quotes. And that would be true, except that usually you can get much tighter quotes than you'd get by simply combining them in practice. No matter to us right now, we're going to learn trading simply, using only the spot month spread to start: May/June.

Now let's set up the action: I see a broker who works for a big brokerage house, and he is bidding $63.50 for the June contract. Because this is a broker, I assume it's a legitimate bid for reasonable size, and I can reach him, and it is likely that I could sell some of these lots to him. Now, how can I try to turn this into an opportunity? Let's look at the spreads again: I know that May/June is 48 bid at 52. The first thing I can try is to buy May contracts at $62.98 or cheaper. How would this help me?

Well, let's assume that I was lucky enough to be standing at the right place at the right time, and let's say that a market order to sell May contracts came into the pit, and my bid was hit at $62.98. Now let's look at what I can do with these contracts, now that I own them.

I could immediately try to sell some of those June contracts to the broker who is bidding $63.50, giving me a spread position in which I am long May contracts and short June contracts at a differential of 52¢. I have done this by doing two separate trades at different times, first buying May contracts and then selling June contracts. This separated trading into spreads is known as *legging into* spreads, as opposed to just buying or selling a spread as a single trade. When I try to unwind this position, it is labeled oppositely: If I take off one part of the spread first, perhaps by selling the May contract before buying back the June, that would be called *legging out* of a spread.

But by initiating this position, considering where the market is being quoted, I have done well and set up an opportunity, if certainly not a guarantee of making money. I have legged into spreads at 52 points, when that spread is already being quoted as being offered at 52 points. I have managed to sell spreads on the offer. Why is this good for me? I could, without further risk, buy spreads at 52 points and retire the position I just initiated without profit or loss, but trading is not about retiring positions without risk—or without profit. No, because I have sold spreads on the offer, I have most probably also sold these spreads to the right of the fair value trade line. Because spreads are already bid at 48 and offered at 52, chances are very good that the fair value trade is in between those two quotes and closer to the 50 points represented on the board in the last trade (and I have told you is true).

I have delivered myself a free shot at making at least something for my good work at legging into these spreads on the offer: I keep in reserve my option of buying back spreads and losing nothing while trying to buy them back more cheaply. If I feel the spread market might be weak or if the offer for spreads looks stronger than the bid,

I might bid 48 with the rest of the crowd, hoping for the spreads to come in. If I were less convinced that the offer of spreads was solid, I might quote higher than the rest of the market, perhaps bidding 50 for the spreads I had just sold, hoping to get hit and take a quick two-point profit on each spread.

Notice two important trading ideas from this simple example. First, because I managed to sell spreads on the offer, above the fair trading value, I am now willing to pay the fair trade value to get out, which normally traders are loathe to do. But the point is always *making a profit*, and sometimes traders will be very willing to do trades at a fair trade value and sometimes even more, in order to lock away profits. Second, notice that at no time during this trade did I wonder, notice, or even for a moment *think* about whether the market was on its way up or on its way down. Direction of the market, as I have said, is usually way back in the list of priorities for good traders of oil (or, for that matter, any market).

Okay, let's go back a step, even before I put the second leg down and created a spread in the first place. I saw that a broker was bidding for June contracts, and based on the spread quotes, I decided to bid $62.98 for May. I figured if I were able to buy contracts at that price, I could sell June contracts and sell spreads on the offer, which gave me a reasonable opportunity, but hardly a guarantee of making a profit. I knew that buying Mays at $62.98 was buying to the left of the black line of fair trade value, knew it beyond even a shadow of a doubt, because of the benchmarks I could take from the rest of the market and how it was quoting.

Okay, so if I am able to buy May contracts under fair trading value, you might rightly ask why am I selling anything? If I am buying value, why am I choosing to sell June contracts and put on a spread in the first place? The truth is, I don't have to do that, I don't have to do that at all—putting down the second leg of a spread is a common way to trade, which doesn't eliminate my risk; it only reduces it. However, it is overwhelmingly the strategy most often employed when traders are trying to minimize risks while locking away profitable opportunities.

Still, depending on how I like to trade and what kind of risks I like to take, once I am confident (through whatever benchmarks I use) that I have bought good trading value, I am free to simply stay long if I like and try to maximize my profits without a second leg—just by staying long—even though I know I am increasing my risks.

Yes, once I have bought May contracts that I am confident are beneath the fair trading value, I have a better chance of making a profit than I do of taking a loss, whether I decide to hedge my bets by putting on a spread or not. Again, *I don't have to wonder or think about where the market is headed, nor should I.* I should only look to make more trades that I am confident are at *better than fair trade value.* The more of these I do, the more money I should make, irrespective of whether these trades are to the left or the right of our fair trading value line and irrespective of whether the market needs to go up or down, or spreads need to go in or out. My probability of success is greater than 50/50, sometimes a lot greater.

I've given you the four most important rules on trading in a few short sections; here's a recap of the most important takeaways, the ones that so few really know about trading before considering what is happening in the markets:

1. **The best traders have no opinion on the market.** They could honestly care less, most of the time, whether the market that they are trading is going up or down.
2. **A trader's only real concern is making the best estimate of what I have called the fair trade value of the asset they are trading at any time.** Traders use whatever advantages are legally (and unfortunately, sometimes illegally!) available to them to know better or access the fair trade value more quickly. The difference between floor traders scalping spreads for a point or two like me and the most long-term macro trader of oil 10 months out on the curve is not the method we employ; instead, the difference is only the *tools* we use to find an advantage.
3. **After finding that fair trade value, a trader's only job is to buy that asset at as deep a discount to that value as he can.** Alternately, he can sell that asset for as strong a premium as he can possibly wheedle out of that market at that moment. The best traders don't ever care a whit which side of the trade they do (although many admittedly have personal biases).

4. *Finally, once the trade is done, a trader has a choice.* He can either hedge that winning trade and its potential profits by putting on some kind of spread in another related benchmark market *or* he can roll the dice for bigger profits by not hedging the trade. Obviously, that choice will be related to the trader's appetite for risk (and his company's appetite, if it's not his money he's playing with).

However, it should be noted that the *vast majority* of trades done by professional traders is almost instantly hedged. A managing director for Morgan Stanley's oil division estimated to me that perhaps 10% of trades on their books are entirely unhedged. Although there clearly were unhedged trades in various asset classes of subprime on many of the bank's balance sheets, I think he's being rather bold, even with that meager 10% call. Why take risk when you just don't have to? You don't, and most of the biggest traders of oil take very little, if any.

Morgan Stanley as Oil Company

Reducing risks and finding edges is what trading is all about. And no one has been more aggressive and more successful at creating edges in the oil markets than Morgan Stanley. It was, perhaps, a natural progression for the world's largest trader in the futures markets to venture into the physical side of the business, especially because of the background of John Shapiro, who was in charge of Oiltrading at Morgan at the time. Shapiro spent time as an executive at Conoco before joining Morgan Stanley and knew from experience how having the pulse of the physical market can help make the right decisions when trading. Together with Neal Shear, head of Commodities during the latter part of the last decade, Morgan Stanley began to amass leases of storage facilities for crude and heating oil.

We've talked about getting an edge and trading is all about advantages, whether you're the smallest local in the pit or the biggest player in financial oil. It's not about doing riskless things, but instead trying to have the chance to be right just a little more often than you'll be wrong. If you can add a few small advantages together, you've got the chance to be right a lot more often. For investment banks like Morgan Stanley, getting involved in physical storage was a way to deliver another not-so-small advantage to their traders back on the desks in Purchase, New York, where the Morgan Stanley oil traders resided.

It is a tremendous advantage, to have the option of buying front-month contracts in the futures markets, knowing you can physically take delivery, if the trade doesn't work out The easiest way to do this is if you control a sizable piece of the official storage facility for NYMEX heating oil delivery, which at one time, Morgan Stanley did. From 2002 to 2004, Morgan delivered more than 60% of all the heating oil in New York Harbor.

There is nothing illegal in what Morgan Stanley did in entering the oil business, although the irony of a purely financial oil company suddenly engaging on the physical side is hard to miss. Indeed, Morgan Stanley took risks by becoming involved in physical trading: I'm sure they needed to sit on inventory while the market went down. Yet looking back in hindsight and comparing the relative successes of oil companies and trading companies, one group did immensely better than the other. It was clear that it was easier to maximize your opportunities in oil by understanding the market first and then venturing to become an oil man, as opposed to being, let's say, a wildcatter from Texas trying to learn the futures and OTC derivative markets. The figures from the investment banks are sketchy, but a report in 2005 put Morgan Stanley's gross profit at somewhere between $1.2 and $1.6 billion on its physical activities alone, never mind what affect the insight of trading all of those physical barrels had on the profits of the traders dealing on the derivative side of the desk (although a principal at Morgan Stanley disputes this figure, reported in the Wall Street Journal at the time).

Morgan Stanley became quite a significant oil company, from both sides of this equation. It took over buying and scheduling deliveries for Denver-based MLP Transmontaigne Partners before buying the company outright in 2006, for example. It has also provided financing for heavyweight MLP Enbridge Energy to build storage tanks in Cushing, Oklahoma, not coincidentally the delivery point for crude oil for the NYMEX WTI contract.

Access to key delivery sites also provides invaluable insight into the direction and trajectory of front month markets, giving already savvy traders at investment banks another big leg up on everyone else engaged in oil. This interesting story completes the cycle of oil market transformation—Oil companies moved to become more and more like hedge funds and trade oil financially, while trading desks engaged to become more like oil companies and find advantages for their trading by dealing with oil physically. These days, it's getting harder and harder to tell the difference.

You're Better Off Without an Opinion, But You Do Need an Edge

Maximizing your reward while minimizing your risks is the name of the trading game. But whether on the floor, the screens, or running a multi-billion-dollar book of business, it all comes down to finding and exploiting an edge. Nobody, and I mean *nobody*, can expect to make a long-term and consistent profit from trading any market without some sort of edge. Whatever it is, and however small and insignificant it might look to someone else, if you've got some sort of consistent edge, you've got a real chance to succeed as a trader. (It's not enough to merely have an edge, of course—money management and discipline count for a lot, too.) And don't tell me your edge is superior insight into the markets you're trading. Please, tell me anything but that. I'd much rather hear of your deep knowledge of the chocolate eating habits of the Belgians during Christmas season that inspires your trading of the cocoa market than about your superior insight into the stocks of certain sectors or the more correct valuation models you're using compared to somebody else's. If you imagine that you or your high-priced analyst can read the charts or public financial statements better than the next guy, I think you're really kidding yourself. Everyone who's got any stake in the markets is trying to do exactly what you are, and you can bet your bottom dollar they've got far superior resources to what you've got at hand. You've got to find something only very few others have. If the information or research or forecast is available to anyone, it's just not going to do you much good. This is just a very simple way to define the idea of market *efficiency*.

Efficiency is a simple but profound idea: All the knowledge that is readily available to the public has been crunched and hammered by the most sophisticated of investment modelers and institutional traders, and the results of all that research is contained in the price of the issue itself. Nothing more in terms of price understanding can be gleaned by merely going over the mountain of figures at hand and coming up with a different interpretation—it's all baked in. But wouldn't all this assume that the price of anything would be static, unmoving— provided all of these fundamental data points haven't changed? It would—and we know that markets do anything and everything except stay still. So what kind of efficiency is that?

Oh, efficiency is real, all right. Fundamental pictures built from readily available data points, accepted projections, growth figures, stockpiles—they represent real numbers and real values. But that's not all that goes into the fixing of a price, not by a long shot. Many other, wonderful, and much less measurable factors of capital, intuition, panic, greed, perception—these can and do impact prices in the short and medium term. And it's been my long experience that those wonderful human factors are so much more important for price discovery: They more often than not swamp the fundamental factors available at hand to the academics and rocket scientists, at least in the short term.

How terrific that turns out for us, as traders. Once we can depend on the unknowable human factors to affect markets in strange and seemingly random ways, we can find motion in price and opportunity in that motion—the outcomes are not written entirely in the code of computer models, but in the souls of the people engaged in the process. Just ask John Meriwether and Dr. Myron Scholes (of the Black-Scholes option model) about the reliability of computer modeling they experienced at Long Term Capital Management, when they lost $4.8 billion in four months. Excuse me for sneering, but I just love that human wild card of trading, especially when it explodes in the face of the experts.

But it is precisely because these factors are so difficult to define and quantify that we need something else to rely on to trade successfully, not the numbers we get off of Yahoo! finance, or the pronouncements of soothsayers.

We need an edge.

On the floor where I made my living for close to 25 years, the major edge for everyone down there was clear: We were at the nexus to the entirety of energy trade. Everyone in the world who wanted to trade oil was ultimately forced to find price in the rings of the New York Mercantile Exchange. As I've already described, oil companies like Exxon, BP, Chevron, and Hess owned seats at the exchange, although in later years they preferred to use independent brokers to execute their business, as opposed to telegraphing their hands by executing with self-owned memberships. The investment banks had no need to be as shy because their books comprised their own trade as well as countless other participants (both retail and institutional) doing both real hedging and speculative trading. Again, as described, all the major houses, including Goldman Sachs, Morgan Stanley, Citibank, Credit Suisse, Paribas, and others maintained floor operations with dedicated brokers. And in the center of it all sat me and about 400 other independents or locals—watching the flow of orders come from all corners of the globe on to the ringing telephones lining the walls and booths of the floor of the exchange.

Those orders would be transmitted to paper and handed to brokers in the ring to be executed. That's a great and descriptive phrase: *order executed*. It sounds like a terminal event, and it really was. Execution was a loud and physical act, in those days merely hundreds done in a minute (today, that speed would be laughed at, because trades easily go by the thousands per second electronically). Yet those hundreds of physically vocalized orders would create a din so incredibly unique.

Let me better set the stage: The community of participants in the pit were the same, year after year—locals and brokers. We had coffee with each other every morning and lunched together in the afternoon. Employees of brokerage houses and new meat (fresh locals) were a rare sight. Every broker became a recognizable face, with an equally recognizable cadence and modus operandi for order execution. They often wanted to put locals off the scent of the orders they were holding by bidding lightly for large orders or yelling more loudly for orders of only a few lots. Other feints and fakes that they used looked pathetic to us—they needed to execute the orders, and most of the time, they just couldn't fool us. We knew them all far too well. When orders of size and importance came into the pit, we could see them coming. And when multiple orders from different sources came flooding the pits, we knew better than to stand in the way. Although on an electronic screen, an order for size is hardly recognizable from the rest of the orders entered into the system, on the floor, it was a screaming signal most of the time: The tone, volume, and activity of the natural rhythm would quicken. This was instantly recognizable to us. It was our edge.

Of course, there were other edges to be had. Merely because new and important trade initiated from the broker's hands and moved outward—paper flow—independent traders often gained a right of first refusal on order execution. There was an unwritten law giving preferential treatment to locals on the floor: In filling an order, brokers would generally favor locals, as opposed to other brokerage orders. At the very least, you could make a strong argument to brokers to be included in the fill, even if you weren't actively bidding or offering at the time, as you technically should have been to be included.

This was another interesting aspect of floor trading. Remember that the exchanges were at that time owned entirely and exclusively by the seat holders—the 816 members of my exchange made up the entirety of stockowners. Of these owners, close to two-thirds of them were locals or were renting their seats for profit. The better the opportunities could be made for the traders of owned or leased seats, the better the seat owners did on their membership investments. The exchanges were little more than a club in those days, little concerned with income or growth, and much more concerned with the earning power that trading with a membership might generate. While open trading continued on the trading floor and orders were rarely violated, it was also an unwritten but understood purpose of an exchange to give seat owners and lessees as much of a legal advantage in trading as they could. The Exchange had a bias, in some cases an obligation, to make profitable trading by independents (who represented a large majority of seat owners) as conducive as possible. In this, they succeeded.

Commercial players from off the floor had their advantages—they were far closer to the fundamental picture than we were. In fact, they often could *generate* the fundamental pictures the rest of the trading community would see. It was a tremendous advantage. Most of the oil companies and many of the mid-stream participants had equal access to the cash markets, where all physical assets were traded for immediate delivery. Here was the hub of pure supply and demand pricing. No one ventured onto those markets unless they were active users or suppliers, and there was little speculation. Obviously, cash market trades were a high-quality indicator of where the futures markets were headed—and the oil companies and others with physical assets had this information in hand far sooner than anyone on the floor possibly could have. We were so far behind in this game and knew it that we didn't even look at cash market prices—almost never. This was the commercial player's edge.

The investment banks' advantage lay in their direct access to real hedgers of energy and the customizable products they offered—they would be the initial point of contact for orders from industrial and other commercial users looking to hedge exposure to the vagaries of daily trade. That unique group of participants and their daily needs from the markets were known only in house and gave the bank traders their own terrific edge. They quoted prices in short- and long-term derivative products to retail customers with one eye on the open markets that we were trading on our exchange, of course always leaving room for a profitable arbitrage to futures contracts if they were unable to complete the other side of any trade in-house—or if their traders preferred, to keep the other side of the trade entirely for themselves. The oil traders at Morgan Stanley and Goldman Sachs made enormous money every year, and most of that money was made by *not* going to an open market like ours to complete a hedge. In any case, whether even a small piece of the other side of that order came onto the floor or not, that flow of retail interest was an immediate and continuing massively lucrative advantage for them.

Even surrounded by these other, much better informed players, we continued to survive and prosper.

It was only because of our edge. We could see the avalanche of buying coming in, or the mountain of selling and hit offers and take bids far faster than anyone off the floor could. But considering our edge and the edge that the commercial and bank players had, we still saw a steady flow of outside interest come into the pit. Dumb money, I called it. Like the payoff to a bad return slot machine, these guys were really behind the eight-ball from the start. They could win in the short term, but over the long haul, they were doomed to fail.

Conclusion

Thousands of articles appear every day on oil, trying to explain the micro and macro movement of prices. Those articles and television spots fling around oft-repeated and accepted ideas of what is *really* driving prices: the dollar, emerging market growth, and peak oil theory, to name only a few. But traders view all of these inputs to price in a far different way than the rest of the public and the news-driven media that report to them.

Now that you have a good idea of what motivates oil traders, it is a great time to view some of these well-regarded influences of oil price as a trader views them: As information that might help generate trading profits. To a trader, *the market* is the one and only important arbiter of value, not the opinions of any economist or oil analyst. Viewed through this prism, many of these well-worn ideas lose quite a bit of their strength—it becomes increasingly clear that the *perception* of these fundamental influences and their affect on investors and traders is far stronger than the influences themselves. Chapter 7 begins to shed more light on this complex but critical piece of the oil puzzle.

Chapter 7

Oil Traders Couldn't Care Less about Peak Oil

Inevitably, if you talk about oil at all or claim any kind of expertise, you are confronted with peak oil theory. So let me be the first to make my complete disclaimer: Despite being a self-professed oil-trading gorilla who has done little notable outside of spending 25 years trading oil in the futures markets, and further having not done any kind of geological or even very intellectual research outside of Internet and magazine reading, I am still a true believer in oil as a limited and depleting resource that will necessarily reach its peak of production sometime in the future.

There.

However, as a trader, and having been surrounded by oil traders all my life, I will make another disclaimer: Oil traders never, ever think about peak oil. Further, the theories and predictions on this limited and ultimately finite resource never enter into any decision on where and what to trade in oil, ever. I have never met a successful (or even unsuccessful) trader of oil mention peak oil theory—not once in my entire career.

Now, with those two statements out of the way, we can talk a little about peak oil theories in the only way that I could possibly speak of it with any authority—in the way that the market currently views the theory. The prices that are being represented tell me about the level of respect the oil world's participants collectively give to peak oil and its rather frantic claims. Whether they are right or not, the collective judgment of the market is that peak oil is not a particularly worrisome prospect at all.

Origins of the Peak Oil Theory

Dr. Hubbert King created the indisputable theory of peak oil in the 1970s, arguing that not only was oil a limited resource, but that our capabilities to find and develop new sources of oil would ultimately dry up and stop. And they did, sometime around 2003; moreover, at the time of this writing, in 2010, it's becoming very unlikely that any very significant new reserves will be found.

The theory continues that there is a current energy appetite that continues to grow at an astounding rate, with more countries that previously used small quantities of energy now (or soon to be) in the midst of industrialized growth and increasing energy needs. This is on top of existing and also growing energy appetites in the developed world. Together, they piece together a dire-sounding and geometrically increasing demand picture for an ultimately limited supply of fossil fuels.

There are widespread and differing opinions about when the peak of this development/demand bell curve is reached, when we will be consuming more oil per day than we are able to extract, but most put the year somewhere between 2020 and 2030, depending on which predictions of growth and usage you go with. After that, the peak oil claimants insist, we are on a steep path downward where resource wars, starvation, and the end of civilization soon will be on us.

One reason they claim that all will be lost soon after the peak of oil is reached is because of our deep dependency on oil, not only for transportation and heat, but for food and manufacture of virtually everything. Once the peak is past, limitations on supply will also limit the ability to develop new energy supplies and restructure our economy and society to accommodate them. The future after the peak is reached, according to adherents, is bleak indeed.

Why Oil Traders Don't Care about the Peak Oil Theory

To argue these points is unnecessary for an oil trader. Books have been written with endless and excruciating facts and figures supplied to support or disprove the trends and theories. It would be impossible for me to begin to take an educated side one way or the other.

I began to hear of peak oil theories in late 2003, as oil rose above $50 a barrel. It was repeatedly spoken of in the press and elsewhere in the media to explain the rising prices of oil. Web sites sprung up to show just how dire the situation was and just why every investor needed to include oil price exposure in their portfolios. Peak oil theory, to me, became just another impetus for individuals to invest in the price of the crude barrel, as opposed to a fundamental reason for oil to be reaching historically new high prices.

And I wondered (and still wonder) how is it that a commodity destined to be delivered inside the next 30 days (as spot crude oil contracts are) are somehow tied to an expected supply difficulty at least 15 years in the future? If oil were like gold, and you could bet on the future price not only with the futures contract, but also by simply taking delivery and putting it in your sock drawer for the next 10 years, perhaps you'd have an argument for peak oil being a driver of price in 2003 and through 2008. But you can't. Storage for oil is impossible (as discussed in detail in Chapter 2), except for the most engaged participant. With oil (and even more so with natural gas), it's use it or lose it. Product delivered today needs to be burned tomorrow.

And the peak oil arguments have spawned that kind of investment in very far back contracts, in oil and in other commodities. It has helped spawn the endless bid. While the traditional users of very far back contracts in the futures markets were the most conscientious hedgers and suppliers, those participants became quickly swamped by long-term investors convinced of the inevitable end of plentiful oil supply.

To put it simply, the market has run out of sellers.

Traded oil price has become more and more skewed as time moves forward through the curve. The less storable the product becomes, the steeper the curve that is generated. Although the curve of prices in crude is a very steep contango, the curve in natural gas has become unfathomable and, to put it mildly, ridiculous.

Later in this chapter, I examine the oil and natural gas curve of prices at length and the unnatural contango that has now become the normal state of energy prices. But as regards the peak oil theory, a quick look at the very long-term trends in prices for the crude barrel becomes very instructive.

The Spread Market Doesn't Believe in Peak Oil

As mentioned throughout this book, the differential between prices is known as spreads, and the spread between the prompt delivery month and the month traded 12 months in the future give us a good indication of the relative values participants put on oil and where they collectively think oil will be priced in the future. For 2009, this 12-month differential, called contango (which I discussed in relation to index funds and exchange-traded funds [ETFs] in Chapter 3), reached unheard-of levels of close to $15. Early in 2009, spot prices briefly hovered in the low $30 area, while prices 12 months in the future were in the high $40s. Although this overwhelming contango was caused by credit market seizure and complete asset deleveraging, it could be considered our worst-case contango, because we shouldn't expect to see such wrenching and unique market conditions often to cause such an outsized back-month premium.

But moving into the start of 2010, a return of a fairly strong contango has reemerged, to upward of $10 a barrel for a 12-month period. While we saw much of the risk return to the oil markets and elsewhere in 2009, the 12-month contango never penetrated less than $5, and generally hovered closer to $8.

Shall we consider this our new baseline peak oil case for premium? If a lessening resource is running up against a world continuing its acceleration of oil use and appetite, then we would expect to see a continuing premium in the price of oil as we move farther afield of the futures prices—farther down the curve. Shouldn't we also expect to see an acceleration of that premium as well, as we near the point at which we find the peak of the peak-oil bell curve, when resources should begin to actually run out? In other words, shouldn't the contango increase with time? If the peak oil theory is to be respected, and in fact, if the predictions that are made of when and where the inflection points are to be reached are true, then the answer must be yes.

But the market doesn't bear this out. In fact, it goes the other way.

For 2009, we saw an average 12-month contango of $8. For 2010, that contango traded around $6. From there, it drops immediately and significantly. For 2011, the differential in December trading prices is $3.50. Indeed, from 2012 through 2018, where the last contract is listed, the 12-month premium is much closer to $2. So, although we have seen more than a $10 contango in 2010, we are in fact seeing a barely doubled $20 contango for the next eight years after that! It is as if the world believes in peak oil in 2009 as a certainty, but yet believes in it less and less as the years progress.

Or is it more likely a case of informed and intelligent participants? Although there are only a few participants in oil contracts that are pricing four, six, and eight years in the future, either they are better informed about the likelihood of peak-oil predictions or the public investor is missing out on the greatest and easiest money making opportunity in the next five to eight years. Of course, the market can always be wrong, but clearly many of the smartest participants don't have much respect for long-term peak-oil predictions.

Peak oil may be absolutely true and the predictions of the most wide-eyed doomsayers correct and inevitable. I don't have the information to either agree or debunk their research and claims. But the market has told me two things in the past seven years:

1. that the total lack of logic and inflation of crude and natural gas prices has been consistently tied to peak oil arguments (both in the press and with investment managers);

2. that a lot of smart people don't believe it and are willing to bet their money against its professed timeframe and inevitability, according to the curve of prices.

Flipping the Curve—The Market Speaks

The market speaks to me as a trader with absolute authority. It is always right in the only way that matters to traders—money. I've written a bit about the oil curve—that is, the difference in prices between delivery months of crude oil futures—but so far, only very little about what the curve of prices can tell us.

For example, is it predictive? In other words, if prices increase throughout the curve, should we continually expect the inflation and weaker monetary conditions that higher commodity prices usually bring? And if prices decline, should we expect commodity deflation in the future, and also expect the recession that deflationary commodity prices normally portend?

The short answer is no: The oil curve has been historically dismal in predicting general economic trends, but it's been terrific in showing where many people think economic trends are going. As a trader, recognizing where the bets are showing can be even more important, however. That is why traders so often concentrate on the spread markets and the curve of prices: They can be the most useful tool in a trader's arsenal. If you can determine where the money has gone into the oil market, it's likely you'll find where the next batch of capital is headed.

All this makes the spread market in oil very, very interesting to examine during 2007 to 2010. It serves a particular interest to me as a proof of the violent dislocations that have been caused by the endless bid in oil. At one particular moment in 2009, the endless bid caused such a disruption to (at least temporarily) destroy the logical framework of the oil market entirely. But to understand this, we need to first understand what a normal curve of prices should look like and why.

All things being perfectly equal, the curve of oil prices should always trend lower. The reason for this is simple: storage. It's a simple case of a bird in the hand—physical oil, ready to be delivered, transported, refined, and used has a ready value and must be dealt with in some way immediately; in contrast, oil in the form of a contractual obligation (i.e., a promise on a piece of paper) has no such immediacy requiring storage. For the majority of my trading career, this was the norm—prices trending (marginally) lower through the curve, a condition called backwardation, or a premium market.

However, even in a normal time, with very little outside affecting the curve of prices, a continual and steady premium market is relatively rare. And it's a good thing that it is rare: Most traders including me, made most of their daily livelihood trading the changing differentials in the curve, trading the spreads. If they were consistently static, at a steady 15¢ to 20¢ a month premium, we would have been out of a job.

No, plenty would affect the spreads and the look of the curve, but many of these things would be readily understandable—for example, a planned refinery maintenance shutdown would spike product prices for a particular month compared to others, or a storm would close down cargo deliveries for a short period. Other measurable events affecting the curve would be seasonal—for example, December was a traditional month for accumulating crude for inventories and would price at a notable premium; gasoline would carry premiums during the late spring and summer months during the height of the driving season; and heating oil would similarly carry premiums during the winter months.

Many of the expected and traditional features of the oil curve changed late in 2007, it seems, forever. Since then, the curve of prices took on a completely opposite pattern than the one oil traders and other oil participants had come to expect: The prices in the front months in crude began to run at a discount to the months further out in the curve. The market now exhibited a contango or discount curve of prices.

The first reaction people outside of oil would have is a lack of surprise: "Of course, the curve of prices changed, the market started going up! It only makes sense that prices further in the future would be higher than they would be right now." Although this may sound reasonable, the problem of storage still makes a contango market totally unnatural.

Indeed, during my interview at Coastal (described in Chapter 4), one of the funny moments I had in the hallways that day was passing by the great Sam Willson on my way to another meeting. During that moment, the crude market was experiencing a temporary and entirely weird discounting, and as Willson passed me in the hall, he asked me, "Hey Dan, when does the contango end?"

Although his tone was casual, the question itself was far from casual, because the physical oil business for Coastal was getting killed by the contango, in essence discounting the costs of storage for them and cutting profits horribly. The company hadn't seen it coming, didn't understand it, and hadn't traded to account for the shortfall. Coastal needed the market to right itself and return to the traditional premium market that it had relied on, and the sooner the better.

I saw the contango then as a trading anomaly, to a far lesser degree than I do now, but I was as stumped then as ever. When was it going to end? How the heck should I know? I fumbled an answer in the hallway, although I knew a believable prediction—whether it turned out to be right or wrong—would probably have landed me the position because Coastal was so mired in discounted inventory. Even at that moment in 1998, there could only be a financial reason that the market was experiencing such a strange and unnatural dislocation—but Willson knew that too.

The real question wasn't why it was happening; instead, the critical question was about when it was going to revert to normal, which is always the most difficult question for any trader to answer. Still, the market reverted to a seasonal premium a few months after my visit to Houston that year, restoring the natural oil markets for producers for a long time.

These days, however, a backwardated market seems a relic of history. And viewed historically, at least using my 25 years of trading history, the continuing contango of oil makes no sense to me. One of the most dependable rules of trading oil that I learned in the first few months after I stepped into the pits in 1982 is about spot market dominance: That the front months always react first and most strongly to market trends. In an up market, you'd get the most bang for your buck by buying the front months, compared to any other part of the curve. In the same way, if you wanted to be a little more conservative and play the spreads instead of outright lots, you'd be an almost certain winner if you bought spreads in an up-trending market; that is, bought front month contracts while simultaneously selling back months. In a down market, the opposite would be true: Front months would almost always move down faster than the back months would, so you'd do well to sell spreads—selling the spot or close to spot contracts while buying contracts further out on the curve.

Much of my daily trade in the pits for the first 15 years of my career was based on this one simple, tired but dependable rule: Early in the day, I might have a hunch on which direction the market might be headed. If I thought it was headed higher, I'd often buy spreads— buy the front months and sell the backs. If I thought it was headed lower, I'd do the opposite and sell spreads. The advantage of using spreads as opposed to just buying or selling the market outright was one of staying power—a single order of any size that came in against your outright position might be enough to scare you out of your conviction. In contrast, holding spread positions would allow you to ride out the big orders that might be betting against you, but which ultimately turned out to be wrong. Spreads are terrific tools for the trader of futures. In comparison, stock traders, even though they have plenty of hedging options, have nothing precisely similar to rely on.

But traders who believed in the long-term upward trend of oil in 2003 or 2005 or particularly 2007 who wanted to hedge their exposure by using spreads got their heads handed to them. They watched in disbelief as the market continued to head upward at the same time that the spreads first began to narrow, then ultimately flip and trade consistently in contango. What happened here?

One thing that happened for sure was part and parcel of the changing cast of players in the oil market: The perception on oil changed into a long-term story of consistently rising prices. Whether it was true or not, peak-oil arguments and the growth of emerging nations pointed to higher prices in the future. To put it simply, no one wanted to sell contracts far out in the future, and they began to demand a heavy premium to do so. We've noted that the curve of oil prices is practically useless in predicting the future price. But perception, as I mentioned at the start of this section, can be much more powerful than prediction.

Supercharged Contango: The Goldman Roll

Another very powerful financial factor also helped to create the new normal of contango oil markets: the Goldman roll. As noted in Chapter 5, long-only commodity funds (LOCFs) have accounted for a large amount of the growth in oil trade, and nowhere were they more influential on the price of oil than in what's been called the Goldman roll. LOCFs invest in a variety of futures contracts, creating a basket of commodities. Energy-related commodities comprise the largest percentage of the contracts held, totaling 50% to 75% of the total portfolio. Energy contracts included in the basket are crude oil, heating oil, and natural gas. Other commodities included in these funds are precious and base metals, grains, meats, sugar, and coffee.

The largest of these funds is the Goldman Sachs Commodities Index (GSCI), with approximately $55 billion invested. Other notable LOCFs include the Dow Jones AIG Commodity Index, the Deutsche Bank Liquid Commodity Index (DBLCI), and the Rogers Commodity Index, but it is the overwhelming significance of the GSCI that earns the moniker of the Goldman roll.

So to understand how all these funds operate, let's look at the GSCI. This fund holds long positions in the nearby futures contract for every commodity in its portfolio. As expiration of the futures contracts approaches, the fund will liquidate (sell) its entire position in the current month and establish a new position (buy) in the next active month. This action of selling the nearby futures contract and buying the next contract month is called the roll, and it's done between the fifth and the ninth of every month. These transactions are automatic and not the least price-sensitive: Positions are rolled whether or not the spread between the spot and next month is favorable.

Despite the fact that this phenomenon is called the Goldman roll, Goldman Sachs itself bears no risk from this mechanical skewing of the futures markets each month. Instead, Goldman's investors are bound by the costs of this artificial investment in oil, and they bear all the risks. In contrast, one of the most famous oil stories involving risk from a forced rolling of positions is one I personally (and successfully) traded and witnessed was the Metallgesellschaft incident, described in the sidebar "An Offer They Couldn't Refuse."

An Offer They Couldn't Refuse

The curve in gasoline prices has always been a little unique. The price curves upward in the spring, peaks to a premium during the summer driving season, then starts to decline again. The months outside any peak period, in gasoline and in other commodities, are known as shoulder months.

So let's rewind the tape to 1993. After the Berlin wall fell, the new Russian republic thought its great oil resource presented a good start to entering the world capitalist economy. Russian crude was readily available, but the Russian refining infrastructure lagged far behind. One government-sponsored group approached a German company, Metallgesellschaft, with an idea—to swap discounted Russian crude for refined gasoline. An entirely new marketing subsidiary was set up inside the German company to create the other side of the swap—selling long-term contracts for crude to end users.

Metallgesellschaft had long experience in these kinds of arrangements, known as forward swaps, but the company had previously used them almost exclusively for currencies and base metals. This was the company's first foray into oil. It would also prove to be the last.

The Russians wanted a long-term arrangement and created some very attractive components to lure the Germans into signing. First, the crude was sold according to the NYMEX curve, but with a significant discount. Metallgesellschaft needed merely to hedge the price outright on the crude market to assure a profit, or to find willing counterparties over the counter (OTC) to take long-dated crude at relatively cheap prices, at least according to the NYMEX crude curve. The company did that part of the trade relatively easily.

The gasoline leg of the swap is what proved problematic. The gasoline market was nowhere near as liquid as crude, and the approximately 3,000 contracts a month that needed to be hedged could not be handled in the far back months at that time. The

(Continued)

An Offer They Couldn't Refuse (*Continued*)

Russians knew this. It was one reason they were not capable of doing this deal without help.

However, in exchange for this risk, the Russians offered to buy the gasoline at a constant summer price, about 75¢, throughout the life of the swap, which represented a 5¢ profit per gallon to the Germans in August and a 20¢ profit in January. This was too good to walk away from, and the Germans entered into a 12-month agreement.

The final step for the Germans to lock in their profits was supposed to be simple as well. As a synthetic short (supplier) of gasoline to the Russians, the Germans still required a hedge. They needed to buy the front-month gasoline contract and then liquidate that position while creating an equivalent long position in the next closest month as the front month expired, an equivalent buy-and-sell operation known as a roll.

In practice, all you need do is buy the spread every month, selling spot as you buy the next month out. The 5¢ profit pad in the first month and the near-20¢ profit at the farthest month should provide an enormous buffer against a price squeeze. All the Germans needed to do was be wrong about the price curve for less than an average of almost 10¢ in 12 months, and they would make a heady profit, which must have seemed near to a sure thing.

When It Rains, It Pours

In the first month, the Germans managed to make a tidy 4¢ profit on 3,000 lots (close to $5 million!) and the best, supposedly, was yet to come. Unfortunately for them, a few traders in the gasoline pits noticed an unfamiliar broker coming in at the end of the month with only one order to fill: over and over, he'd look to buy a lot of spot spreads.

In the second month, a few traders were watching for this broker to appear. He did and found that he had quite a bit more trouble getting his roll accomplished, although he still netted the Germans a tidy profit.

An Offer They Couldn't Refuse (*Continued*)

By the third month, the game was up. Pit traders inflated prices in the days before expiration and blew out the front month spread in preparation for the broker's one-sided orders, helping to see that his orders were filled as expensively as possible.

Hey, what can I say? Traders are in it for the money. I remember feeling particularly sorry for this broker. It's impossible to play poker when everyone at the table knows what cards you're holding. I imagine the reports he had to give his German clients at the end of a day weren't very happy ones.

By the fourth month, the entire floor was in on this monthly gift. Almost every NYMEX trader had a few gas spreads waiting for this poor guy. Remember, too, that the Germans had little choice but to try to cover their gasoline risk. The upstairs desks were also aware of the Germans' problems and were even less likely to buy their bad swaps positions. Other fundamental factors also skewed the curve against them. When it rains, it truly does pour.

Needless to say, the German firm did not survive the life of this swap arrangement: By the sixth month, it was bankrupt.

Modern position rolls for commodity indexes carry little risk for their providers, and for a long time, they also had little impact on the curve of oil prices. But as investment in indexes increased in size, the influence of the Goldman Roll did as well. Traders are no dummies either (as you can gauge from the Metallgesellschaft story): They recognize an opportunity when it arises, so the mechanical and dependable spread selling that entered the pit each month became more and more noticeable and a lot more actionable. Traders began to anticipate the roll, skewing the natural shape of the oil curve. As a few traders caught on to the coming roll, they'd sell front-month spreads a day or two before the orders from the index owners would come in.

But as more and more traders caught on, and as more and more indices became popular, traders began to anticipate the roll even earlier, selling spreads many days before the scheduled program selling would arrive. The combined effect of the rolling of index positions with the opportunity trade from independent and commercial traders finally altered the traditional curve once and for all, where now the contango condition seems to be the natural state for oil futures.

The mechanical and inevitable monthly roll from indexes (and recently from ETFs), which created a sharp new upward sloping curve in oil prices, over time helped to overemphasize whatever fundamental arguments for rising prices there were. A self-fulfilling prophecy of rising prices was being represented by the curve. No matter what the nature of the economy, stockpiles, storage, or geopolitical events, the crude curve continued to exhibit its unnatural contango. But nowhere did the silliness of the constant contango become more ridiculous than in the first few months of 2009. Unnatural premiums applied to oil's curve of prices finally run up against the most obvious wall: It becomes a money-losing proposition to ever sell a real barrel of oil in the prompt market. This is what happened in the early months of 2009.

As the crude oil market experienced the most violent deleveraging in its history in the late summer and fall of 2008, spot oil prices fell from a high of $147 a barrel to a final low of $32. This historic drop in the price of the crude barrel was caused by the perfect mirror image of the same forces that had seen oil rise in price sixfold in five years. All of that investment money—in the form of index investment, hedge fund, and individual trading and commercial speculation tied to easy credit—disappeared, practically overnight. But what remained was the longer-term real hedges established by commercial producers and end users. The effect on the curve of crude prices was not only illustrative of the power of all of this capital on price; it also threatened to call into question the value of the market itself.

As the air came out of the oil bubble, all of the speculative money disappeared from the front-month contracts, where they had always come for liquidity and immediacy, while many more of the back-month participants had legitimate hedge reasons or longer-term investment commitments to stay with their positions. As the market first dropped under $80 and then $50 and $40, the contango in the curve got more and more pronounced. And because it got more pronounced in a market where the prices were so much lower, it multiplied the actual differential of the contango on a percentage basis to an amazing degree.

In January 2009, I appeared on CNBC to report that the contango for a 12-month period in crude oil had ballooned to close to $15—unheard of in the history of oil, particularly with crude trading in the mid-$30 region. And I explained that this dislocation was creating a very weird but unique opportunity for physical oil (at least, physical West Texas Intermediate [WTI] oil): You could make a very decent profit (actually a ridiculously huge profit) just by storing oil, instead of delivering it.

The math on this was simple. If you bought oil on the open futures market at $33, where the spot month was then trading with the plan of storing it, you could simultaneously sell futures contracts 12 months down the road for $47. This amounted to a 36% return on investment, minus the storage and credit carry costs. In an environment of deleveraging assets and recession, even depression fears, this was a terrific opportunity.

Storage at the Cushing, Oklahoma delivery point for WTI quickly reached its bulging limits. Stories began to emerge of crude tankers being cannibalized from transport duties to storage, both in Europe by Royal Dutch Shell and in the United Stated by Koch energy. Other integrated energy companies simply withheld delivery of WTI crude oil from delivery wherever they had the option, although most had obligations they couldn't ignore. Any time you could avoid selling prompt barrels, whether for a day, a week, a month, or a year would be rewarded with instant profits. It was an obvious trade. It was obvious, but it was far from simple. Although interest rates were hovering near 0%, finding the credit to borrow against future deliveries for most participants was impossible. So too was finding storage: Independent tanks reached capacity, and further advantage from this backward carry trade was available only to those few who had storage capacity of their own that remained unfilled. Because so few could take advantage of this crazy dislocation in the curve, it continued for an astoundingly long time.

During 2009, as oil began its investment-inspired run up from $32 to $82, the contango began to lessen, in real dollar terms but particularly in percentage terms, which made the oil carry trade at the beginning of the year so lucrative. But besides index investment that continues to skew the contango through the rolling of positions, the wide-scale growth of commodity and oil-specific ETFs are adding to the contango dislocation. Toward the end of 2009, oil took a breather, moving from above $80 a barrel to close to $71. During that 10% selloff, much of the same ballooning of the contango as happened early in the year repeated itself. The oil market again saw $11, $12, and $13 discounting over 12-month periods, giving physical partici-pants with access to storage and credit the opportunity to bank absolutely free-money arbitrage—all on the paid backs of index and ETF investors who were willing to pay for exposure to oil at seem-ingly any price at all. As of this writing, the money continues to pour in, making money for the physical trader and shills for these flawed financial products.

Of all the many proofs of the diabolical effects of the endless bid on legitimate markets, the crazy contango of 2009 still ranks as the most definitive, literally taking hundreds of millions of dollars out of the pockets of consumers and handing it to those few with lucky access to storage.

The Dollar's Influence on Oil is Highly Overrated

Finally, any discussion of oil pricing in the last decade will naturally also involve a discussion of the dollar. I argue about the non-fundamental factors driving oil price to crazy levels, but the devaluation of the dollar in the last decade is a fundamental impossible to entirely ignore: see Figures 7.1 and 7.2.

Since 2000, the dollar has been clearly trending lower by both benchmarks of the dollar versus the European Central currency (the Euro) but also using the dollar index (DXY), a basket of currencies measured against the dollar.

This matters, obviously, because crude oil is priced in dollars on every exchange and in the majority of swap and OTC contracts. If you are an international buyer, relying on a benchmark product priced

Figure 7.1 Tracking the Monthly Price of DXY, The Dollar Index from 2001–2010
SOURCE: Barchart.com

in dollars, your purchasing power for oil also relies on the value of the U.S. dollar that you must use to price it.

Therefore, it is just impossible to ignore the factor of dollar weakness in the rise of crude oil prices. But the dollar's fall has been far too universally and singularly used as the most important factor in oil's price rise, by some analysts as the only important factor. This is a

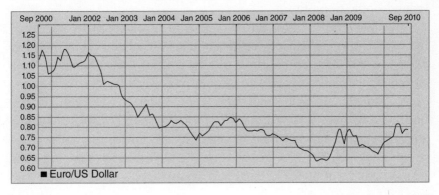

Figure 7.2 Tracking the Price of the U.S. Dollar versus Euro from 2000–2010
SOURCE: Barchart.com

mistake, and an oversimplification. Let's analyze this relationship a little more closely and see why.

In trying to make the best case for the dollar as the most striking influence over commodity prices, it is common to use the absolute height of the dollar's strength in 2001 as a starting point. This is unreasonable, because it captures a moment in time when U.S. expansion was at its strongest, recession was a distant memory, and emerging markets had not really begun to expand. In 2001, the dollar index stood touching 120, and the Euro could be bought for 85¢. These are outsized numbers and not representative of the dollar's history, a far more reasonable benchmark might be a dollar index of 100 and a 1 to 1 parity to the Euro. But for argument's sake, let's take the extremes and debunk the influence of the dollar using those benchmarks. Surely if we can weaken a case for the extremes, the medians should fall rather easily.

Firstly, for deals taking place in the domestic United States, the dollar price should really not matter at all. The correct relationship between purchasing power and the dollar for trading and physical buying and selling should not be the dollar index at all, but the inflation rate—as it is with all other domestically purchased goods and services. A moderate inflation rate of 3% from 2001 to 2008 can hardly account for much of the six times price inflation that oil saw in those years. And a sizable majority of trading and swaps activity is initiated around domestic positions.

But let's even assume that all valuation of oil on every exchange (no matter the participant or the ultimate use of the trade) is being executed through the window of the dollar metric. Even at these extremes, the dollar's decline can only take weak and partial responsibility for the monster multi-year rally. Even if we figure in the outsized doubling in the value of the Euro compared to the dollar and a much more significant but still large 42% decline of the dollar compared to the basket of currencies in the dollar index that still only manages to account for a meager portion of oil's six-fold price rise from 2001 to 2008.

Let's do some simple math to prove this. Let's take oil price at the absolute height of the dollar index, in early 2002. At the start of that year, oil was trading very close to $25 a barrel. Let's now take the dollar's lowest moment, in the second quarter of 2008, when the index reached a low of about $72. Even with every barrel priced with dollar sensitivity, this 41% dollar devaluation could account for a $16.67 increase in price—a $41.67 benchmark, not the $125-plus per barrel prices we saw during the spring and summer of 2008.

Of course, we could skew these numbers to minimize the dollar's effects even further. Oil traded very close to $30 a barrel both at the start of 2001 and the start of 2004. But the dollar index stood well above 110 in the opening months of 2001, yet closer to 85 at the beginning of 2004. If we used this 2004 figure as a benchmark with crude oil at $30 a barrel, we would expect the dollar's influence at the height of 2008's blowoff to be a meager 29%, adding about $8.82 to oil's price, or giving about $38.82 a barrel dollar-adjusted benchmark.

And so many interesting moments from 2001 through 2008 point to an astounding yet complete decoupling of the dollar from oil. For example, in 2005, the dollar staged a mighty rally, with the index moving from around 80 to over 92. That same year saw some of the biggest gains for oil on a percentage basis, starting the year just above $40, yet ending it approaching $70. In a world where the price of oil is so closely tied to the dollar, is such a move possible? Apparently, in 2005, it was.

Although impossible to completely dismiss, it is clear that far more influential of price than the movement of the dollar has become the universal perception of the dollar's motion on the price of oil. After witnessing the lockstep motion of the dollar and oil's price during the first decade of the twenty-first century, it isn't apparent to me that the connection between the dollar and the price of oil is very strong at all.

What is clearly apparent is the enormous strength of the now rampant and widespread dollar/oil trade. It is impossible for two markets, even two assumed as closely related as oil and the dollar to trade so absolutely, inversely together as they have in 2007 to 2009 particularly, as shown in Figure 7.3.

Far more than the dollar moving oil, it now seems that program trading and hedging systems are perpetuating and, in fact, creating this inverse relationship. Trade systems are buying oil and now hedging

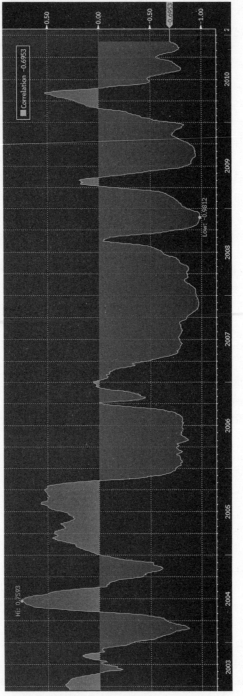

Figure 7.3 Correlation between Oil versus Dollar, 2007–2009
SOURCE: Bloomberg.com

with the dollar, selling oil and buying the dollar. Indeed, the dollar/ oil trade has become a buzzword in financial media, the hot method to hedge oil bets and a simple and understandable story for oil's motion from day to day.

And yet this relationship seemed to be rapidly disintegrating through 2009 and through much of 2010. It has shown a strong recent rally of more than $10 while the dollar has also shown relative strength, moving from under 75 to trade above 78. European monetary difficulties in 2010 weakened the Euro, simultaneously strengthening the dollar rapidly, without a concurrent deflationary effect on the crude barrel. Like in 2005, there are still moments when the dollar's influence on oil can weaken and disappear. One thing is for sure: Drawing a straight line between oil's price and the dollar's price is a facile and mostly wasted effort. As with most markets, nothing bends to quite such simple rules so easily.

Conclusion

We've looked at some of the fundamental arguments that have had a strong influence on the price of oil in the past—whether truth or perception, the market remains the only important arbiter. Now might be a great time to have a look at some of the fundamental arguments that look likely to have tremendous impact on oil price in the future and see how the oil markets are treating them. We're getting closer to fully understanding Oil's Endless Bid in all its forms and all of its problems. Chapter 8 begins the discussion with alternative crude oil sources.

Chapter 8

Alternative Sources of Oil

Why Investors Should Care

etting a lesson on the many varied non-conventional sources of physical crude oil from a career day trader of futures is like taking a lesson in animal hunting and pelt gathering from the midtown fur salesman at Saks. Yet even as unqualified as I am, it is clear to me from the way that the market trades that these alternative sources of crude oil (which are already a significant part of the physical market) are projected to be even more substantial in the future.

Remember our discussions of the curve of oil futures prices in Chapter 7? Even very far into the future, quoted prices for crude oil barely keep up with a standard 3% to 4% rate of inflation. Therefore, the consensus of those betting on the oil market in the medium term doesn't anticipate much of a supply problem arising, at least until 2025.

Of course, the market's predictions could be entirely wrong, as markets often are. It seems, though, that non-conventional sources of crude oil are the reason that our longer-term curve of prices doesn't slope more upward than that simply tracked by the route of pretty common raw materials inflation.

Moreover, examining new sources of the supply of oil has two important purposes. First, it can help you understand just what less-conventional sources demand of the oil barrel price in order to make them cost-effective. For example, if conventional importing of crude oil, from Saudi Arabia let's say, holds a break-even cost of $5 a barrel, while historic prices for crude have hovered under $25 a barrel (at least until 2001), we can assume that a $20 profit margin was a market-driven and reasonable expectation for the oil industry. Conventional crude sources continue to dominate global production, but the nonconventional sources we outline here continue to increase their share of global supply. One would expect, however, that the profit margins for these newer supplies would remain mostly in line with the traditional sources they now augment. Therefore, should we expect even ultra-deepwater-drilling production, which is only in its infancy, with about a $35-a-barrel break-even cost, to fundamentally support a price much higher than $55? It shouldn't, particularly because the break-even costs of accessing deepwater supplies (the most costly non-conventional supply to get at) will continue to drop, as experience and technology continue to advance.

The second important purpose of examining less-traditional oil supplies is in some ways to debunk supply-side arguments for increasingly volatile and oft-times steeply increasing prices. We have seen that global supply of crude has been a fairly elastic number: As global growth has demanded more supply, sources have emerged to satisfy those demands rather easily. Although there surely is a limit on what the earth can ultimately provide, these unconventional supplies of crude oil represent resources capable of powering the planet for many centuries to come.

And although many technological and environmental difficulties are yet to be surmounted, it is clear that the science, finances, and will are rapidly moving toward enabling these supplies to be slowly, but inevitably, unlocked. Any shocks in the price of the crude barrel are difficult to blame on global supply restraints; instead, it has been the perception of these supply difficulties, felt through financial instruments, that have had the most immediate and telling effects on the price of oil.

So let's examine these false perceptions by showing how the many new, alternative supplies of crude oil are abundantly capable of providing for any energy shortfall until truly alternative means of energy are ready to take their place.

What Constitutes a Nonconventional Source of Oil?

What do I mean when I refer to nonconventional sources? These are all the sources of crude outside of traditional free-flowing land wells, which most of us imagine when we speak of crude oil. Most people conjure up the image that has been replayed a hundred times in movie scenes: A down-on-his-luck wildcatter finally strikes it rich and does a little Wallace Beery Treasure-of-the-Sierra-Madre jig, while getting showered in black gold in front of his spewing wooden rig. "It's a gusher, fellas, it's a gusher!"

Yet many sources of crude other than from simple onshore wells are being accessed today. Technology advances have played a significant role in the discovery and ability to extract crude from less obvious and more complex situations than the simple, 1920s-era image of a wooden derrick and a rotating drill. It's important to understand a little bit about these less-traditional sources of crude oil, if only to understand just how rich our planet still is in fossil fuels and how deep our supply options still are.

We are simply not being held hostage to the Ghawar oil field (which is the largest single crude reservoir in Saudi Arabia and its reserves), as many in the peak oil camp will argue. There are new methods to get crude out of places we never thought accessible, and there are new technologies to get more crude oil out of places we thought were completely empty from previous extraction efforts. In addition, there are unconventional sources of crude oil, like oil sands and oil shale (which I discuss in detail later in this chapter), that have been largely ignored because of the relative ease of conventional crude extraction. Together, these sources can deliver a reliable and more domestically derived supply of crude oil and other fossil fuels to power our economy much further into the future, when truly alternative sources of energy will be ready to take the place of fossil fuels.

Why Do We Still Depend on Foreign Sources of Oil?

We've been spoiled in the ease with which we've been able to find energy sources, and that ease has inspired our runaway addiction to oil. For most of the last 100 years, crude oil has been found and extracted very easily. In the United States, where the volume of crude extraction and usage has, per capita, enormously outpaced all other countries worldwide for almost a century, ease has entirely dictated our choices for where to get our supplies. The simplest source has been to harvest as much crude from U.S. fields as possible, using as little excess energy as possible—in essence, drilling a hole in the ground, adding a pipe, and allowing the intrinsic pressures of oil reservoirs to empty. This simplest form of oil well reached peak production through the 1960s and continues to actively produce today, although at lesser levels.

As domestic wells began to run drier and our appetite for cheap energy exceeded what those resources could easily support, we've looked to increase recoverable percentages from existing wells, but more often, we have concentrated on other sources of easily flowing crude (often in the Middle East), and we've paid to have it imported. The only metrics in deciding where to get our fuel supplies for the past century have been ease and cost effectiveness.

But it gets clearer all the time that our relationships with exporting countries and our political standing with other developed and emerging nations have been changing those simple equations. Creating effective alliances for crude oil imports from Saudi Arabia, Kuwait, Iraq, Venezuela, Nigeria, and Mexico—six of the top 15 importers of crude to the United States—was a far easier task in the 1950s, 1960s, and 1970s than it is today. OPEC's flexing of supply muscle during the oil shock of 1973 was our first indication that political forces could affect our ability to import oil cheaply. Two gulf wars and continually changing political stability in Nigeria and Venezuela continue to haunt our ability to be sure of overseas resources as being reliable.

In light of all this, it is surprising that the United States continues to rely substantially on foreign sources of oil in 2010. In spite of the fact that every administration since Richard Nixon's in the early 1970s has promised to take drastic steps to reduce our dependence on foreign sources of energy, we have, in fact, moved backward in the last 40 years. In 1970, 24% of our oil came from imported sources; in 2010, that number stands slightly above 53%.

The reason for this is simple: money. In a country that has a greater appetite for oil than any other by far, we have continually chosen the simplest and cheapest route to supply, wherever it can be found.

Offshore Drilling Opportunities

Drilling for crude oil through water has a long history, dating back to the middle of the nineteenth century, but it has been only since 1960 that significant production offshore has been secured, and only since 1990 that production in the U.S. offshore has overtaken domestic onshore supply. Overseeing this massive resource is a federal responsibility, because individual states' control of shorelines disappears outside of three nautical miles from shore and reverts to the Federal government. Licensing and leasing of offshore drilling rights are under the aegis of the Materials and Management Service (MMS), a division of the U.S. Department of the Interior. In the United States, the waters outside California, Alaska, Louisiana, and Texas comprise the vast majority of producing wells, with the Western Gulf of Mexico providing almost 25% of the total amount of domestic crude oil supply in 2008.

Three rather generalized classifications exist for offshore drilling production based on water depth (see also Figure 8.1 for a comparison of these three types of production):

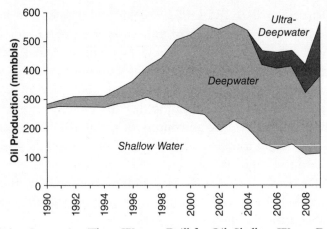

Figure 8.1   Comparing Three Ways to Drill for Oil: Shallow Water, Deepwater, and Ultra-Deepwater
SOURCE: Mineral Management Service, Energy Information Administration, and Office of Oil and Gas

1. Shallow-water drilling includes depths up to 1,000 feet. Shallow-water drilling in the Gulf of Mexico comprised more than 90% of all the production until about 2000, when the technology problems of dealing with the intense pressures and lower temperatures of deepwater environments began to be conquered.
2. Deepwater production is between 1,000 and 5,000 feet. Since 2000, deepwater production has begun to overtake shallow-water production.
3. Ultra-deepwater drilling is classified at depths of more than 5,000 feet. Since 2005, ultra-deepwater drilling has pushed drill bits further and further under water to find ever-larger reservoirs and continue to increase production from offshore drilling, now double what it was in 1990.

Of course, costs were the most significant reason that shallow-water drilling dominated offshore production in the Gulf of Mexico until 2001. The day rates for leasing offshore rigs tells only part of the story of ratcheting costs as depths increase: A jackup rig can lease for anywhere between $30,000 to $100,000 a day, whereas the most well-equipped ultra deepwater drill ships and semi-submersibles will lease for as much as $150,000 to $500,000—in other words, five times that of the shallow rig equipment.

At deeper depths further offshore, crews must be helicoptered in for two- to five-week shifts onto rigs that are floating hotels as well as workplaces, because it becomes impossible for crews to sleep onshore and work offshore with units that sit 50 to 100 miles off of the coast. As depths increase and more expertise is required, wages also must increase.

But it is not simply the cheaper costs and reducing production of shallow-water drilling that is spurring the drive for ever deeper and more risky drilling in deep and ultra-deep water. There is a clearer understanding, as we move further offshore and further down beneath the sea, that enormous undiscovered and unexplored fossil fuel deposits still wait to be found.

A prime (but certainly not lone) example of this is the huge Tibor oil field find, only discovered in September 2009. This field lies 250 miles east of Galveston, Texas in water between 1,300 and 5,000 feet in depth. It is estimated to contain between 3 and 5 billion barrels of crude. Ironically, the first rig to drill down into the Tibor field and create a producing well in 2009 was the $2 billion Deepwater Horizon rig owned by TransOcean, the same rig that caught on fire and sank in the Macondo well disaster in April of 2010.

That disaster has brought into question the risks of offshore drilling versus the obvious gains, but only for the moment. Much of the growth expected to satisfy ever-increasing demands for oil relied on deep and ultra-deepwater drilling. It seems highly unlikely that even a disaster as far-reaching and destructive as the Macondo well spill can have a very significant effect on the future of drilling in the Gulf and elsewhere. Technological advances have enabled us to only recently explore and find wells as rich as the Tibor oil field. Exploration procedures are equally in their infancy that can deal with near-freezing water, pressures of 3,000-plus pounds per square inch, and dense rock and salt formations to unlock the reservoirs held deep under the oceans and even deeper inside the earth's crust. Right now, the MMS regards the Tibor well as at best only 20% to 30% recoverable, perhaps yielding only 600 to 800 million barrels of oil.

Further advances and experience at drilling in ultra-deepwater is more than likely to greatly enhance the recovery rate of new finds, much as injection technologies have reinvigorated old land-based wells thought emptied and dead. Currently, close to 4,000 wells operate in the Gulf of Mexico, and 40,000 have been successfully drilled. With ultra-deepwater drilling only beginning, we can only guess at the new supplies this nonconventional source can and will ultimately deliver.

Another Alternative: Oil Sands

Other less traditional sources of crude oil do not involve accessing free-flowing reservoirs contained in the depths of the earth's crust; instead, they involve separating crude from other mixed products. For example, oil sands are viscous crude deposits, known more commonly as bitumen, mixed in sand and clay fields.

By far, the largest deposits of oil sands are in the Athabasca region of Alberta in Canada, with the second largest source located in the Orinoco deposits of Venezuela. The proven reserves of oil sands in these two regions alone are stunning: Each deposit—individually—is more than the total worldwide proven reserves of conventional crude. Between the two is an estimated 3.6 trillion barrels of potential crude, compared with a total worldwide reserve of 1.75 trillion barrels of conventional supply.

Oil sands are an intriguing way to reassess oil supply equations, because they represent such an enormous and promising supply of future crude. However, so far, they have attracted relatively little attention, except in Canada.

The mechanisms for harvesting bitumen are different from conventional crude wells. Because the bitumen does not flow as rapidly as crude from conventional wells, it either needs to be strip mined (like other rock-enfolded commodities), or forced to flow using injections of steam, solvents, hot air, or combinations of the three. However, these techniques require large amounts of outside water and energy.

In addition, because of the very heavy (sulfurous) nature of these deposits, the resultant crude needs to be pre-processed to prepare it for a conventional refining, a process called upgrading. Again, these hydroprocessing procedures require even more water and energy inputs. Finally, the crude is ready for transport and use.

You can see where this equation is headed. Although the technology already exists to turn these enormous oil sands deposits into useful crude, the costs of mining and processing have been the limiting factors to tapping these huge resources. Canada is far ahead of everyone else on actively mining and processing unconventional bitumen in the Athabasca region, and currently 47% of all the oil the Canadians produce is from oil sands. As oil prices rocketed upward after 2003, oil sands as an alternative source of crude have become more and more worthy of development: In fact, several dozen companies are planning almost 100 new oil sands projects in Canada, totaling nearly $100 billion in capital expenditures.

But even with a projected high price of crude as incentive for increased development of oil sands, other hurdles remain. Current technologies for extraction including surface mining, cold flow, Cyclic Steam Stimulation, Vapor Extraction, and Steam-Assisted Gravity Drainage all depend on energy and water, with their inherent environmental and resource-intensive questions to answer. Oil sands extraction contaminates enormous quantities of water, which must be isolated in tailing ponds, are holding pools for the toxically polluted water. Finding ways for reclaiming and reusing this water has taken on great importance. In 2009, Suncor energy announced a new and promising process called tailings reduction operations, which could reduce the time for water reclamation in tailing ponds from years to weeks.

Other issues are equally pressing. Strip mining of bitumen carries the same environmental effects as other mining operations. Recovering and preprocessing oil sands emits far more greenhouse gases than with conventional crude. In short, there is a long way to go to be able to safely maximize the recovery of this alternative source of crude in an environmentally conscious way.

Right now, 1.25 gigajoules of energy are needed to extract a barrel of bitumen and upgrade it to synthetic crude. That energy is mostly generated through the burning of natural gas. A barrel of oil contains about six gigajoules of energy; therefore, there is a 5 : 1 energy efficiency for oil sands production. But the history of oil technology suggests that this number will do nothing but increase, and quickly.

Injection technologies and processing chemistry have leapt forward since 2004, sparked, of course, by the increasing price of the crude barrel and the relative profit possible from alternative sources, and not only oil sands. But Royal Dutch Shell released in its 2006 report that its Canadian oil sands unit had made an after-tax profit of $21.75 per barrel, nearly double its worldwide profit of $12.41 per barrel for conventional crude. Clearly, profits spur innovation.

Conventional oil wells have been similarly revitalized by newer injection technologies to produce crude again, even though they were considered depleted by the old technology standards as recently as 2000. Costs associated with natural gas and oil extraction technologies decrease every year. The possibilities continue to expand. By current methods, only 10% to 15% of oil sands from recognized deposits are so far recoverable. As technologies continue to expand, these percentages are sure to increase, as they have with conventional oil supplies.

Although Canada is the only country now even beginning the harvesting of this enormous new supply of crude, proven reserves of oil sands have been located in the United States in Utah, as well as in Russia and African nations. The American fields are relatively small compared to Canada's Athabasca, but they still hold an estimated 85 billion barrels of harvestable crude—which alone is enough to deliver the entire crude oil supply that the United States will need until 2020 or so. Both these smaller fields, as well as the enormous Orinoco field in Venezuela, remain relatively untouched.

The reasons that huge fuel resources promised by oil sands have been left relatively unexplored have both practical and perception problems associated with them. It is not only the three-fold increase in greenhouse gas emissions compared to traditional crude extraction and the huge water requirements in processing the tar sands that has slowed the permitting process here in the United States, although these are admittedly substantial hurdles. It is the dirty perception caused by the bad odors and foul mining operations that have slowed progress. This country loves its oil, but it does not want to admit the foul nature of its extraction. Extracting and processing tar sands is a foul process indeed.

Technology again is cutting the costs for both extraction and processing, where oil sands break-even cost is now slightly under $30 a barrel. Even with its environmental hazards, tar sands represent a domestic (or at least North American) resource that is quickly becoming impossible to continue to ignore. If there is one thing that the BP Macondo well blowout and Gulf of Mexico spill should have taught us, it is that off-shore drilling, although not right in front of our eyes, hardly shields us from the environmental dangers of pursuing nontraditional crude sources.

Another Alternative: Oil Shale

If you were looking for a domestic source of nontraditional crude, with equal if not greater potential supply as oil sands, you couldn't find a more promising candidate than oil shale in the United States, which was almost completely ignored until 2009. Deposits of shale containing large amounts of Kerogen, a crude-like hydrocarbon, are found in enormous supply in the Green River formation, located through Wyoming, southeastern Utah, and western Colorado, as shown in Figure 8.2.

Once Kerogen is dislodged from the shale, it can be processed into a synthetic crude oil through a chemical process known

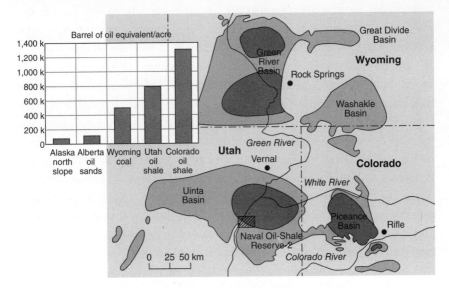

Figure 8.2 Map of Oil in Utah, Wyoming, and Colorado
SOURCE: Energy Information Administration, www.eia.doe.gov

as pyrolysis. But getting at the rock is the first and most difficult hurdle. Up until about 2007, the only available process required strip mining the rock and transporting it for processing—a primitive method that did not excite the big-money oil companies into further exploring this oil resource. Only little Estonia had created much of an industry for mining and exploiting oil shale.

But again, technology has begun to find ways to unlock these crude supplies using less antediluvian tactics. Shell was the first large oil company to gain testing licenses to explore in-situ methods of oil shale extraction and methods of separating the useful kerogen deposits, extracting them from the earth without mining out the rock. Most processes being explored do not call for injection of gases or water (as with oil sands), but with heating the rock to allow the synthetic crude to flow freely away from the shale.

However, the hurdles to oil shale extraction are similar to oil sands, including waste water disposal and an increase of greenhouse gas emissions. In addition, trying to flow oil away from shale has created a problem of possible pollution of intrinsic aquifers that provide drinking water for the surrounding states. Shell has been working on a project that attempts to freeze the surrounding water around oil shale wells, so that aquifers cannot become compromised. So far, the major Shell project in Colorado, in Rio Blanco county, has been restricted to experimentation and not opened for production yet.

In 2010, however, a very interesting company has become involved in oil shale as a nontraditional crude source. IDT, a telecom company that soured to lose more than 90% of its share value, has come roaring back because the company's entrepreneurial CEO, Howard Jonas, has focused on the oil shale deposits in Colorado. Although it's difficult to have confidence in a telecom CEO when it comes to oil extraction technology, the IDT method of extraction seems to make a lot of sense. The rock gets traditionally heated, but the natural gas that is initially expelled from the shale gets reinjected back into the ground and ignited—in essence, using the shale's own energy supply to further heat and liquefy the crude components so they can flow. The oil then gets pumped out directly from the rock formation, which is at depths below the aquifer, avoiding the threat of water contamination. IDT claims that its ability to use energy from the shale to help extract the oil from the rock puts its break-even costs at about $25 a barrel, below that of oil sands extraction and offshore drilling.

It's hard to say whether the IDT method will ultimately have the kind of success to unlock this resource safely, but the company does hold one of only three leases from the federal government to explore and experiment in 160 acres of Colorado shale, with an option, on further success, to leases on 5,000 further acres. Moreover, the giant French oil company Total has already committed whatever further capital IDT will need to complete its development.

If any of these technologies ultimately prove their worth, or another new idea comes along to unlock this resource, the potential is absolutely massive. Proven reserves of oil shale in the Green River Basin alone could amount to as much as 2 billion barrels of crude— which is approximately equal to the entire global conventional supply. In oil shale (as with natural gas), the United States holds far and away the largest proven reserve, with 62% of the total.

Determining the Relative Value of Crude Oil and Refined Products

Crude oil supplies have reached far beyond the conventional sources that most people imagine. And while the most traditional sources of land-based wells are undoubtedly running shorter (although their supplies are also underrated), there continue to be fresh and mostly untapped resources for energy in conventional crude oil through offshore drilling as well as oil sands and oil shale. Believe me, my arguments of ever-increasing supplies of crude (albeit ever more expensive to access) are not intended to condone profligate use of energy, or to continue to advocate that 4% of the world's population (the United States) continues to consume more than 25% of the world's production of fossil fuels. Indeed, it would make no one more delighted than me to see fewer 115-pound soccer moms driving their children to school in 7,000-pound trucks that get less than 15 miles to the gallon, and I believe that the quicker we, as a nation, can get off the addiction to crude oil, the safer, more independent, and better off we will be.

Fundamental arguments, we have seen, are less about supply and demand realities than about how they are perceived by investors and traders. These perceptions then feed Oil's Endless Bid to wreak havoc and cause unfathomable dislocations in two areas particularly—with crack spreads that determine what refiners can charge for finished products and with natural gas. The next two chapters describe each of these proofs of the power and destructiveness of Oil's Endless Bid.

Chapter 9

Proof of Oil's Endless Bid: Crack Spreads

You'd never expect an unstable and generally high oil price to hurt the oil companies, but Oil's Endless Bid has actually forced many of the refiners and dedicated natural gas firms to rethink their business models and pushed some close to the brink of failure.

During much of this book, I've spent most of my efforts concentrating on crude oil, its many varied sources, and alternative supplies. We tend to refer exclusively to the price of the crude barrel when we are trying to gauge current and future energy costs—it is the single price that streaks by when watching CNN or CNBC.

And yet, crude oil by itself is a useless asset. You cannot use raw crude as a fuel for anything. It is only in the refined products from crude oil (like gasoline and heating oil, among many others) that crude has any value whatsoever. The financial relationships between crude oil and its refined products have changed massively because of the endless bid redefining how refiners make—and now lose—money. Now would be a good time to examine those relationships and see how financialized oil surprisingly hurts oil companies.

Two massive energy market dislocations, most noticeable since 2006, have clearly shown just how powerful the endless bid can be—in the traded relationship between crude oil and refined products, (what are known as crack spreads) and with the crazy divergence in the price action between crude oil and domestically traded natural gas (as we'll see in Chapter 10).

Crack spreads are the shorthand way that all market participants use to gauge the relative value of crude oil and the refined products that are made from crude oil. Crude oil in and of itself, no matter what grade, is of absolutely no use to anyone at all. You can't burn it or drink it or use it for lubrication. It's obvious to point this out but still important: It's only because you can make something out of crude oil—something you can burn, or use for lubrication—that gives the crude barrel any value at all.

In other words, it's the products of refined crude oil that we really worry and care about—including gasoline to power our cars and recreational vehicles, heating oil to heat our homes, jet fuel to make our airplanes fly, and so on. It's also important to note that no one should care one whit if crude oil costs $4 or $40 or even $400 a barrel. What matters is how much gasoline or diesel fuel will cost when the raw crude that it comes from costs $4 or $40 or $400. That's what crack spreads measure: the relationship between crude and refined products.

On the New York Mercantile Exchange (NYMEX), in addition to the West Texas Intermediate (WTI) crude oil contract, there are also very actively traded New York heating oil and unleaded gasoline contracts. Each of these contracts exists separately, but there are important and obvious connections between them.

When crude oil is taken to a refinery to be broken down into component refined products, that process is known as cracking— hence the term crack spread. When most sweet grades of crude are refined, for every three units of crude oil, approximately two units of gasoline and one unit of distillate product (like heating oil or diesel fuel) are created (along with other less important hydrocarbons). This

3 to get 2 and 1 ratio is far from perfect, and it depends somewhat on the refining process and the grade of crude being used. (Also, sometimes, these ratios aren't applicable at all.) But it doesn't really matter.

Here's what does matter: Merely as a convention, the 3:2:1 ratio has been adopted by the industry to standardize the connection between the traded markets and the physical refineries. If we were a refinery or marketer and wanted to perfectly hedge our crude and product exposure, we'd certainly have to deviate from this 3:2:1 ratio, but for simply following and trading the relationship between crude and refined products, the 3:2:1 crack works wonderfully well. For quoting and trading, the 3:2:1 crack dominated trading on the NYMEX through much of the 1980s and 1990s.

But as trading of the cracks became more important than having cracks that approximated real-world refining realities, simpler ratios of 1 crude unit to 1 refined product unit (i.e., 1:1) were adopted to quote and trade them. I point all this out for a reason: Although all crack spreads that I refer to and that are talked about by energy analysts nowadays are these simpler 1:1 crack spread, this 1:1 ratio is just a simpler convention, but it doesn't represent the reality of refining, which is far closer to a 3:2:1 ratio.

More important still is to realize that the 3:2:1 ratio implies how much more important gasoline is to the refining process and the refinery business than distillate products. The 3:2:1 reality of refining implies that gasoline products are around twice as widely produced and the profits on gasoline are twice as important as other products refined from cracking. So because gas is twice as significant to refiners, it becomes clear that the gasoline crack spread will be far and away the most significant part of the crack spread to keep an eye on and analyze.

Charting the prices of 1:1 gasoline crack spreads over the last 15 years gives tremendous insight into the oil market and also the disastrous and detrimental influence that the endless bid had in these interrelated markets.

Figure 9.1 is a monthly chart of the 1:1 quoted gasoline crack spread from 2005 through 2009. Although it may look like a crazy wavy line to you, let me show you how simple it is to understand.

First, gasoline is a cyclical commodity. In the summer, as driving ramps up, demand for gasoline ramps up as well, and we should expect prices for gas and the premium for gas compared to crude oil to be higher. With just that information alone, you now would expect the historical crack chart to look like a multi-humped camel, rising in the summer months while fading somewhat in the winter. And that's what you see, mostly.

But in the years 2004 to 2007, what happened? During these years of intense economic growth (both in the United States and in developing nations), we would expect the premium for refined products (i.e., those energy products that have real value as opposed to crude) to increase. And they do. With that information, you would now look at Figure 9-1 and expect to see the same multi-humped camel, but this time that camel should be walking slowly up a hill. If we get into a moment of overheated, or hyper-inflated growth (as in the massive amount of emerging nations growth we saw in the years from 2004 to 2008), we would expect our camel to not just walk up a hill, but to look like he's climbing up a mountain! In those particular and spectacular years, we'd expect the value for refined gasoline would increase overall and throughout the entire year, but also carry an outsized and unusual premium in the peak months of the summer season. Finally, if demand is extremely strong during these moments while refineries are at or close to their limits on what they can produce—what is called full utilization—which can occur particularly in the summer months, we might not be surprised to see a summer squeeze of gasoline, sending the crack values in those summer months soaring.

Now take another look at Figure 9.1.

With some variation that any market will give you, our seasonally humped camel is making our expected and pretty steady walk up a small hill until 2005, 2006, and 2007. Then, we see our camel reach what seems to be the foothills of the Himalayas and start to tromp his way up the Mount Everest of cracks. These years of overheated growth saw incredible spikes in the crack spreads over the summers. Even for experienced gasoline traders like me on the floor, these years were astonishing to see. Where previously I had expected summer crack spreads to fall somewhere between 15 and 20 based on previous

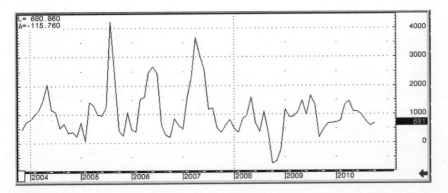

Figure 9.1   Monthly Chart of the 1:1 Quoted Gasoline Crack Spread
SOURCE: CQG

history, instead, we saw a peak crack value of 42 in 2005, a peak of 28 in 2006, and 38 in 2007. Many small fortunes were made on the floor in the summer of those three years (which were also the last few great trading years on the floor, before much of the volume began migrating onto the electronic platforms).

I made some extra money those years too, if only because buying gasoline during those summer ramp-ups in price was difficult to miss, even as a day trader. You'd have to be a total dummy not to be long gasoline while that train was blasting through the station. And even I wasn't a total dummy. But I missed the really big money made by the smarter gas traders I stood near who recognized this for the water-shed trend it was and traded around a consistent long position of a couple hundred (or more!) gasoline cracks each.

Give a Trader an Even Chance, and He'll Look to Manipulate It

Four guys in particular were just awesome at maximizing their posi-tions and profits during these summer crack squeezes: I'll call them Rob, Bobby, Steve, and Mike. They were also all pretty good friends who compared notes about attacking the gas markets during these summer gas fiestas. They pulled out all the stops at their disposal to make the gas market seem as powerful as they possibly could, pushing the potential profits of their positions by helping to drive up the settlement prices for gasoline every day on the close. (Settlement prices are the final prices at the end of every day, which are used to universally value all open positions; because of that, they are also the most significant prices for traders. A bad price reported and traded during the day only implies a loss or gain on a position, but even an unlikely or undependable settlement price at the end of the day creates a real and reportable paper calculation of a loss (or a gain), a real exchange of money, an equity swing, and perhaps a margin call for more capital to support a position.) So it is clear than one can wield tremendous psychological pressure on the market and market participants by marking up or marking down prices on the close, and these guys did all they could—all inside the rules and legally—to mark positions in their favor.

Our outsized influence on settlement prices was another great perk of being a floor trader. I often saw settlement prices that I couldn't believe, given the nature of the real buying and selling during the day. And if I was looking askance at some settlements as they got reported, I can only imagine what many of the participants outside the floor trade must have thought of some of them. They cursed us regularly and complained to the exchange constantly about the legitimacy of settlements.

But in the end, what does it really matter if any price (settlement or otherwise) represents the true balance of buyers and sellers at one time and is really legitimate or not? Once the price gets translated into real capital profits or losses (with its attendant glee or anxiety for the position holders), it's become plenty real enough for me. You want to play the settlement game? First pony up your money, and don't forget to write all of your complaints on a small folded paper and leave them in the box by the door—where no one will look at them or care.

One trick the smarter floor traders would use to advantageously mark positions and make a few extra dollars in the process was by placing trade at settlement (TAS) orders. I've told you how important settlement prices are: they are the daily benchmark that gets printed in the paper, quoted on the news, and marked in accounts for profit and loss. Many customers trading in the commodity markets are so sensitive to settlement prices that all they really want is to capture the settlement price. They initiate a position at a settlement price, adjust it at another settlement on another day, and unwind it at settlement on a third. That's why you'll see the common market on close (MOC) order. It's designed to get prices, whether buying or selling, as close to settlement price as possible.

But customers are an untrusting lot (sometimes rightfully so). When putting in specific orders for the close to try and capture settlement prices, they assume or expect that they will be taken advantage of and not receive execution very close to the final settlement price at all. During my trading days, the advantage that local traders got during the closes was little different than the advantages they expected and got during the rest of the day; however, most customers tend to remember the orders that were filled off settlement that weren't in their favor far more often than orders which were filled in their favor. That's just a fact of brokerage life. Yet despite what I saw as a broker's best intentions, it's just impossible to expect an executing broker to be a mind reader and market genius on the close, trying to measure where in that brief two-minute period they should fill a customer order to capture a price as close to the final settlement as possible.

And yet, it seemed brokers are more often yelled at and threatened by customers about on close orders and settlement prices than for any other time or any other order. It was because of this pressure from customers to try to assure execution close to, or optimally at, settlement prices that the TAS order was created by the exchange.

It sounded like a great idea.

You simply announced your desire to buy or to sell your desired number of contracts at the settlement price of the spot month at any time during the trading day. A broker would come into the pit and yell something like buy 20 TAS, indicating his desire to buy 20 contracts at the final settlement price yet to be determined at the end of the trading day. If you found a partner on this trade, they would be the sellers of those contracts, also at the settlement price.

Through this trade, a customer would be assured of receiving the settlement price. No more worries about executing orders during the chaotic and unpredictable closing range of the last two minutes of the trading day, no more arguments with brokers, no more explanations to clients about fills that were executed far away from settlement.

Everybody should have been happy.

But, with tremendous irony, TAS turned out to be one of the greatest edges ever given to the locals of the floor community, to the detriment of the outside customer. Although it was created to accommodate participants in the futures markets who were looking to limit the advantage of locals in the closing range, instead, it increased that advantage. It took only a few short weeks from the onset of the TAS trade for some of the savviest traders on the floor to figure out a way to manipulate the orders in their favor, augment their odds on the close, and give them far greater insight into the probable direction of the market as each trading day came to an end. Here's how it worked in practice:

During the very hot summer months when speculative orders in gasoline would reach their peak, many TAS orders would come into the market. Every day would yield a fresh crop of paper. And, with TAS as an option for trading, we on the floor could gauge just how much selling and buying there would be on the close. That's because you'd never get the same amount of TAS buying and selling on the same day. And that information would give the floor traders a terrific edge.

Let's say that 500 TAS lots would come in during the day to sell on the close, but 4,000 lots came in to buy. Obviously, after the 500 lots would match up in the pit, there'd be a large leftover amount of buying that still needed to be done. Adding to this obvious insight for the floor traders was the general tendency for the TAS orders to often outline other regular closing range orders yet to be entered at the end of the day. In other words, if there were a lot more TAS buying than selling during the day, it was more often the case than not that traditional orders being entered on the close would have much more buying than selling too.

Making money in a situation like this for a savvy floor trader gets very easy. All you need to do is position yourself to be long in the close and do whatever you can to force the overwhelming amount of buying in the close to pay as high a price as possible.

And you do this, counter intuitively, by initially selling the TAS paper during the day.

By selling the TAS on a day where there's more buying in the pit, you've become obligated to sell at the closing price, which should have some terrific pressure already to go up, as the buying is forced to chase on the close. Now, all you need to do is help that along.

So, if you've sold 300 TAS lots, you now need to be long about 200 lots going into the close. And then, when the closing bell rings, you've got another 100 lots that you can use to push prices as high as you can, forcing the remaining buying to chase the close. Some of the lots you buy in the close will be above the final settlement, to be sure—but you will almost certainly still have an average buy price far below settlement because of the 200 lots you bought earlier outside the range.

Follow now the whole trade: you've bought 200 lots already, near the price being traded before the bell rings to begin the closing range. The two-minute closing range will generate the settlement price by taking the volume-weighted average of prices traded during the range. Now, during the close, you pay as much as you can for the last 100 lots, pushing the weighted close and settlement price as high as you can. (Of course, you have other traders who are helping, too.) By the end of the closing range, hopefully you've managed to create a closing average significantly above the 200 lots you've bought prior to the close and probably above most of the 100 you've used as ammunition during the close. At this moment, the 300 total lots you've bought will get matched with the 300 lots you've earlier committed to sell TAS—at the settlement price you've just helped jack up. Got it?

And, besides making a nice extra bonus with the TAS trade during the day, this device can be incredibly helpful to your longer-term crack position—because you've also helped inspire an advantageous settlement price for the other longer-term cracks you continue to hold.

I'll get back to cracks in a minute, but the TAS story really describes a lot of interesting and important ideas about the oil market. First, it proves how difficult, even impossible it can be to level a playing field among participants in any free market. Based on access and insight, someone will always have an advantage—in this case, the floor traders. Despite all intentions to deliver to the public a mechanical and fair settlement price vehicle, the TAS trade tended to do entirely the opposite—deliver a far less legitimate and easily manipulated settlement price where customers often paid far more (or received far less, if they were sellers) than they otherwise should have.

(As an aside and because I can't resist, government regulation in complex markets looking to level out playing fields for other participants often has similar results, despite best intentions. I talk more about this in Chapter 11, when I discuss what possible solutions to the uncontrolled oil market are available to us.)

During those golden years before 2007, TAS trading and other devices were used on the floor to generate higher and higher summer crack values. When much of the trade moved from the floor to the electronic platforms and these kinds of floor tricks were no longer available, cracks in the summer never again reached the lofty levels they did in those years.

But the levels we have seen since 2007 have been as unbelievable and unrealistic as the lofty crack levels we saw in the summers of 2005 and 2006. Since those years, the summer cracks have been unrealistically tiny and represent an entirely different game being played. Let's try to figure this out. Have a look at Figure 9.2, an historical chart for cracks moving forward from 2007.

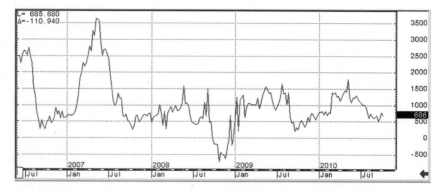

Figure 9.2 Historical Chart for Cracks Moving Forward Since 2007
SOURCE: CQG

What happened to our camel? He's disappeared back to the desert, leaving a very flat and uninteresting line. Whereas cracks spiked to pretty lofty heights during the summer prior to 2007, now there seems little premium to be found for gasoline cracks in the summers at all.

Maybe the gasoline cracks in the summer had gotten a little out of hand, spurred by an overheated global growth story and over-heated traders pushing the momentum in them as far as they could go. Maybe the move of crack trading away from the floor and onto electronic platforms has brought a more legitimate margin of crude to gasoline.

Well, certainly the advent of electronic trade took a little of the steam out of the summer crack craze, but the numbers in 2009 and 2010 just don't make any intuitive sense. The peak 2008 crack value of 15 is 70% under the average that we saw even in the years prior to 2005, and the peak 2009 crack value of 15 is equally dismal. And remember, this occurred in a year when the price of the crude barrel was travelling up—to a heart-stopping $147 in July 2008. Does it make sense that gasoline is at its cheapest price relative to the crude oil that it comes from precisely when crude oil is most expensive?

Simply put, the price of gasoline relative to crude oil continued to go down as crude oil got more and more expensive during 2008. Something very interesting seems to have been happening here.

But even more strange, not only are the premiums slight in the traditionally gasoline-poor and high-demand driving season we also saw gasoline cracks in late 2008 go below zero and actually trade a negative premium. Think about how strange that is for a minute.

Imagine you are a maker of applesauce and the apples that you buy to make your sauce are traded on a regulated market. You can't choose what price you pay for your apples; instead, the market deter-mines what both a seller can charge and what the buyer must pay. Let's also imagine that the price for the applesauce you manufacture is likewise openly traded on a regulated market. Not only can't you really negotiate a price for your raw input of apples, you are also at the mercy of the market in how much you can charge for your end-processed product (applesauce).

Now imagine that the price that the market says you are entitled to for your product (i.e., the price you get for running your expensive factory, for hiring people to grind and process your apples, for bottling and boxing your finished product, and for making it ready to be delivered to local food stores) is less—less!—than the price you paid just for the apples that you started with!

That is what refineries are looking at when gasoline cracks trade at a negative value, as they did in 2008 and often in the spring of 2009.

Refineries have long-term contracts with retail gasoline stations that round off the edges of a bad month or two of margins. Therefore, even a negative crack value (which indicates a loss on gasoline sales) cannot sink a refiner or force a shutdown—unless it lasts quite a long time. Still, negative cracks (and, to a lesser extent, depressed cracks under $15) in the summer are strange events that make no sense, yet they have become the norm since 2008, with poorer and poorer margins seen through 2010. Refinery shares during the last two years of these preposterous market margins on gasoline show just how brutally their business has been impacted: For example, have a look at the weekly charts for two independent refiners, Valero and Tesoro, shown in Figures 9.3 and 9.4.

Although the stock market as a whole was certainly under pressure during the 18 months from January 2008 to July 2009, the major market averages lost around 47% while Valero and Tesoro posted 70 and 72% losses to their market cap, respectively. And notice how the disaster in these refining shares began to occur as oil ratcheted up

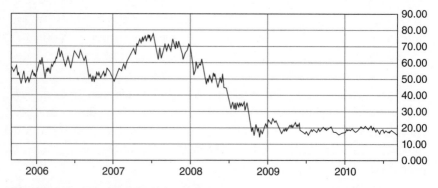

Figure 9.3   Weekly Chart for Valero
SOURCE: www.quotemedia.com

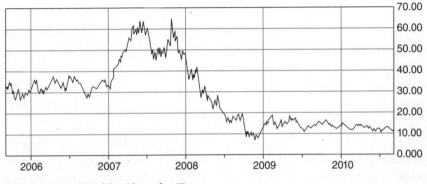

Figure 9.4   Weekly Chart for Tesoro
Source: www.quotemedia.com

during the summer of 2008. Apparently, the high price of oil wasn't of much good to the refiners: in fact, it worked directly against their profits. So much for the myth of high oil prices benefitting gasoline companies!

So what can we say accounted for the strange and unfathomable disconnect between crude oil and normal refinery margins, represented by crack spreads?

Certainly, some of the added liquidity as the markets moved onto electronic platforms and the lessened ability of gasoline traders to work some advantageous tricks with settlements and other price action helped to smooth out the curve. But just the motion to the electronic platforms cannot account for the total destruction of refining margins since 2007. No, it seems clear that the price action in crude oil has disassociated itself with the refined products that are made from it.

Although gasoline and distillate products are traded using the same exchange and the same mechanism as crude, no investor or investing manager seems to care much about the prices in these products (as I discussed in detail in Chapter 6). When investors look to gain exposure to energy, it is clear where they have been going for that exposure—to the crude barrel. After stocks, investors don't look to invest in the price of gasoline, or heating oil—it is doubtful whether they even know that these products are traded as openly as is the price of crude oil. We see that the interest in crude oil (as represented by the volume and open interest as reported by NYMEX) has skyrocketed; in contrast, although the volume and open interest of gasoline and heating oil contracts is increasing, they have had far less of a percentage gain. Volume and interest in over-the-counter (OTC) swaps show similar overwhelming growth in crude without a similar growth in gasoline. The price motion in crude oil from investor interest has been overwhelming and destroying the traditional and fundamental relationship between gasoline and the stuff that is used to make it. With that information, when you look at Figure 9-2, the new normal of crack values start to make a little more sense. When crude oil rallies strongly, gasoline cracks respond slowly as the end product struggles to catch up to the massive buying being done without regard for price. Crude goes up, margins go down.

And because we have a new influx of dumb money, looking for exposure without looking equally for value, there's a new market reality created: dislocations between markets, previously thought impossible, can now last for weeks, months, and even years.

Professional oil traders continue to buy gasoline while selling crude oil, buying cracks and getting killed, as the logic of negative cracks turning positive never seems to come true. Even as crude got murdered during the monster deleveraging that occurred in the eight months between July 2008 and February 2009, cracks refused to significantly recover. Fundamental demand destruction in gasoline usage of the recession was immediately felt in futures markets as sales took a nose dive. Meanwhile, although crude prices were falling more steeply than they ever had before, they still generated enough investment interest on the downside from amateur traders betting on an economic recovery to not fall as sharply as products did.

In essence, the average guy who was looking for exposure into the energy market was again suckered into buying crude oil futures through indexes and ETFs—even though no professional would invest a dime at prices that indicated such a ridiculous premium to the refined products that were being priced at the same time.

But what else would you expect from this army of amateur traders? No plain Joe investor that I've ever met who desired commodity exposure into oil would ever think to check out the relative prices of gasoline or heating oil before investing their hard-earned capital. And most of their so-called professional money managers were equally oblivious to these key markets. During the times of dislocated crack prices I've described, oil was a far worse investment than it even normally is.

Simply put, one market (the refined product) trades more fundamentally than the other (crude). The crude market becomes an investor's inflation hedge, dollar hedge, commodity bet, and recovery wager, while less viewed or less accessible product markets respond to what we might consider to be regular economic rules.

Cracks are one new example of this, but we can view the very same phenomenon in the curve of oil prices, in storage and in natural gas, where its relationship to crude has, because of the endless bid, become bizarre. So let's take a look at natural gas.

Chapter 10

The Fuel that the Endless Bid Forgot: Natural Gas

Natural gas poses a fantastic contrast from crude oil and with it, another proof of the power and truth of the endless bid. Natural gas is an equally accessible, perfectly viable nonrenewable energy source, and it has only one characteristic that distinguishes it from crude: Its lack of ability to be stored. That is a very significant difference, however.

Of all the subjects I've tried to tackle in this book, natural gas becomes the most interesting, because it has so much in common with crude oil, yet because it is more difficult to be stored, it has responded so differently to the endless bid. It is in the contrasts between oil and natural gas that make a little history in the pricing and trading of natty worth touching on here.

Natural gas is a fossil fuel, like crude oil. Geologically, it is often found in the same places. It is mined from underground, like crude oil. It uses similar tools and technologies to bring it forth from underneath, and most companies that work to find and extract crude oil naturally extend themselves to be part of the natural gas business as well, because at many places where you can extract crude, you often see a pocket of natural gas above it. Yielding this natural gas is almost a side benefit of oil extraction, something large oil companies often get just on the way to getting at the crude deposits.

When you take into account the differing costs of extraction, the more intensive need to refine crude oil into usable products, and the increased difficulties in utilizing natural gas, most energy experts would agree that there's little advantage, at least in terms of energy yield, of one to the other. In environmental terms, however, there are plenty of advantages for using natural gas whenever possible: A much smaller carbon footprint for processing and burning makes natural gas a far cleaner, greener fuel.

Trading Natural Gas Is Very Different from Trading Crude Oil

I'm a trader, so the differences I saw between crude oil and natural gas represented themselves to me in which guys and which companies endeavored to make their livings from gas, as opposed to crude, and in how the market traded. Despite being on the same floor and accessible with the same yellow NYMEX badge, the markets couldn't have been more different, and neither were the characters who chose to trade one over the other.

Natural gas traders were the most eccentric of the oil traders, much more accustomed to even quicker profits and losses than the already lightning motion of crude oil. Some of the characters were legendary. For example, Sandy was not only a seat owner and a natural gas trader but also the owner of a large independent natural gas brokerage company. In other words, he had natural gas covered from every angle, yet he would only appear in the pit when the market got particularly hot. Most of the time, he presided over his businesses from his office above the trading floor, its walls covered with pictures of thoroughbred horses that he either partially or fully owned. His badge, TROT, affirmed his passion outside of the commodity world.

Eric Bolling, now a host on the Fox Business Network, was a massive natural gas trader and a good one. After appearing on the cover of *Trader's Monthly* magazine in his trademark open-collared shirt and free-flowing blond mane, he began his on-air career appearing for CNBC as an energy analyst, doing spots for them right above and in earshot of the natural gas pit. An original trader chosen by CNBC to star on its Fast Money show, he was given the moniker The Admiral. Apparently, as Eric was doing spots for CNBC, the traders in the natural gas pit would joke with Eric and chide him while he was on camera above the ring. Bolling claimed that the group was chanting his nickname—"Admiral! Admiral!" However, the traders in the pit later claimed that they were chanting something slightly phonetically different.

Another colorful trader was Drew (who would become a partner of mine in another business venture). Although Drew was born and bred a Jew from a famous publishing family in New York, he routinely sported expensive cowboy boots and oversized silver buckles for his trousers. He owned a working ranch in Colorado for many years and even in the pit he was known by everyone as Drewbob. You couldn't find quite so interesting a crew as those you'd find trading natural gas.

However, there was also a less-entertaining truth about natural gas trading at the New York Mercantile Exchange (NYMEX): Because of its incredible speed, natural gas tended to attract traders with a weaker moral compass, for lack of a better phrase. Natural gas traders were more likely to use advantages to secure quick and sometimes shady profits in the dust clouds that the fast trading of natural gas futures generated. I stood trading in the unleaded gasoline ring no more than 30 yards from the natural gas pit, and almost daily, I heard stories about fortunes made and sometimes lost in a matter of moments. The crude oil and crude product traders were rendered slack-jawed (whether out of envy or disdain) by the tales of quick hits that emerged from the natural gas pit when natty was on a roll, which happened almost biannually in 2000, 2002, 2004, and 2007 but particularly during the big spike of 2005.

Why Trading Natural Gas Is Different: The Problem of Storage Affects Supply and Demand

Much of the extra shenanigans that went on in the natural gas pit, but not in crude oil or the refined products rings, were possible only because of the physical nature of natural gas: It isn't easily stored. In contrast, crude oil is a steady-state liquid, so if you want, you can store crude practically forever in a Dixie cup, with little to no ill effects. The national Strategic Petroleum Reserve (SPR) consists of four main storage sites near the Gulf of Mexico, basically converted salt mines that can hold a maximum 724 million barrels of crude. The first injections of crude oil into these reserve sites were more than 30 years ago, on July 25th, 1977. The SPR has taken a few breaks in its filling cycle over the years. Since filling of the SPR began, there have been about a dozen cases of significant amounts of crude oil extraction in the 35 years since, both as sales and loans of oil, the most recent case immediately following Hurricane Katrina. There have been no reports that this long-term storage of crude caused any degradation of quality. Because it is in the ground, crude can be kept literally forever without a problem.

In contrast, electricity sits at the other end of the energy spectrum and is the least storable of the major energy supplies. I suppose one day battery or capacitor technology might reach a point where electricity will have practical storability, but for now, it's basically use it or lose it.

Natural gas runs in the middle of these two on the storage scale, yet natural gas resembles electricity more than crude. The options for storing natural gas are few, expensive, and require complex injection and extraction processes. With crude oil, all you really need is a container and a funnel. In contrast, gas requires quite a bit more.

- Pressure is always needed to both inject and retrieve gas, and as wells run dry, the pressure will drop, making a certain portion of a gas deposit unrecoverable.
- Delivery through pipelines also requires pressure and therefore constantly full lines; consequently, there is inventory inside the pipes as well that serves as a base and cannot ever be used.

- Getting natural gas to a plant or home requires direct access with pipes or exchanging mechanisms. As opposed to crude products, you can't run to the local station with a steel can and fill 'er up.

These differences of storage and transport between natural gas and crude oil account for the most important market difference between them as well: volatility.

With a prompt product that constantly needs a ready place to go and be used immediately, and with few and expensive options on storage, even small fundamental changes in supply and demand needs can have enormous effects on prices for natural gas. If you schedule a certain quantity of flowing gas for customers in a Northeast area in the wintertime, and if instead, you get an unusually warm stretch of weather, then you're going to see a surplus of gas waiting at the wellhead and at the pipeline nexus points. Lots of gas with no place to go is going to require some really cheap prices to incentivize someone to push it through an alternative pipeline where it can be used or stored. In other words, tiny changes in the weather reports, new finds both on land and offshore, and inventory numbers will have much larger affects on a percentage basis to gas prices than you would ever see for crude.

That kind of inherent fundamentally generated volatility and large percentage price swings was the allure for many energy floor traders and fund managers to engage in gas that the crude oil market just didn't quite attract. To see just how different it was trading natural gas on the floor, let's take a look at Figure 10.1, which shows the explosiveness of the price over a few years.

Natural gas volatility not only attracted the least risk-averse and wild men to trade it in the pit, it attracted the same swashbuckling, intensely hungry and morally relaxed traders outside the pit in the trade houses and hedge funds as well. On the floor, we heard of several oil companies that had tried to make the transition to trading companies (as in the local case of Northville, as described in Chapter 4), but instead of finding success, they crashed their boats on the rocky and volatile trading shores of natural gas. In almost all cases, the natural gas sirens became very difficult for these groups to resist, because of the inherent speed and potential profits of trading it. Besides the

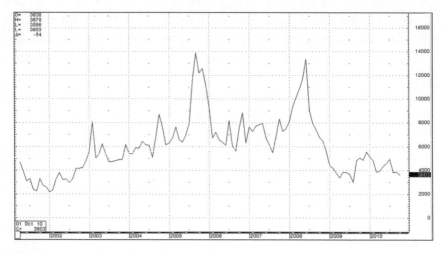

Figure 10.1   Natural Gas Price
SOURCE: CQG

merger fever of natural gas exploration and production companies at the start of the decade, the quick shifts in the balance sheet from trading that most in the industry believed they needed to be competitive helped kill many share prices, including natural gas majors El Paso, Williams, Duke, and Coastal. Natural gas was and remains a trading game only for the most intrepid.

How Natural Gas Seduced a Hedge Fund that Wasn't Even Interested in Energy

Amaranth Partners came to represent the ultimate symbol of the wildness and unrestricted risk contained in the natural gas market. Interestingly, the Greenwich-based hedge fund was not even in the energy hedge fund space at all.

Founded in 2000 by the Greek trader Nicholas Maonis, Amaranth made most of its investments for the first five years of its life in convertible bond arbitrage, doing very well indeed. But with most strategies that involve riskless arbitrage, the opportunities never last forever. Although more and more money came stream-

How Natural Gas Seduced a Hedge Fund that Wasn't Even Interested in Energy (*Continued*)

ing into the fund, fewer and fewer bond trades became available. So Amaranth searched for other money-making opportunities, becoming what is now known in the hedge fund business as a multi-strategy or diversified fund. Funny how increasing risk away from truly hedged opportunities makes you more sophisticated. It actually just makes your investments riskier. Amaranth began to center more of its efforts on its new energy desk, run by the Canadian Brian Hunter, a trader being given ever more responsibility and incentives to take greater and greater risks in the energy markets. And for the greatest amount of volatility and possibility to score big, nothing quite equaled the opportunity in natural gas.

Hunter had apparently made big money for the fund in 2005 by getting long spreads in the peak months while selling spreads in the months with less demand, known as the shoulder months of the curve. Helped enormously by hurricanes Katrina and Rita, Hunter made a fortune, earning himself a reported $75 million bonus. In 2006, Hunter planned for a repeat and perhaps even more stellar performance.

Although I wasn't trading natural gas, I can recall being on the floor and hearing every day of the wild number of spreads that were being bought in the pit in the summer of 2006. March—April, March—April, every day, hundreds and hundreds of spreads for delivery in 2007 were being bought by a couple of brokers, but—the rumor was—for one particular customer. When you're trading on the floor and somebody comes in with a singular and seemingly endless appetite, there isn't a trader in the world willing to stand in the way. Most traders were smart enough not only to refuse to sell these spreads, but to *buy spreads* alongside the Amaranth beast themselves, relying on the hedge fund to support their positions with ever more volume, appetite, and need to mark up their positions with massive and frantic purchases of spreads during every closing bell. Traders in natural gas made their own fortunes by

(*Continued*)

**How Natural Gas Seduced a Hedge Fund
that Wasn't Even Interested in Energy (*Continued*)**

forcing the fund to pay the pit traders a premium to initiate the
monster positions.

Joel Bush, who at the time was clerking for Sandy Goldfarb
in the natural gas pit, was my conduit for the daily update on the
March—April spread: Where it was trading, how many spreads
had come in and how often, and how the boys were making out
on the avalanche flow of paper. Joel had seen a lot in his long
history on the floor, having been one of the original brokers
working for Sal Calcaterra, one of the original NYMEX independents, along with Mel Miller, Dick Leeds, John Tafaro, and a few
others. Joel had seen it all, yet he still related it to me breathlessly,
"You've never seen anything like THIS, Danny!"

But no man makes the market. You can fool it for a while,
but not forever. When it became clear that 2006 was not going
to be a repeat of 2005, the collapse in the peak/shoulder spreads
and specifically the March—April was fast and vicious, moving
from $2.50 to about 50¢ in less than a month in September.
Amaranth had reportedly lost close to $6.5 billion in the space of
a few weeks. As bad as the collapse was, it was clear to me that
more than NYMEX was involved in the hedge fund's demise.
Even a catastrophic $2 move in the spread could not account for
such a loss: To account for $2 billion of losses, you would need
to fully own 100,000 spreads at the top of that $2.50 price and
only fully liquidate positions at 50¢, without participating in any
trade in between at all.

In fact, there weren't anywhere near that many contracts available to be bought. The open interest in the March and April 06
and March and April 07 contracts were far less than 100,000 all
together. Rarely did open interest in natural gas contracts exceed
40,000 in outside months.

Someone was helping Amaranth to their enormous exposure,
through swaps and other derivatives not being cleared on our open
exchange. Someone was also writing options on NYMEX spreads
outside of NYMEX, while using other over-the-counter (OTC)

How Natural Gas Seduced a Hedge Fund
that Wasn't Even Interested in Energy (*Continued*)

markets to clear and hedge those bets. And more than likely, they were helping them create that excess leverage in that position for a reason: a counter-bet of their own.

In Amaranth's case, it's difficult to know exactly who profited from their fall. The hedge fund Citadel and Goldman Sachs eventually bought the positions from Amaranth at a tremendous discount, and Amaranth sued JP Morgan, its clearinghouse, for interfering with that sale and costing the fund an extra billion dollars. In fact, both Goldman Sachs and Morgan Stanley admitted to using Amaranth as part of some of their in-house fund of funds, so they bore some of the Amaranth losses themselves. But those were the results of the unwinding of positions, not the initiation of them.

The Amaranth questions are about more than one hedge fund's bad wagers. More important, it was about such an overwhelming position being created through derivatives that represented far more product than could be physically accounted for. It's about who was delivered the leverage to be able to make or lose such a staggering amount of money in so short a time frame. And it's about a participant unengaged in any way with the physical markets or physical pricing, who was singularly controlling one side of the entire interest in that product, and therefore (by definition) manipulating it, even if only for a short time.

Amaranth continues to operate as a hedge fund in Greenwich. Even Brian Hunter, despite his disastrous wager with Amaranth, was easily able to resuscitate his career as an energy trader and start a hedge fund of his own in 2007 called Solengo Capital Advisors. But the mechanisms that allowed him to bet so broadly into the energy market in 2006 haven't changed one iota.*

*As of December 2010, Brian Hunter reappeared in the news as Peak Ridge Capital Group, the current owner of Solengo Capital assets and advised by Hunter, was sued by Morgan Stanley for more than $40 million dollars for bad trades in—you guessed it—natural gas.

Clearly, natural gas is a wild and wooly trading market, much more volatile than even crude oil has been since starting its monumental run in 2005. But natural gas doesn't trade in a vacuum. It is an energy source, as noted, that is similar in many respects to crude, and its prices have traded with a very strong correlation to crude prices. The NYMEX contract for natural gas is specified to deliver to the Henry Hub in Erath, Louisiana, much as NYMEX West Texas Intermediate (WTI) crude is specified to deliver at Cushing, Oklahoma. During the time that both contracts have traded side by side since 1989, the price ratio between the two contracts has stayed relatively constant and reliable. A common industry convention compares the prices of these two by looking at the ratio of natural gas, priced using dollars per million British thermal units, and crude oil, priced at dollars per barrel. Historically, this ratio has held with crude oil pricing about 6 to 10 times more expensively than natural gas. Figure 10.2 provides a more detailed comparison.

Natural gas price versus crude oil was constant and reliable, that is, until late 2008 and throughout 2009 and 2010. Something happened to natural gas: it no longer follows crude oil any more, not even closely—and we have to wonder why. Let's take a closer look at when natural gas prices changed and what happened.

Natural Gas Prices No Longer Track Crude Oil Prices

Natural gas followed crude oil, if probably only sympathetically, in the spring and summer of 2008, reaching a high price of almost $14. The many fundamental arguments for higher prices for crude oil during that spike made far less sense when applied to the fundamentals for natural gas: Clearly, no growth in developing nations could account for price gains in a U.S. domestic energy supply, nor could a weak dollar be used to excuse a run-up in a commodity that cannot be easily transported and whose prices are therefore local and not global. Still, the correlation between prices of natural gas and crude oil seemed to hold true—a spike to $14 is right inside the eight to ten times range that crude oil, being priced at $150 at the top, would imply.

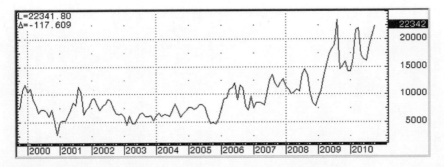

Figure 10.2 Natural Gas versus Crude Oil Price Ratio
SOURCE: CQG

But after the massive deleveraging of stocks, bonds, and oil in the fall of 2008 and through the winter of 2009, all asset classes began to recover, including and certainly not last or least, crude oil. And yet, natural gas has not experienced much recovery at all: While crude oil has nearly tripled since its lows of early 2009, natural gas hovered around $3 at its trough and briefly touched $6 before settling in to trade throughout 2010 at closer to $4. That's a price truly worthy and indicative of a recession.

The ratio of the price of natural gas to crude oil has hovered between 6:1 and about 10:1 during the times both have traded side by side. And yet, since the energy lows set in March 2009, we've seen crude outpace natural gas and run ratios of a low of about 15:1 to a high of as much as 28:1! How can another energy source like natural gas, even after being the historical wild west of energy markets, trade like such a pussycat in the midst of a rocketing oil market? Why is natural gas all of a sudden trading fundamentally, without interest in the financially driven crude oil market—for clearly the very first time?

Although I tend to focus on the financial influences on price, one fundamental factor is hard to ignore: Natural gas technologies have made tremendous strides, particularly since 2008, and have opened up brand new resources that very few imagined would be accessible. The recent findings of natural gas lodes locked inside shale deposits have changed the balance of provable reserves tremendously. Estimated natural gas reserves rose to 2,074 trillion cubic feet in 2008, from 1,532 trillion cubic feet in 2006, according to a report issued by the

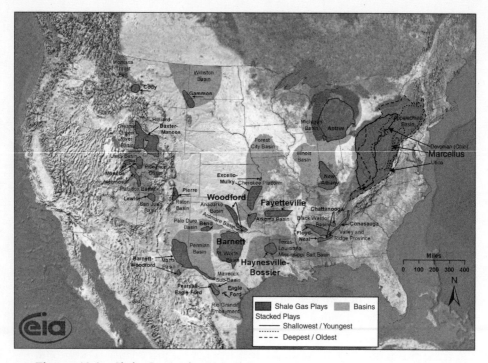

Figure 10.3 Shale Gas in the United States
Source: Energy Information Administration, www.eia.doe.gov

potential gas committee, an authority on domestic supplies. Most of the increase in this supply is not due only to the new findings of shale gas in the United States, but much more significantly to the giant leaps forward in the extraction technologies of shale gas since 2006: see Figure 10.3.

There's a lot to be happy about in the recent shale discoveries in the United States. Enormous new finds of natural gas should make our country far less dependent on other nonrenewable sources of energy from outside sources. Shale gas has truly made our country the Saudi Arabia of natural gas.

But there are a number of environmental hurdles to overcome to access this rather new and almost limitless source of fuel. The most common new injection technology to get at these shale deposits of natural gas requires copious amounts of pressurized water, a process known as hydraulic fracturing, or fracking. Fracking can threaten drinking aquifers above shale deposits. Also, water used for fracking becomes compromised and polluted and needs to be trapped in ponds. How to treat that water correctly and hopefully return it to the biosphere has become a sore spot for the advocates of fracking technologies.

In addition, shale mining looks very similar in equipment and infrastructure to coal mining and is exceedingly ugly and unappetizing. The largest deposits of shale gas in the Marcellus region (shown on Figure 10.3) include less-rural areas of New York, Pennsylvania, and West Virginia, all of which are politically sensitive areas for environmental concerns. These more affluent communities are less in need of blue-collar job growth and more concerned with keeping smelly and loud industry activity away from their middle-class, well-groomed homes. The point is that although natural gas supplies in shale areas look like a very promising source of energy, there are still simpler ways of obtaining energy at cheaper political cost—both with offshore natural gas drilling as well as continued imports from up North. North Slope natural gas from Alaska, a proven reserve of 35 trillion cubic feet, and a more modern pipeline to push it south into the Continental United States continues to be pursued, despite the fact that Marcellus shale gas reserves alone have been estimated at more than 10 times that—Approximately 363 trillion cubic feet. Like crude oil, the most politically expedient and cheapest sources of natural gas continue to dominate supply choices. Viewing them purely as they trade physically, crude oil and natural gas, not surprisingly, retain many similarities.

We must, however, circle back to the financial influences on price of this apparently overabundant fuel. After all, natural gas has been priced using the same mechanisms and Chicago Mercantile Exchange (CME)-controlled electronic markets as crude oil. And yet, the ratio of this equally capable fuel has ballooned to unfathomable multiples. Even with an admitted abundance of available supply, and even with greater potential supply of natural gas available, it is hard to imagine the relative price of the fuel shrinking two and half times since 2008 when compared to crude oil. Although the potential supplies for gas remain vast, currently environmental hurdles and a less-than-enthusiastic Obama White House put the access to these supplies many years away, if not decades in the future. And of course, it's not as if crude oil hasn't been in constant oversupply during this period as well, seeing stockpiles in 2010 at their highest levels since 1990.

Conclusion

We must conclude that natural gas is trading with a much greater respect to its fundamentals, its large supply and lagging demand, and with far less influence from the financial market forces that have plagued the price of crude oil since 2003 and markedly since 2008. Again, it is storage—or instead, the inability for natural gas to be stored—that primarily makes this so: There can be no carry trade, no way to significantly alter scheduling done many weeks or months in the past, and fewer physical manipulations one can use to take advantage of a quick change in market price. Natural gas market gyrations in the past have consistently outsmarted and beaten up many of the best energy traders. At least today, to the benefit of the natural gas market, few large trading interests engage in the speculative activity that inevitably magnifies market moves and price skews in both directions. And finally, natural gas is a much smaller component of the financial instruments that we have seen influence the price of crude: For example, the natural gas component of the Goldman Sachs Commodity Index (GSCI) is a little more than 3% of the index, whereas crude oil components make up nearly 50%.

In short, players care less about the price of natural gas than the price of crude. Overwhelmingly, when outside participants have sought exposure to a rising price of energy, they have reached for exposure to the price of the crude barrel.

It is in the perfectly understandable and *fundamentally* driven price of natural gas—which is cheap during times of recession and expensive during times of growth—that we get one of the most compelling proofs of the endless bid as it influences the price of crude.

Part III

WHERE ARE WE HEADED?

Chapter 11

What Needs to Be Done

We've lost control of our oil market. Of that, there can no longer be any doubt. Controversy raged during the summer of 2008, when I and one other lone voice, Mike Masters, were talking and lobbying about the activity and effects of speculation and investor interest in the oil market, yet most other public figures in the media were confidently advancing fundamentals as the source of rising prices. *("Oil is expensive because we're running out!")* Or they were minimizing the cause and effect of speculation on price. *("Sure, there are guys just betting—but for every buyer there's a seller, isn't there? So, how is it possible that even numbers of buyers and sellers can bias a market one way?")* Or they were free market capitalists who saw effects but were willing to see them play out because they believed in the sanctity and purity of market dynamics. *("The market may get temporarily skewed, but they always work themselves out—what, you want more government involvement? You know what that means.")* Or they just didn't see much wrong in unnecessarily paying two or three or five times more for a gallon of gas than it should cost. *("Hell, shouldn't we all be driving tiny hybrids like the rest of the world anyway? High oil prices? Bring 'em on!")*

When conversations turn to oil, all of these arguments and more get mixed up, and we lose sight of the simple truth: It would be useful for everyone to have a reliable and trustworthy oil price—even for the environmentalists.

The conversation is changing rapidly. As I write this late in 2010, the voices on the side of markets unbiased by capital effects and of fundamentally fuelled oil volatility are fading fast. For example:

- Timothy Geithner, the Treasury Secretary under the Obama administration, has made no comments on either the fundamental or speculative nature of oil trade, as his predecessor Hank Paulson so famously did. There is a message in his silence.
- Paul Krugman has recently recanted his dismissal of speculation in oil since winning his Nobel Prize and has gone back to considering the many economic issues of the global bailout.
- Boone Pickens is mostly silent, licking his wounds from extensive investments in wind farms and an ill-timed bet on the price of natural gas. You hardly hear a peep about the Pickens Plan anymore, although Boone has had so many big wins and recovered from so many big losses that I do not expect to have heard the last from him.
- Commodity industry insiders, those who run the commodity exchanges and Futures Industry Association, are still lobbying fiercely against interference from regulatory agencies, but they are far less apt to talk of a market purely priced based on fundamentals. Their public assertions are of a different color now—of keeping the routes to legitimate hedging open and easy and of the fantastic opportunities to be gained from access to new financially engineered derivative products. America is all about innovation, they argue. Wouldn't it be a shame to lose all the progress that's been recently made to the benefit of the futures market customer?

Traders know. Everyone has a position and talks it—both in the pit and outside of it.

It's heartening to see the ideas I advanced on speculation—which got me in a lot of trouble with colleagues and industry professionals—now gain wider acknowledgement.

The latest report from the Commodity Futures and Trading Commission (CFTC), which was released in July 2009, retracts the earlier conclusions of September 2008 that there was "no evidence" that investment flows had a material impact on prices. Previously, CFTC staff members doggedly maintained that physical supply and demand factors could explain all the observed volatility in oil and other commodity prices. However, the latest report blames *speculators* for a significant role in price spikes in 2008.

Of course, once the government admits a problem, we expect it will take action to try and fix it. That changes the question from whether to limit the impact of investment money on commodity markets to one of how to limit it. Now I'm frightened.

I'm frightened because the CFTC is ill-equipped to fix anything, even if the ideas about how to do it were very good, which they're not.

I'm frightened because the actions the CFTC will take are likely to do more harm than good to the operations of the market and the industry dependent on it.

And I'm frightened most because politicians and administrators, despite their best intentions, do not have the insight or experience to calculate the effects of regulating complex markets. I suppose it's lucky that the political will for change in the derivative markets doesn't extend very far. But there are sure to be actions in the next several years, and we need to know which ones are likely to have a positive effect and which are likely to have a negative effect.

Let's take a look at the tools that the government has at hand to try and get a handle on our broken oil market and how it has attempted to come to grips with possible solutions.

How the CFTC's Commitment of Traders Report Measures Speculation in the Oil Market

I believe the CFTC to be an organization made up of very hard-working, intelligent, and well-meaning individuals. But they have always been in a difficult spot.

They have to measure the good of the nation against the good of the industry they serve. They are forced to constantly balance the wishes of the current administration, the political agendas of barking congressmen, and the lobbyists for the futures industry.

They try to enforce regulations that hopefully lead to a level playing field and a fair market. They oversee virtually all trading and accounts on futures and derivatives, a monumental task, all with very limited funds and manpower.

They wrestle with a constantly changing market and a slew of new financial instruments both for trading approval and oversight. They are naturally opposed in their efforts to understand and regulate these products by the people who create and market them, the people in the investment banks and clearinghouses and derivative trade organizations. And the people in those positions inside the banks and independently trading and marketing commodity funds are some of the most innovative, smartest, and richest people in the country.

That creates a situation where the CFTC is like the most impressive group of second-graders you've ever seen trying to oversee the work of college-level physics students. They mean well, but through no fault of their own, they're just not up to the task. Incompetent? No, let's instead be charitable and say that the CFTC is woefully *inadequate* for the enormous task it is charged to do.

One small example will illustrate the point. The CFTC is obliged to maintain records of the positions of participants in all of the domestically traded commodities at regulated exchanges. This is known as the Commitments of Traders Report, or the COT.

The COT has been provided as a regular service by the CFTC since 1962. The idea behind it is important and critical to the CFTC's tasks: It tries not only to quantify the number of participants in each futures market, it also attempts to *qualify* these participants, as hedgers or speculators. It does this by forcing participants to file with the CFTC in every market where that trader or trading entity exceeds a fairly low threshold of positions held.

The layout of this recurring document is simple in idea and incredibly complex in its scope. Until its attempt at reform in August 2009, the COT report attempted to lump every participant who maintains an overnight position (not the day traders, therefore) into one of two categories. A *commercial participant* was supposedly a legitimate hedger and, as defined by CFTC regulation 1.3(z), has very specific engagement with physical assets. A *noncommercial participant* is everyone else. The idea makes a lot of sense, or at least it did for a very long time in the history of COT reporting. If you owned an oil well, or a refinery, or a storage tank, and you could prove it, you were classified as a *commercial participant*, and your engagement with the futures market was considered legitimate hedging.

Unfortunately, these simple definitions have failed utterly to differentiate between *real hedging* and *outside speculation*. Indeed, once classified as a commercial participant, your status became permanent, so virtually every traded contract passing through your desks became classified as commercially motivated and therefore initiated (at least as far as the CFTC was concerned) for pure hedging reasons. Even for the most intensely physically engaged oil company like Chevron or BP, the idea that every contract held overnight and reported to the CFTC is directly related to a tangible unit or an intended unit of production over the next 12 months (as stipulated by CFTC guidelines) is patently absurd. And these are the futures participants most directly engaged in the physical markets.

A more ludicrous but instructive example is Morgan Stanley and its oil company: Morgan Stanley Capital Partners (MSCP, described in Chapter 4). Suffice to say that because of its MSCP connections, Morgan Stanley is listed as a commercial participant in the futures markets, and therefore, all of its proprietary positions in the overnight oil markets are classified as hedges. Commercial status is also held by virtually every other investment bank, with even less direct but clear exposure to physical assets.

Remember, the COT report has been used as an almost exclusive benchmark for measuring the level of speculation in the oil markets. Both the exchanges and the futures industry leaders have quoted the figures as proof that the level of speculation has not significantly increased since 2003, since the percentage of commercial participants has similarly increased. In short, the COT report is a useless benchmark.

An Attempt to Reform Trading in the Oil Market

The CFTC realized how little light its weekly report shines on futures participants: In October 2009, it revised its classifications of traders for the COT. Instead of commercial and noncommercial participants, the CFTC instituted four new classes:

1. producer/merchant/processor/user,
2. swap dealers,
3. managed money,
4. other reportables.

The CFTC now uses these four classifications in its report, along with the traditional or legacy classes of the old report. Little (if any) greater transparency is gained by using this system as opposed to the old. Although at least now there is a separated swap category (which was previously always aggregated with commercial interests) and a managed money category (which is, not surprisingly, always overwhelmingly long on a percentage basis).

Although the CFTC still uses the old form 40 to have participants (in essence) classify themselves, the CFTC now is permitted and entrusted to check up on any desk it likes, with the option of classifying participants in any category it deems fit. Information on this new attempt at transparency is so far very thin, yet it is still very clear that understaffed and inexperienced agents at the CFTC are unable to do much more now besides *trust* the industry participants to describe their reasons for participating in the futures markets. In short, not much has changed. Nor is it likely to.

Possible Governmental Regulations to Prevent the Endless Bid

Besides trying to keep track of the participants engaged in oil trade, the government can add financial burdens and try outright to limit participation, through increased margins and position limits. But how useful are these efforts? Let's take a look at those regulatory options now.

Complicated problems don't often lend themselves to simple solutions, and the uncontrollable mess that the oil markets have become is certainly complicated. But when talk about fixing the commodity market begins using new or sterner regulations, two ideas are almost always mentioned: increased margins and position limits.

My thesis throughout this book has been simple: Oil markets no longer represent fundamentals because the players engaged in them are more interested in the financial opportunities of the markets rather than the *underlying assets* represented by them. As a floor trader, I was the ultimate speculator: I cared little about the oil barrel and merely wanted to buy (or sell) it well, keep it for as short a time as possible, and sell (or buy it back) for a profit. All markets absolutely need people like me, called liquidity providers (very generously in my view), but the oil markets are now overrun with them.

Therefore, all attempts at reestablishing control of oil requires a whittling away of betting interests, either by reducing the number of people like me or by increasing the number of commercial participants, or both. Although the pool of legitimate hedgers has definitely increased, we've seen how much more quickly the pool of speculators has grown. More onerous margin requirements and position limiting look to restrict the speculator alone. Let's take each one of these suggested solutions separately.

Can Increasing Margins Limit Speculation in the Oil Market?

In and of themselves, and when applied to any asset class, margins have a unique purpose: They are designed as *cash guarantees*. They are intended to protect the clearinghouse, but mostly to protect other traders in the market and the integrity of the market as a whole.

Margins for commodities come in two flavors, applied to members or nonmembers of an exchange. Members have significantly cheaper margin requirements than nonmembers, because it is assumed that members are less likely to risk default. Margins have always been a moving target. As volatility for commodities has increased over the years, margins also have increased to protect against the added risk. Margining has maintained its one and only purpose: To help indemnify each participant equally against risk of default.

But now, margins are being asked to accomplish a different task in trying to somehow single out speculators and limit their involvement. Never before has the margining of positions been intended to try and establish the motives of the traders behind the trades. Margins are universal and, except for the member/nonmember difference, untargeted.

So what is the idea behind increasing margins to limit speculation?

It is imagined that the speculator alone will have to make a judgment on the capital intensity of trading oil. A hedge fund or investor of commodity indexes or even a day trader like me will be faced with higher margins and will either limit his positions or seek out better leverage and better returns on his investment of dead capital. Conversely, it is hoped that the legitimate commercial hedger will not abandon the market as quickly as his or her need of risk management is assumed to be necessary to his or her business. It is assumed that hedgers will bear the extra costs of hedging, while speculators will look for greener pastures to invest their money. Increasing margins for everyone is a shotgun approach blasting away in a wild spray, yet attempting a surgical, targeted result.

The reality of increasing margins is vastly different. The increasing volatility of the oil markets has been consistently met with concurrently increasing margin requirements. During that time, the number of hedge funds, exchange-traded funds (ETFs), managed futures accounts, index funds, and trading shops devoted to oil have increased astronomically. Apparently, increasing margins haven't helped limit the influx of speculative accounts into the oil market. [It's almost like the old joke of using bug spray at the picnic: "Don't spray that stuff around these insects out here," the hardened outdoorsman warns the Sunday picnicker. "They've gotten so used to the spray that they've learned to *like* it!"]

So it seems the case with increasing margins. The participant who was most forced to change his trading habits in light of ever more onerous capital requirements has been the independent floor trader (i.e., people like myself). Margin calls for single independent traders have forced many of us to maintain open-ended financing relationships with our clearinghouses and more and more ready capital in our accounts in order to stay in business (if we were even able to stay in business). Many of the single independents have been forced to close shop and find other work, not the least because of the increasing universal margin burdens that we as a group have been least able to withstand. An even sharper and federally inspired increase in capital requirements in the futures market will surely force the rest of us entirely out of the game.

On the contrary, the participants who are most easily able to accommodate higher capital requirements are (of course) the participants who can most easily access capital—prime brokerage clients like hedge funds, ETF managers, and the proprietary accounts of the banks themselves. If margins on oil were tripled overnight, liquidation would occur across the board, but those accounts that are most engaged in high-volume speculation would likely be *least affected*.

Even with this explanation, increasing margins is such an obvious tool to draw on for trying to rein in the excesses of all capital markets, that it is difficult for me to entirely dismiss the idea. New regulation for other financial derivative markets (particularly for credit default swaps (CDSs) and other real estate securitizations that were blamed wholly or in part for the economic collapse of 2008) center on two central themes: transparency and increased capital requirements and reduced leverage. At least in the futures markets, we've got one of these—transparency—already in place, leaving an adjustment of capital requirements as one of the very few regulatory tools left.

In the oil markets, there has been enormous growth in over-the-counter (OTC) contracts reliant on the regulated futures markets and driven by them, but compared to other more recently demonized markets, transparency is far less of a problem. Prices are posted every moment and settled every day. Positions are not open to accounting interpretation, and there's no debate about mark to market. It's an absolute fact. Every contract cleared on a regulated exchange is subject to being reported to the CFTC after the close of every business day. In the futures markets at least, we've seen in some ways through a clearer lens what true transparency can bring—and transparency alone hasn't been able to avoid the problems of markets pushed and pulled by speculative forces.

It's just not clear that increased capital requirements—margins—could have any more instantaneous palliative effect, either. Or, let me at least qualify that: The increase of capital requirements necessary to have the desired effect of chasing enough of the bad money out (with obviously a lot of the good money also leaving) would seem to me to also risk destroying the well-developed market for everyone.

We still have legitimate needs and uses for oil trade. We still have a futures industry that employs thousands gainfully and for good purpose. The types of onerous capital requirements needed to clean up Dodge City, for example a 30% or even a 50% margin on nominal value, certainly is highly unlikely and entirely destructive.

I expect the march of margins to continue upward, accompanied by regulators who will take credit for getting tough on the market manipulators—but those increases will in fact be shrugged off.

Margins alone will ultimately have little effect in restoring a fundamentally reliable price for oil. So let's take a look at limiting positions.

Can Limiting Positions in the Oil Markets Help?

It would seem patently obvious to control any one participant's overwhelming influence in any market, not just futures or derivatives. When you can own a majority of shares of a company, or control a majority of open contracts, or even have the most chips in front of you in a game of poker, you can maneuver the game to your advantage and change the fundamentals. In a truly open market, that's the opposite of what we want.

To give a simple example, let's say you were trading the publicly traded Widget company, where the owner, W. L. Widget, controls 70% of the shares. And let's say you thought that widget sales were going to be horrible for the next quarter and wanted to bet on the decreasing sale of widgets by shorting the stock. Sure enough, reports for the quarter come in, and widget sales are indeed down by almost 30%: You were right! You're now expecting to see a deep discounting in the shares of Widget stock, allowing you to buy your shorts back for a tidy profit.

But instead of seeing a *decrease* in the price of the stock the day of the quarterly report, Widget shares are in fact *up* a bit. What is going on here?

A couple of things might be happening, but one thing is surely happening: W. L. Widget has decided he doesn't want to see the share price of his company go down. Because he owns 70% of the supply of stock, he can virtually assure that Widget shares won't devalue so fast, if at all. Besides refusing to sell any of his shares, thereby removing 70% of the inventory of possible shares that you could use to cover your shorts with, he could also use company money to initiate a buyback program or find further investors to increase his ownership of stock, putting bids in at many levels underneath the market. These might not have a permanent effect, and Widget shares might ultimately decrease, but for the moment—and it could be a long moment—you're stuck.

And if you're stuck, chances are others are stuck too, wondering how long to wait out Mr. Widget in his perhaps economically foolish attempts, but practically very potent efforts to keep his company's stock price strong. That stock is not going down right now, and I'll bet you're going to think hard about staying short. If you're like me and most other traders, you'll actually opt to cover, leave Mr. Widget to his machinations, and move on to a different stock that's being more honestly priced, where your correct judgment of value will be justly rewarded.

That is the point of position limits, a potentially very potent tool that exchanges and regulatory bodies can use to limit the influence of any one individual or group in any market. Force a limit on the number of shares—or, in the futures markets, on contracts you can hold—and you prevent an undue influence of any one participant on the traded prices.

Futures exchanges are well aware of this powerful tool and have always had fairly stringent position limits to begin with. As the futures markets have grown, so have maximum position limits. When I first entered the markets, limits were set at 500 contracts for any single participant. Those numbers have ballooned, of course, but they are still sufficient to prevent too much influence from any one account. At the New York Mercantile Exchange (NYMEX), reportable limits are 3,000 contracts for the spot month, with a 10,000 contract limit for any single month other than the spot month, and a total limit of 20,000 contracts.

This may sound like a lot, and it is—but even 20,000 contracts of crude oil spread out across the entire curve gives influence over less than 2% of the more than 1.3 million contracts that were open as of September 2010, a very representative number. And it's not quite an arbitrary figure that the exchanges, along with the CFTC, try to apply. At $70 oil, 20,000 contracts will leverage $1.4 billion of crude, which is sufficient to deal with most of the pure hedging interest of almost all multinational oil companies, and certainly any commercial end user. Even with these limits, CFTC exemptions exist for anyone capable of proving a greater pure hedging need than the 20,000 contract limit, an exemption I believe has never needed to be legitimately applied for nor granted.

In terms of simple position limits on futures, the exchanges have historically had and currently continue to have a good handle on any possible over-influence of any one participant.

Unfortunately, what we have seen in oil is not one particular participant, looking to corner a market or otherwise influence prices; instead, we have seen a new breed of participants, moved solely by financial imperatives and creating an avalanche of homogeneous buyers (and occasionally sellers), impacting the oil market all at once. If there were only one company with the desire to buy and hold 20,000 contracts of crude oil, their position and intent would be utterly transparent and easily controlled. But imagine instead 200,000 investors all wishing to hold one contract apiece as an investment in the futures market. Position limits obviously can do nothing to prevent this.

Moreover, as we have seen, individual investors do not access oil futures directly through individual accounts. They exert their influence in the futures markets indirectly, through commodity index investing and with futures-based ETFs. Exchanges have undone position limitations by helping index funds gain unfettered access to the futures markets as their trading does wonders for monthly volume figures. Not surprisingly, index funds are exempted from limits, and they engage as much as they need in order to properly track the underlying commodities, including oil. Futures-based ETFs share this advantage. In short, in the case of indexes and ETFs, position limits don't even try to slow investor interest in oil.

As for other speculative accounts, the ones that we might normally fear will try to gain better influence on price by continuing to increase position size, exchange position limits have little effect here as well. Although exchange rules specifically state that two separate accounts with even 10% shared interest must be aggregated in position counts, there is a very difficult, if not impossible, path for tracking down connections between two or more accounts with the same owner and intent. With many possible clearing partners and accounts that can be labeled through subsidiaries and other offshore partnerships, it would not be very hard for anyone with the will and capital to establish 100 accounts that would look entirely unrelated, yet share the same intent and ownership.

But speculative players in the futures markets don't even need to go to these extremes to increase their exposure to oil beyond exchange position limits, if that is their desire. Again, it is in the unregulated OTC swaps markets on oil that their hands are freed to establish virtually as deep a position as they would like. Outside of a regulated market, no position limits exist, and the extent of any one fund's exposure is only limited by one's ability to find a counterparty who believes in your ability to make good on your wager. For example, we saw in Chapter 10 where Amaranth Partners was capable of accumulating the equivalent of 100,000 spreads in natural gas, even though the limits on natural gas are even stricter than with crude oil: a maximum of 12,000 contracts with no month's exposure exceeding 6,000 contracts. Clearly Amaranth was able to establish such a position only through the more lax reporting limits of the secondary derivative markets.

It would seem a difficult, if not impossible, challenge in trying to establish and extend position limits into the OTC oil markets, and not one that will be met with much support and help from the brokers and dealers of those markets.

So although the intention of position limits is a good one that makes a lot of intuitive sense, it is also true that, in practice, they have been of limited and practically toothless effect at limiting access to the oil markets and therefore influence on oil's price.

Unreliable oil prices hurt everyone, whether their unreliability is expressed in a market that is unreasonably going up, or in a market unnecessarily going down. The United States is ultimately responsible for the veracity of the oil markets and benchmark prices: not only are both the Chicago Mercantile Exchange (CME) and Intercontinental Exchange (ICE) businesses under the regulatory control of federal agencies, but the vast majority of OTC trade in oil derivatives originates here.

It has become clear that even OPEC nations are beginning to doubt the ability of U.S. regulatory agencies to control the financial manipulations being exerted on the oil market, even if those manipulations have largely led to higher and not lower prices for their valuable resource. Still, Saudi Arabia, the largest OPEC exporter, has seemed uncomfortable at having pricing power remain exclusively in the United States.

Saudi Arabia Tries to Change the Way It Prices Oil

Unsure of America's ability to continue to provide a reliable pricing mechanism with continued relevance, the Saudi Arabian national oil company Aramco has begun pricing its oil exports into the United States using a different accounting benchmark than NYMEX-traded WTI. As of January 1, 2010, Aramco oil exports were priced using the Argus Sour Crude Index (ASCI).

Since 1993, the Saudis have used WTI as a pricing benchmark because it offered the most liquid and transparent model. Because of OPEC's commitment to WTI, other derivative products were developed to connect the sour grades of crude that dominate OPEC exports to the WTI and Brent sweet grades of crude. These financial products connecting these grades of crude are known as *basis swaps*—the differential of price between sweet grades of crude (WTI and Brent) and sour grades (Mars et al.).

Sour grades of crude have more sulphur and therefore have the disadvantage of being more difficult to refine. In the United States (where sweet grades of crude dominate), the sour grades require specific and costly refinery conversion to be utilized, and even after conversion, they cost more to refine into finished products.

Consequently, sour crude grades should *always* be discounted in price to sweet grades of crude, sometimes by as much as $5 a barrel, but rarely less than $2 a barrel.

Correctly hedging a crude position on a Saudi import of sour crude would require a position in the WTI futures market as well as a basis swap of WTI to sour crude. These two financial contracts in combination would mitigate the risks of these two related crude prices moving too far out of whack. We have seen large and unprecedented movement in the benchmark price of WTI crude, while the Saudis and other OPEC members have been perfectly willing and content to continue to price their oil resources through the sweet crude benchmarks and the U.S. exchange mechanisms. This is for two big reasons: First, because the largely American assetization of crude oil has contributed to a very healthy price premium, and the Saudis and other OPEC member states know it, and second, because the basis differential between WTI and most sour grades of crude has been very reliable and steady. So while oil prices have gone up and down, sometimes violently, the difference between the sweet and sour grades of crude hasn't seen anywhere near that same kind of volatility, as shown in Figure 11.1.

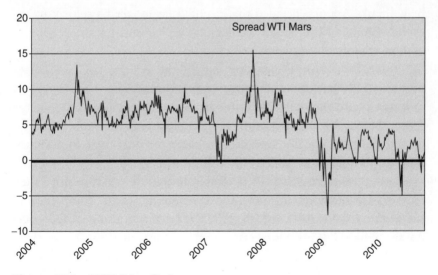

Figure 11.1 WTI/Mars Basis
SOURCE: Platts

Well, they hadn't seen the same kind of volatility—that is, until 2009. The intense and unprecedented deleveraging from assets during the fourth quarter of 2008 and first quarter of 2009 annihilated the price of West Texas Intermediate (WTI) crude on the NYMEX. From July 2008 to the lows in March 2009, fully 78% of the market price disintegrated in eight months' time. But while the prices of sour grades of crude also fell precipitously, they did not fall anywhere near as hard as the benchmark sweet grades. During the great crude price collapse of 2009, sour grades of crude actually sold at a *premium* to sweet grades on the cash markets, a practical absurdity. As WTI reached its interim low of $32 a barrel in 2009, the dislocation between WTI and Mars sour reached its most stunning apex: An unprecedented premium of $12, another incredible financial anomaly in a year of many other unfathomable markets, not only in crude oil.

During those months, however, Saudi and other OPEC member imports into the United States were still tied to the NYMEX futures and were being priced $5, $7, and for a brief time as much as $15 below where the cash markets in sour crude grades indicated they should be priced. An enormous, unprecedented amount of OPEC oil revenue was lost because of their continued loyalty to the WTI benchmark. Aramco decided that it could no longer be subject to the capital whims of the American market mechanisms for the pricing of its lone exportable resource.

If we have proven just how surely the endless bid had caused immense problems from unnecessary price inflation for the economy as a whole and problems for domestic refiners even inside the energy space, the quick retraction of the endless bid and fast deflation in prices caused another equally difficult problem for the overseas, Middle Eastern producers of crude.

In response, the Saudis have chosen to use the ASCI to price their exports. Invented by the oil-quoting Argus group (a competitor of the industry stalwart, Platts), the ASCI is calculated using traded prices on the sour crude *cash* markets, not the futures market. It uses three different grades of Gulf of Mexico traded sour crudes, including the by far most common and quoted sour grade, Mars crude. While the index still relies heavily for liquidity on WTI, both the NYMEX and the ICE have rushed to create new ASCI futures products to try and capture this new Saudi benchmark. Time will tell which, if any, U.S. exchange will capture this new market, but the fact that the Saudis have now moved away from the NYMEX and ICE sweet benchmarks to price their inventory indicates explosive change about to occur to the future of oil trade.

For one, the Saudi's drift away from WTI indicates a loss of confidence in the pricing mechanisms employed by the U.S. exchanges. The move to a cash market index, as opposed to a single product priced in the futures market demonstrates that the Saudis want product priced based on real sales in cash markets, unencumbered by derivative products and derivative influences and manipulations, whether they are momentarily beneficial to OPEC members or not.

It also strongly suggests that OPEC members do not continue to be entirely comfortable pricing oil exclusively in dollars. Once oil trade begins to move from U.S.-dominated futures markets, it is a small step to begin to transact physical trade of oil in something other than American greenbacks. Further, once oil benchmarks begin to move from U.S. and European sweet grades of crude and begin to be dominated by Gulf of Mexico sour grades, it is even a smaller step to moving the entire pricing mechanism to another exchange outside of the United States. The differentials between sour grades of crude continue to remain steady, and there is minimal basis risk in trading the Argus sour crude index as opposed to, let's say, the Dubai Mercantile Exchange's Omani and Dubai sour crude grades.

In essence, the move of the Saudis and OPEC to the ASCI represents a pushing of the reset button on the trading of global crude. Although U.S. exchanges continue to hold primary control, *they must once again compete for a share of a new market that might ultimately dominate trade—and a market that they risk ultimately losing.* And although crude pricing in the United States is subject to capital and other manipulations, crude pricing in the center of the Middle East would increase the influence of OPEC member states on that price tenfold.

You'd think at least OPEC members would appreciate the advantages of our broken oil market, but even they don't entirely. Even with years of financially inflated high prices increasing their profits, Saudi oil ministers continue to worry about similar financial manipulations robbing them of profit margins when prices move to the other extreme. It seems that *no one* wants an unreliable and wildly volatile oil price.

Wish List for Solving a Broken Oil Market

It's time to suggest ways to fix oil's screwed-up pricing mechanism. Make the price of oil more reliable, and you'll end up with an economy with far better long-term growth and hope.

My thesis throughout this book has been about the participants engaged in oil pricing. We moved from a group of players who had direct physical interest in the price of the crude barrel to a dominating group of players engaged in financial oil with little to no interest in the physical product. Although the implementation of any reforms will be very, very difficult in the complex world that oil has become, the road to reform is not difficult to see: *we've got to change the market back closer to the way it once was.* We need the dominant responsibility for the pricing of oil to be returned back to the people engaged in the pricing of physical oil: *the oil producers and users.* In short, we need to give the oil market back to the oil companies, the way it was when I first set foot on the trading floor in 1983, until around the last half of 2001.

We can use both aspects of the market that the government and the exchanges have control over—which are trading and clearing—to put oil pricing back in the hands of the oil companies. Explaining the how of giving pricing power back to those who own and use oil is fairly complex and wonky. However, the path to that goal is, at least in theory, surprisingly simple.

First, the immense OTC secondary market in oil needs to be brought under the same umbrella and supervision as the primary futures market and be subject to the same regulations.

Second, access for trading oil needs to be limited only to participants who need the hedging functions that the futures and OTC markets offer. *Access to trading oil can no longer be a universal right for everyone.* We need to find a way to remove the purely speculative participants (who are interested only in financial oil) and do it without destroying the liquidity that legitimate hedgers need. Although this is a draconian proposal, it is actually incredibly simple to do and would go a very long way toward finding out what oil is really worth.

I have a friend who is even more cynical than I am (if that's possible). Whenever I talk about regulation of oil, or regulation of anything on Wall Street, he just shakes his head. "It's like a family relationship, between Wall Street and the politicians," he says. "No matter what they say, the government just won't ever do anything to hurt Wall Street and their business."

I certainly hope that's not true, but it's become more difficult to have hope. The original bill for bank regulation in the wake of the 2008 financial crisis made its debut from the Obama White House in August 2009 and looked to make sweeping changes, sounding to me nearly like a restoration of the banking acts of 1934 known collectively as Glass-Steagall. These intelligent set of regulations (which had been put aside during the Clinton administration in 2000), kept our capital markets safe and relatively panic free for 70 years. Since their repeal, we've had 10 years of almost bi-annual meltdowns, culminating with the 2008 catastrophe that nearly sent us all into a forced reprise of the Great Depression. The proposal, which Secretary of the Treasury Timothy Geithner at the time touted on the CNBC and Fox Business network trail, would move virtually all derivatives to at least be cleared through regulated exchanges, and others that represented systemic risk to be traded at exchanges as well. This bill looked to be a game-changer for bank business as well as hitting at the heart of the real problems that caused the massive overpricing and subsequent collapse of so many assets connected to the 2008 meltdown.

Bank lobbyists quickly went to work on watering down the proposals and seeking support of Congress to euthanize the concepts before they even got written up into a debatable bill. The public rage against the big five banks—Citibank, Bank of America, Goldman Sachs, Morgan Stanley, and J.P. Morgan—continued to reach a fever pitch throughout the rest of 2009 and into 2010 and made it impossible to fully destroy the important ideas being advanced by Geithner and Obama. And yet they still were able to take much of the strength away from the proposal before a law was ready to be advanced. The bill to emerge from the House of Representatives Banking Committee and its chairman Barney Frank was already a much weaker bill than the Geithner proposal had suggested, but eyes were more keenly focused on the bill that would emerge from the Senate.

After months of wrangling with Republican leaders on the Senate Banking Committee, Connecticut Senator and committee chairman Chris Dodd threw in the towel on bipartisanship and advanced his own version of banking reform in March 2010. When he advanced it, he couldn't get one Republican on the committee to support him, although the bill he finally proposed was rather tame, and a far cry from what Geithner envisioned back in August 2009. The major sticking point of the bill for opponents was where to house the newly created consumer protection agency for financial products—whether inside the Federal Reserve or independently outside of it. That the conversation about the important changes necessary to prevent another meltdown like the one we saw in 2008 had devolved into a question of *where to house* this frankly unnecessary agency is testament to the strong influence that the banking lobby had in the eight months since Geithner first spoke. Although oversight of consumer loans and consumer protection is a laudable idea, it goes nowhere near the sources of our collective grief on the near financial Armageddon we experienced.

This is a book about oil, yet I keep talking about the much larger capital markets and their failures for an obvious reason: Because oil is headed down the same road, using the same financial innovation tools, the same access to cheap credit, and the same profit centers of dark-pool OTC markets to end up with a very similar looking, dark, and foreboding stew. And oil, of course, has much more diabolical risks of disaster than other capital markets precisely because it *isn't* a capital market; it has only been made to *look* like one.

So, after exploring the problems with the modern oil market—how it works, where the money goes, and how it fails us—the question finally arises: How do we try and fix this?

It's time to do a little reconnaissance on regulation, first. We need to first ask: what *can* be done?

There are two pieces to every modern derivative market—the trading of an asset and the clearing of an asset. Clearing is a more arcane, less understood concept, so let's tackle that one first.

We Need to Change the Way Oil Trades Are Cleared

When you buy a share of stock, you take ownership of a piece of a company. Clearing happens with stocks after a sale is completed, but with shares of stock, the process is far less complicated than clearing oil futures, because with stocks, a change of ownership is recorded and money exchanges hands, and that's pretty much it, in terms of clearing stocks. In contrast, oil futures and other oil derivatives don't represent any real ownership, but are instead merely a promise, often from anonymous counterparties to make good on a bet, no matter which way the bet ultimately goes.

Bets with counterparties can rightly make some people pretty suspicious and jittery. *"How do I know that the guy on the other side of my bet is going to pay off if I'm proven right? Even if he means to be honest, what if my bets are so right that I bankrupt the other guy? Can I still get paid?"* This is the scariest part of this type of clearing, known as *bilateral clearing* (discussed in detail in Chapter 4): You are at risk to the counterparty himself to get paid. The truth is that bilateral clearing works very well, and although there are examples of people skipping out on bets that go bad, they are pretty rare events. The other truth is that when it doesn't work so well, the results can be disastrous, as in the case of Long Term Capital Management. Most clearing of OTC derivatives on oil is bilateral.

Centralized clearing, used for commodity futures, is significantly different. I tried to outline some of the practical differences in Chapter 1, with my story of Jeff and others. With a centralized clearing system, participants apply to be approved as clearing members of an exchange. There are strict capital requirements. If approved, a clearing member promises to be responsible for the capital obligations of every person they clear trades for, ultimately agreeing to the exchange that they will take the responsibility to make good on any trade that any of their clients are unable to honor. Even more, every member firm and clearing member at the exchange make up a greater safety net: They are obligated to protect the integrity of the clearing mechanism and engage their own capital to prevent any default. In essence, every clearing member is ultimately responsible to a certain degree for the behavior of every other member. So every clearinghouse is responsible for its customers' actions, and every clearinghouse is somewhat responsible for every other house—they're all in it together. Clearing members are also obliged to report on a daily basis to the exchange and the exchange's regulatory body on position changes and position limits.

Two very important changes take place when participants are forced to engage in centralized clearing, as opposed to clearing bilaterally.

1. Because a clearinghouse's own capital is at risk, it is much more likely to choose very carefully and monitor very closely the people that it accepts as customers.
2. Because the clearinghouses have the Securities and Exchange Commission (SEC) and CFTC looking over their shoulders, it becomes much more difficult for any client to silently accumulate a large enough position that will pose systemic risk.

Shared responsibility and the implicit transparency of the clearing system used by regulated exchanges holds almost immeasurable advantages to the bilateral clearing used to process most OTC derivatives. My bias is based on observation—I have been a participant and have seen the relative lack of systemic problems emerge from the use of this system for the last 25 years, compared to the many crises, all of which surrounded derivative contracts that were bilaterally or independently cleared.

However, despite central clearing's many advantages, there is a hurdle: Increasing the scope of regulated clearing has been limited by the number of capital organizations still willing to do it. With ever-increasing accounts and participants, and ever-decreasing fees that can be extracted for the service, more and more financial institutions have been happy to cease being clearing members at exchanges, if their clients will allow it and just let the other guy take the risk. I can't say that I blame them, but commercial capital must be incentivized (yes, by the government, if necessary) to continue to engage and enlarge their scope in the clearing markets, and share the risk responsibilities, not abandon the system. Being even peripherally responsible for the actions of all engaged has been proven to have a remarkably salutary effect on the system. Safer, more measured, more reliable. Centralized clearing just works better.

Let's now turn to the other tool at our disposal for dealing with our broken oil market: trading.

We Need to Change the Way Oil Is Traded

I've outlined in depth how trading has changed since I first began to engage in oil in 1983, and it can be summed up in one word: access. When I first started at the exchange, you had to overcome some pretty daunting hurdles to even be permitted to trade oil futures. Besides the guarantees of capital that were obvious, we had to pass exams at the exchange and pass through a business and moral profiling procedure. We needed two members of the exchange to support our bid for membership with sponsorship and provide extensive data on our relationships, previous employment, and where we had lived. For the overseeing CFTC, we had to register ourselves. I can remember walking into the local Nassau County police station and submitting myself to fingerprinting, which was to be kept on file at the FBI, a necessary step for anyone who wanted to trade in the futures markets.

Clearly, there were some people in the government and at the exchanges who wanted to be pretty careful about who they were granting access to the markets for oil trading. They not only wanted to know who they were, but they wanted to know exactly how to find you if they needed to in the future.

Compare that with today, where a futures account can be opened and used pretty much on the same day, from a countless number of clearing suppliers with little more than the answering of a question-naire. *("I have had 5 years' experience trading futures: check!")* If you choose to access the oil futures market through ETFs, even that is unnecessary; your online stock account will suffice, limiting you only by the amount of money or margin you can swing.

It Should Be Difficult to Access Oil

So there are two distinct aspects to oil pricing through the oil markets: trading and clearing. Whether we encounter the futures markets, the

ETF market, or the gigantic OTC derivatives market on oil, both of these aspects (trading and clearing) will be the key parts of how oil prices are discovered. Neither trading nor clearing can be considered a right given without prejudice to anyone under the Constitution. Both the ability to trade and the access to have your trades cleared are a *privilege*, delivered to individuals and institutions by all three entities that oversee the market: the exchange, the clearing member, and the government's oversight agencies.

More important, there are multiple examples, one of which I outline in the Appendix, pertaining to the silver market, where the exchange, the clearinghouse, and the government have used their authority to change rules, limit access, alter contract specifications, impose further regulation, increase margins, and mediate disputes without recourse from the parties involved.

Here's the point: The people involved in the running of the oil markets have both the precedent and the authority to adjust both the trading and the clearing of oil in any way whatever in order to protect the integrity of the market they oversee. The only thing they require to take action is *the will to do so*. We need to remember this when opponents of increased regulation begin their campaigns claiming draconian, anti-American, anti-free market measures: *Re-regulating the oil markets is a question of will alone and nothing else.*

Oil is overpriced, we know that. We also know that oil's high price is a constant burden on the middle class and on business, both small and large.

Instead of predominantly benefiting the large oil companies (as the common man on the street would intuitively think was the case), the high prices of oil much more directly benefit our foreign suppliers from OPEC nations in the Middle East. Massive profits are being made by the traders of oil in energy hedge funds, managed futures, and indexes, through management fees on ever-growing assets, even if they can't predict where it's headed tomorrow. But if we map the returns on capital, one group stands apart in reaping outsized profits off of the increasingly high and volatile price of oil: The sales and trading desks of the five largest international investment banks. Inside that powerful five, two have created themselves a special and most beneficial niche in oil: Goldman Sachs and Morgan Stanley (as discussed in Chapter 4).

It is because these two 500-pound gorillas make so much money trading oil that we are faced with such a difficult (and maybe impossible) uphill battle on regaining control on price. We have seen proposal after proposal attempting to deal with the banks relating to the crisis in credit, real estate, and other derivative markets. All of those markets and the repercussions of the collapse of those markets have had a much more immediate and tangible effect on the economy and the typical consumer as compared with oil. And yet, most of the more serious proposals to emerge (including the Volcker plan which was designed to separate again the trading arms of the banks from the lending arms) have been all but abandoned in favor of piecemeal and superficial regulatory reform efforts.

The proprietary, in-house trading accounts of the big five investment banks make an estimated *eight times more profit* from trading than they do from the fees generated by their more traditional investment banking roles; roles that include private and public placement, fixed-income origination, and mergers and acquisitions (M&A) advisory services. These are the services that we associate with investment banking: The accumulation and redistribution of capital that makes business run and helps fuel their growth. Yet again, to reiterate the key point, the trading groups inside those banks' walls are making money eight times faster. Adding to the resentment and recent outrage at the investment banks, these profits seem hardly tied to the success of the U.S. economy at large—2009 proved to be the most profitable year on record for both Goldman Sachs and Morgan Stanley, in spite of global recession, increasing unemployment, continuing unhealthy credit markets, and freshly repaid TARP loans.[1] In short, since 2000, for the banks, it has been a case of *"heads I win, tails you lose."*

It is hardly surprising, then, that any reform that would attempt to restore the barriers between the lending purposes of these powerful

---

[1] Troubled Asset Relief Program—undoubtedly necessary, but still a clear bailout program of Government loans that prevented bankruptcy of financial institutions but was also perceived as an implicit safety net that rewarded bad trading behavior.

banks and their in-house investment programs (as was the 70-year tradition of the 1934 Glass-Steagall bill) would be resisted fiercely, despite the claims of Vikram Pandit, Lloyd Blankfein, Jamie Dimon, and John Mack of their commitment to financial reforms in front of various Congressional committees. These four CEOs of Citbank, Goldman Sachs, JP Morgan, and Morgan Stanley (Bank of America is the last of the big five) maintain one of the most powerful lobby groups around the Beltway.

Finally, as if the barriers aren't high enough, Washington is today engaged in perhaps the most partisan bickering in its long history of contentiousness. Even superficial proposals to come out of the 2008 meltdown that only look to establish simple consumer protection are being met, as noted, with partisan fighting. The discussions never seem to be about what will better help America, but what victory can be claimed for one party and what defeat can be saddled on another.

Looking at this bleak picture of government posturing and relative inaction at reregulating a financial industry that nearly brought on a global financial disaster, can we have any hope for a better result when it comes to fixing the broken oil market? Should we even bother to suggest possible solutions?

We should. Short of the extreme seizing of the credit market we saw with the fall of Lehman Brothers in late 2008, nothing should scare America and America's business leaders more than a runaway price for oil, a sure outcome if everything is left the way it is today. Even looking at the direct correlation that oil price has had recently with the stock market indexes, it is inevitable that a solid economic recovery (if we get one) will coincide with an oil price at least approaching the highs of the summer of 2008, and will move higher from there. This push/pull relationship will be difficult to break out of without reform and more difficult to endure: High prices for oil will derail a recovery, causing mini-busts that just add volatility. This will all happen when steadiness is needed the most.

But more than that, nowhere has both the consumer and business world been so innocently victimized as in the oil market. We might be able to put some blame for subprime's collapse on people taking low-interest loans that they knew they would be unlikely to repay.

We can blame Fannie Mae and Freddie Mac for being willing partners. We can blame GM for kicking the can so far down the road
on pension liabilities that the first big downturn in sales was going
to send it into bankruptcy. We can blame institutional and government pension managers for blindly following bank salespeople into
buying questionably rated securities without doing real risk analysis.
And we even might blame individual investors for both believing in
the constant, never-ending uptrends on both the housing and stock
markets.

But no one gets a choice on energy. It costs what it costs,
and everyone needs it: some more and some less. Every day, like
it or not, everyone has to open their wallets and pay. Not everyone owns stocks. Not everyone owns houses. But *everyone needs oil*.
That alone would make oil seem like a priority if we are to seriously
tackle any of the many problems of our increasingly complex financial
world. On the plus side, because the issues surrounding oil are in
entirely different capital markets, populated by fewer participants,
and with relatively tiny capital invested compared with other asset
classes, those factors should make it much easier to find and enact
solutions.

It is because of this—because oil is so relatively puny compared
to all the other traditional capital markets—that I still have my hopes
of seeing energy priced fairly and honestly. So far, the number of
people and businesses reliant on the profit engine of commodity
product sales and the trading of oil and oil products is relatively
small—even the largest banks with the most dedicated desks to energy
garner less than 10% of their profits from it. The number of people
likely to be hurt by enforced restrictions on access to oil pricing and
oil trading are far, far outweighed by the benefits that reliable prices
will have on the consumer and big and small business alike. If there
were one market we might try to remove from the endless cyclone
of financial innovation and the daily trading frenzy, I suggest oil as
the perfect candidate and the most beneficial for everyone.

But where to start? Again, we are left with the two mechanisms
inside of oil pricing where we can exert control: clearing and trading.
Let's discuss how we can bring centralized clearing to *every* aspect of
oil trading and how that will help.

Centralized Clearing Is the First Step

On September 25, 2008, I wrote an article for thestreet.com and appeared on CNBC suggesting that the quickest and surest way to wade through the morass of questionable real estate bonds and credit default swaps was to place them all on public exchanges and allow open and transparent pricing on them. Those that couldn't be standardized, I suggested, needed to be cash settled and retired, but I also suggested that the vast majority of bonds could be graded and collated into tradable, standardized products. (Moreover, Bill Gross of PIMCO actually volunteered to do it.) Of course, at that time, the last thing the banks and insurance companies wanted (and perhaps, in retrospect, the federal government as well) was to see this enormous stinking pile of securities get priced at fair but fire-sale rates all at once. Although the OTC Credit Default Swaps market has gained a little (and I mean a little) traction at getting cleared by public exchanges, there is little hope that any standardized tranches of CDOs are going to appear for trade at the CME or any other regulated exchange anytime soon.

Suggesting that all the securitized mortgage bonds be moved en masse to the CME and the NYSE might have been a bit more than anyone could chew at the time. It is, however, the only road to real transparency. Transparency is the strongest advantage of the regulated exchanges over the opacity and lack of oversight of OTC markets. The CME already offers clearing of many OTC oil contracts, having chosen the most commonly quoted and traded contracts on Mars and Brent grades first and quickly growing their offerings over the years. Today, it offers clearing on literally hundreds of OTC oil products.

But clearing is all it offers. And it is entirely optional. If you enter into an OTC contract through a bank or an OTC broker, you can choose to clear your trade through the NYMEX or not. You can trust the bank and broker and ultimately the credit-worthiness of the party on the other side of the trade, who you may or may not know. The vast majority of OTC contracts are cleared bilaterally, so your bet is only as good as the ability of the other guy to pay—an arrangement that saw a little bit of trouble recently with a small insurance company known as AIG—a little trouble costing $180 billion.

In oil, that option needs to be taken away. All OTC products need to be cleared through a regulated exchange mechanism, where each clearing member in the system shares at least some responsibility for the obligations of the actions of every other participant who engages in that system. There just hasn't been any history of a blowup under a regulated clearing structure that caused systemic risk ever, whereas the enormous failures in unregulated OTC markets (including the recent AIG debacle) are many. That should be reason enough for regulators and the rest of us to demand the migration of every swap, swap option, or other derivative of derivative variant on oil to a regulated exchange. But there is more than shared responsibility for the use of a marketplace at stake.

It became painfully clear to me and every other floor trader during the last half of the 2000 decade how far OTC markets had gone to replace regulated floor markets for price discovery. Advantages were shifting away from the participants trading at the exchanges and moving to the brokers and dealers of swaps and other contracts. There are so many recent examples of dark-pool markets being a catalyst for manipulation that it hardly seems worthy of taking the time to explain why transparency in these markets is a necessary next step. AIG's disaster in credit default swaps is clearly the largest example causing systemic risk and affecting everyone.

But even in energy, two recent cases of manipulation come quickly to mind: In 2007, BP paid a $303 million fine to settle allegations of manipulations in the propane market while controlling much of the storage and pipelines business in the specialty gas as well as the trading of it. And the electricity crisis of 2000 and 2001 in California and the West was at least enflamed if not entirely a creation of manipulations by Enron traders in Enron-controlled markets in newly created OTC power swaps, egged on by a fly-by-night cottage industry of one-room power-marketing sweatshops peddling the notes to anyone who would buy.

There are other smaller examples, but the point should be clear: Self-regulated markets breed temptation and opportunity for manipulation. If instead we can see the positions and particularly the large, one-sided ones get reported, we have a chance to catch a big problem before it happens instead of after. Someone needs to be watching.

The OTC oil market has become very deep and very complicated. It's hard to even know just how big it has become, because most contracts don't have reporting obligations. The salesmen and brokers of these instruments are understandably quiet about how much capital is engaged in off-market trading for oil. Estimates for the OTC derivative market for all assets range upward of *$600 trillion—which is 6 times bigger than the entire market cap for traditional stocks and bonds.* Although it is difficult to know the full nominal value of OTC contracts that have oil as one of their component parts, we can be sure that it is in the many trillions of dollars, dwarfing the size of the futures markets, on which they rely, by several hundred times. It is a very big problem trying to bring this behemoth under control, with plenty of component parts that need to be considered. Gary Gensler, Chairman of the CFTC, has been making the same case as I have here: These products need to be moved to regulated exchanges. Besides the problems associated with migrating a market of such mammoth size, there is one other even more difficult issue to overcome: The customization of the majority of products now being held.

Why am I suggesting this then? Why should the government undertake destroying a fully formed market in off-exchange products in oil? When I first entered the floor and learned about oil pricing, it was clear that the cash market, where real barrels of oil were bought and sold, was where pricing was decided. Later, it became increasingly clear that the source of prices was coming from the futures markets that I engaged in, with the cash market following along—a true case of the tail wagging the dog. Even more recently, it has become increasingly clear that the massive growth in standardized and custom oil swaps (in indexes, for example) have been the primary movers of the futures markets and then of cash prices. This is the hair on the tail of the dog wagging the dog, I guess, except that the tail hairs of this dog are hundreds of times longer than the dog itself. We cannot get to the root of oil prices moving without regard for fundamentals unless we begin by arresting oil's OTC markets first.

The pushback from the OTC community on truly following through on this proposal is sure to be stunning. The CDS market shows us to what extent the participants are willing to go to protect their self-regulated, dark-priced, and big-profit markets. In late 2008, then-Secretary of the Treasury Hank Paulson demanded, correctly, that the CDS market that forced the enormous AIG bailout should be migrated to a regulated exchange to increase transparency, generate centralized clearing, and mandate Federal regulatory control. It was a correct proposal and a stunning one to come from an ex-chairman of Goldman Sachs. The CME, at that time, had a viable CDS contract in which it had already tried to establish traction for more than two years before Paulson's proposal. It seemed an obvious next step that the Federal government would therefore mandate the migration of credit default swaps to the CME, as well as require a quick way of either converting or retiring the custom contracts that could not be basis-priced using an exchange instrument.

It didn't turn out that way: While Washington dithered, the investment banks created a shadow clearing organization named The Chicago Corporation, designed as little more than a pass-through clearing organization wholly owned by the same banks to marginally satisfy the clearing mandate that they did not think they could possibly wheedle out of. They did not believe that in any case would the government ever actually require open pricing and real government oversight of CDS trading, so they made no contingent plan for that at all.

The banks turned out to be right. As of this writing, not only hasn't the CDS market been forced out of the dark pools where they have always traded, but the Chicago Corp. lingers without purpose— the Treasury has not yet followed through with its demands even on centralized clearing. The bank and OTC brokers' lobby in Washington is demonically strong.

For oil to succeed in finding transparency where credit default swaps for now have not, a bill will have to be crafted specifically for oil, mandating full migration of every OTC contract into a centralized clearing pool on regulated exchanges. If the product is so specialized that it cannot be centrally cleared, it needs to be retired, and construction of any new such customized products needs to be made illegal.

Migrating and retiring a big part of oil's OTC market is not enough to ensure proper pricing of the crude barrel. In order to do that, we will need to control who is trading oil as well.

It has been the investor and speculator who have become the dominant players in oil and the most significant influence on oil's price. To put it simply, if we want to get to a fundamentally correct price for oil, we need to remove most, if not all, of the investors and speculators from their access to trading oil.

Two quick fixes can be made to get closer to this goal immediately: The prohibition of commodity index investing and a further prohibition of oil ETFs that engage in futures.

Earlier in the book (in Chapter 3), I described the unnecessary influence that index investing and ETFs have had on the price of oil—a negative influence that inevitably leads to higher and less fundamentally supported prices. It seems difficult to believe, but I have engaged in an argument with a famous CNBC host on an individual's right to invest in the price of crude oil. I won't do it here, it is just too silly an exercise. *A fair price for a gallon of gas for everyone who uses gas is undoubtedly more important than someone's right to bet on it.* To truly do that, you need to entirely eliminate investment vehicles that use the futures markets.

That means no more commodity index products that contain energy components, whether accessed directly through the CME or more often through swaps provided by the investment banks. This must target the biggest index funds, most notably the S&P Goldman Sachs Commodity Index (GSCI) and the Dow Jones AIG commodity index fund (DJAIG). It also means an end to the approved charters of crude oil ETFs, most notably the United States Oil fund (USO) and the iPath Crude oil total return fund (OIL), to name the two largest.

That's a simple start, and no one will suffer for it. There are other proxies for the price of the crude barrel that can easily be substituted that will not impact the traded price of it, including stocks of integrated oil companies, refiners, and oil service companies. Except for the monumental spike in 2008, there's been a fairly close correlation between the share price of integrated oil companies and the price of the crude barrel—have a look at the telling chart, in Figure 11.2.

That's how we all should bet if we want to bet, on a rising price for oil—with stocks. You know, those pieces of paper that were designed to be invested in. But just removing these two investments

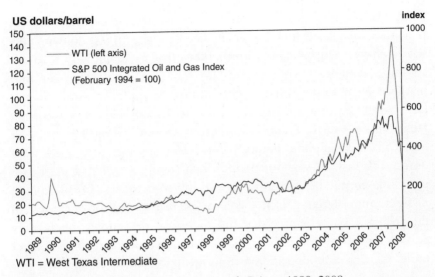

US dollars/barrel   **index**

Figure 11.2   Oil and Oil-Company Stock Prices, 1989–2008
Source: International Monetary Fund

in oil doesn't quite give back oil trading to oil producers and end users. No, to really finish the job, we'd need to establish a gatekeeper to limit participants in the futures markets themselves. A license would have to be issued from an overseeing agency, presumably the CFTC, to even trade in centrally cleared OTC and established futures markets in oil, and the volume of daily trade and particularly the positions one could hold would be determined and limited by each individual participant's physical commitment to the products represented by each market. This makes it very simple to assure that those most engaged in physical oil production will have the strongest influence on the traded price of the crude barrel: indeed, Exxon, Chevron, Shell, and BP again would be the biggest possible fish in the oil trading sea, just as they were when I first set foot on the floor of the NYMEX back in 1983.

Of course, liquidity is still critical to the smooth operation of the oil futures markets, and further licenses to qualified liquidity providers would also have to be issued, but with strict volume and position limits. We need to prevent any financially driven participant from being able to overwhelm and dominate the price discovery of the legitimate, physically driven players. Liquidity is sure to be a first topic of argument when ideas of limiting access to oil markets are discussed. It is often suggested (but has never been proved to me convincingly in my 25-year engagement with markets) that more liquidity is always an improvement. *Deeper* markets do not necessarily make for *truer* markets, even though that might intuitively appear obvious. It is a facile argument for unfettered access to trading—to sticking one's rapacious nose into a cookie jar where it doesn't belong. I never, ever heard a complaint about liquidity in oil from any legitimate participant during my first 20 years of trading it, despite the fact that there was very little engagement from funds and investors, not an OTC product in sight, and a fraction of the volume there is today. In fact, most of the traders I knew appreciated the slightly wider quotes where they could take a legitimate risk to split the difference and drive market trade. Clearly, nobody suffered from a supposed lack of liquidity. No one certainly seemed to mind the rock steady and low prices of oil during those years, certainly no coincidence.

What I'm suggesting is admittedly a lot to ask. Applying this model of transparently clearing secondary trading and restricting access to the primary markets to other larger and better established capital markets might be understandably laughed at as impossible.

My case for oil being the first and perhaps lone market for this kind of scrupulous regulation is two-fold. First, I hope I've made the case that oil is a universal need and affects everyone, whether they are directly engaged in the trading of it or not. But secondly, oil has only begun its march down the same road as we've seen played out with corporate bonds, credit default swaps, and subprime mortgage-backed securities. It's a small market, and fully regulating control of it would harm so few while protecting so many. If we are to draw a line in the sand and force the banks and the proprietary traders and the index managers and hedge funds to back off somewhere, shouldn't it be with oil?

It should.

Appendix: December 2010

The manuscript for this book was due to the publisher at the end of September 2010—a deadline I absolutely approved of and worked hard to meet. We had a very topical issue to discuss and a book that would have the greatest impact the sooner the publisher and I could reasonably get it to print. The last substantive chapter, Chapter 11, describing the possible action and solutions to oil's unreliable pricing mechanism was therefore written in the summer of 2010.

On July 21, 2010, President Obama signed into law the Wall Street Reform and Consumer Financial Protection Act (commonly known as the Dodd-Frank financial regulatory bill), which was designed to bring under control the many varied financial markets and market makers that the Federal government deemed to be wholly or partially responsible for the great financial meltdown of 2008. This massive piece of legislation affected the information provided in Chapter 11 because the bill included two key components that could have a major effect on the solutions for oil that I had already committed to the text. The first was a version of the Volcker Rule—although weakened—designed to divest the investment banks from their proprietary trading desks of all sorts of assets. And the second was a frontal assault on over-the-counter (OTC) derivatives of all types and their dark pool lack of transparency and oversight.

Both of these provisions of the bill had the potential to initiate some of the major reforms I have already outlined in Chapter 11 as necessary to get the oil markets under control.

Maybe this new bill wasn't just a significant start. Maybe this was an honest fix, a reapplication of the Glass-Steagall guidelines that had been repealed in 2000. Watching the legislation beginning to take shape into laws during the fall and early winter of 2010, I wondered whether it was time to take my pen and go home, happy that the Federal government had so clearly seen the problems as I had and was now working to ensure that financial influences would never again trump fundamentals in energy.

Well, maybe—but most probably no. First, I have to give credit where it is due to the Commodity Futures Trading Commission (CFTC)—and specifically to Chairman Gary Gensler and ex-Chairman and Commissioner Bart Chilton. Both men have made specific and frequent statements declaring how seriously the CFTC views the legislation and will look to implement the Dodd-Frank reforms with as wide an umbrella as they can wield—in spite of incredible pressures to instead take the easy road, pay lip service to the frankly vague definitions and designs of the bill toward commodity derivatives, and pretty much let business go on as usual.

And the pressures to do just that have been enormous. Pressure has come not only from the investment banks and their traders, but almost as strongly from the advocacy groups of industry traders in crude oil, natural gas, and other refined products, whose profits also derive significantly from the trading of oil, not just the selling of the stuff. Whether that is a business model worth continuing to pursue is not really at issue, at least not yet—most oil companies and natural gas dealers engage to an enormous degree in the trading of energy, taking the profits when it works and passing the losses down to their consumers and stockholders when it doesn't. That's just the way Oil's Endless Bid has played itself out: very few in the industry have wanted to be left out of the profits to be had from the financialization of oil.

The CFTC has taken the vagueness of the Dodd-Frank bill and applied a very logical and measured method of implementation into commodities. It has isolated 30 separate and specific areas of rulemaking that it needs to create and define. It is important to understand just how massive a project this will become, as the CFTC tries to take some oversight control over a derivative marketplace that is— depending on whose figures you use—at least 8 times and perhaps as much as 30 times larger in nominal value than the ones the CFTC has already been charged with overseeing. The CFTC has undertaken to:

- Define what a swap is just to know what contracts must be under CFTC oversight and need to be centrally cleared.
- Set clear guidelines as to who can deal in these instruments as brokers and traders.
- Define how clearinghouses are to be run, who can own them, and what capital requirements need to be met so that new derivative houses are not mere pass-throughs for OTC trading, doing the bare minimums of compliance.

Finally, there are other rulemaking areas in complex issues involving trading, reporting of trades, and enforcement.

Caramba. Each one of these 30 rulemaking areas has been opened up by the CFTC for public input and discussion before decisions will be made on precisely how to implement their newly written rules, using public meetings and welcoming comments from all interested parties. Needless to say, the commission has been quite literally overrun by opinion letters by industry advocacy agencies such as the Futures Industry Agency (FIA), the National Futures Association (NFA), and the Securities Industry and Financial Markets Association (SIFMA), to name only a few of the largest. Virtually every bank, every hedge fund behemoth (such as Blackrock and Pimco), and every major oil corporation has participated in the dozens of external meetings scheduled by the CFTC to discuss specific sections. During the third quarter of 2010, the number of lobbyists hired to represent corporations, associations, and other interests to the CFTC rose by 22%.[2] Not included in these figures is the avalanche of lawyer requests for meetings with CFTC attorneys and staff from such bank and industry firms as Alston & Bird; Gibson, Dunn & Crutcher; Patton Boggs; Sullivan & Cromwell; and Skadden, Arps. Since the CFTC began publishing its meetings starting in July, firm attorneys have met with agency staff on at least 50 days leading to November 2010, with some days holding multiple meetings.[3]

Still, statements from the commission indicate that they are (at least so far) trying hard to hold the line and believe reforms of the derivative markets for all commodities and particularly oil should be as inclusive as possible. They have a daunting task ahead of them as the voices from the other side are weaker: There are very few groups arguing the case for the consumer, and their resources are more limited (although one group—Stop Oil Speculation NOW (S.O.S. Now)—is composed of an interesting blend of consumer groups, growers' associations, airlines, and convenience store associations).

And there is reason to believe that it won't matter much anyway. Michael Lewis, author of *Liar's Poker* and *The Big Short*, recently

---

[2] According to the Center for Responsive Politics, a consumer advocate organization that tracks lobbyist disclosure forms.

[3] According to a Capital Business analysis of agency records.

opined that banks are divesting themselves of proprietary desks well in advance of specific orders from the CFTC and the Securities and Exchange Commission (SEC) to do so. They are apparently not waiting around to be forced to do it, but are instead doing it voluntarily and rapidly.

Why?

They clearly are not throwing in the towel on trading profits, which have been far and away the source of the majority of profits earned in the last 5 years. Lewis believes that banks are in the process of rebranding their proprietary desks as agents of client and outside investors. Through a vague definition of principal interest outlined in the bill, Lewis maintains that any trade that can be rationalized as done, even marginally, on behalf of a client or investor removes the trader from principal status. For the banks, this is a simple task: raise a little capital from any outside trading group or private investors, rehire in-house proprietary trading teams as new members of this newly created vehicle still under the umbrella of the bank, and voilà! The Volcker rule is side-stepped. No one needs to even move a desk.

And while the magnifying glass has been placed on the investment banks as they begin whatever sleight of hand they can to retain what trading interest they can, there are other rapidly growing groups ready to fill whatever vacuum the banks leave behind. Independent trading houses of commodities continue to grow and gain capital support. For example, Swiss group Glencore, now the world's largest privately held commodities trader, raised $2.2 billion in a convertible offering in December of 2009 and is reportedly headed for a $10 billion IPO in the second quarter of 2011. The multiple opportunities for traders of commodities are matched only by the insatiable appetite for capital to satisfy and profit from them, whether they appear at or outside of the trading desks of the banks. Glencore has been in discussions for this partially public financing plan with—yes, that's right—Citigroup, Morgan Stanley, and Credit Suisse. In the end, the massive effort put forth by the CFTC may have only one real effect—decentralizing the major trading power in commodities and oil away from the dedicated desks at the banks, but hardly arresting the engine that drives the ridiculous prices we are seeing in cotton, coffee, copper, corn, and of course, oil. As a zero sum game, commodity trader profits from big price moves may take a long road, but must ultimately come out of the pockets of consumers.

All of this works hard but never settles on targeting the real symptom of this disease. One specific area that the CFTC cannot define and regulate is the underlying *motive* of any trade, the only way to be entirely sure whether a transaction adheres to the originally designed purposes of the futures and derivatives markets.

Simply, and as I asked Mr. King during my interview at Coastal: is it a hedge? Or is it a bet?

If it's a hedge, it has legitimate purpose in the market not just as a financial tool, but more important, as a component of a true price.

And if it's a bet? Then it serves as an unnecessary and illegitimate influence on the prices you and I pay.

I don't minimize the great and correct strides being taken by the CFTC, above and beyond what is mandated by Dodd-Frank reform. This joust and parry of rulemaking will continue for the next three years at least—by most estimates—until any real reform is ready to be enforced. Even if the players are too smart for the system, water down the final rules through intense lobbying and high-priced attorney activism, and move traders into different spheres and vehicles out of the purview of oversight, there is a good reason to believe that the final results will help slow the influence of traders on commodity prices, even if they go nowhere near eliminating them. Dodd-Frank will certainly help.

But I titled my book *Oil's Endless* **BID**, for a reason. While traders are the *amplifiers* (i.e., the superchargers on top of the engine of wild price movement and higher prices), the *fuel* for this runaway engine remains the investment interest in oil. And this new and insatiable desire to consistently own oil like a stock or a bond (i.e., the *bid*) is coming from index speculators, managed futures accounts, commodity-specific hedge funds, exchange-traded funds, and personal futures accounts in discount brokerages all across this country and around the world.

Dodd-Frank, unfortunately, has nothing to say about any of that.

As I write this at the end of 2010, oil is up a measly 23% on the year. So maybe I should have written instead about *coffee's* endless bid, which is up almost 60%; or *corn*'s endless bid, up 40%; or *copper*'s endless bid, up 27%; or *cotton*'s endless bid, which had almost doubled on the year before falling back to be only up 57% on the year.

While the traders have magnified every one of these moves this year, this across-the-board price explosion in all publicly traded commodities has *not* been caused by economies running at 6 to 8% growth, either here or in emerging nations, nor by worldwide drought or unexpected freezes. As with oil, they've moved *as large amounts of capital have attempted to invest in relatively small and delicate markets that were never designed for investment.*

Until we find a way to regulate that, the endless bid will continue to dominate prices of oil and all the other products we depend on daily.

Epilogue

Oil's Endless Bid Appears in the Gulf of Mexico

There is a live feed of video running on the screens in my office, and I can't help myself but obsessively scan back to it every few minutes during the trading day. It doesn't change, but every time I scan back, I am hoping it will. It is the BP live feed camera of the open-riser pipe in the Gulf of Mexico, spewing a black cloud of oil and natural gas in an unrelenting stream into the ocean.

It is day 35, two days before the attempt of the planned BP top kill effort to force heavy mud into the wellbore that is supposed to staunch and ultimately kill this runaway well, 50 miles off the coast of Louisiana and a mile down. I am starting to fully comprehend just how important this story has become—not only for the ecological nightmare it is causing and will continue to cause for the next weeks, months, and years—but also for how it now will dominate the oil markets that I am following and trying to predict and trade. I have been called to do a CNBC spot on oil and analyze where prices might go, right now on the low end of a 2010 trading range. In this short 3.5-minute segment, I cannot seem to think or talk about anything except the nature of the leak in the gulf and how it is overwhelming every other aspect of what are normal inputs for crude prices.

If I were looking for another (or better) proof of the endless bid— that is, the financial influences overwhelming the fundamentals—I could not have generated it with my wildest imagination.

It is an unwanted proof of my theories of oil pricing on the back of an unbelievable catastrophe. Coast Guard Admiral Thad Allen, the U.S. Government's access point and spokesman for the ongoing operation and fallout, comes on TV news show after news show with a teddy bear look always on the verge of tears.

I am on the verge of tears myself. I have been engaged professionally only on the financial side and not ever the physical side of oil, and I know as little about the mechanics of ultra-deepwater drilling as anyone you might meet on the street. I personally have never met even one man involved in the procurement and transport of crude oil locked inside the deepest recesses of the earth miles beneath the sea, for British Petroleum or any other oil corporation. And yet, I feel guilty, ashamed, and powerless. I have made a living and a success in the oil business, even if it is the most removed part of that business from the part that has screwed up so royally and will leave Gulf coast residents and businesses with a mess that will take them years to recover from. But I am still connected in a small way, and I also feel somehow responsible. However, like everyone else staring mute into the live BP feed, there's nothing I can do.

Tony Hayward, the current BP CEO, has spent the three years since May 2007 as the head of the company trying to overcome the truly horrifying safety record of the third-largest multinational oil company, lagging in size only behind Exxon-Mobil and Royal Dutch Shell. The previous CEO, Lord Edmund John Browne, had spent much of his tenure pushing BP as a green energy company, beginning a worldwide campaign of commercials starting in 1997 featuring women with strollers chatting casually about alternative energy: "How wonderful would it be to see our world moving away from fossil fuels as our primary source of energy?" they wonder aloud to the camera.

These fine pictures of concerned parents were followed by BP graphics of the investment efforts of the company into wind, solar, and other renewable technologies, followed by a big picture of the then-new green sunflower logo for the company. "BP," it shone in big letters: "Beyond Petroleum."

These commercials play in stunning disregard for the facts. BP has accumulated the worst safety record in the industry by far, and it has long been the reason that many oil analysts have tended to recommend BP less often than other oil integrated companies in the past, in spite of BP's consistently sector-leading dividend history. BP accumulated hundreds of violation citations for its drilling and refinery operations over the last years of Lord Browne's stewardship, while other oil companies had counted violations only in the single digits. That record culminated in the Prudhoe Bay 200,000 gallon oil spill from BP's Alaska North Slope pipeline in 2006 and in the disastrous 2005 Texas City refinery fire, which killed 15 BP workers and injured 170 others. In the aftermath of that fire, the Chemical Safety Board (CSB) found a raft of violations and previous safety problems that had been left unaddressed by BP before the accident, an unfortunate but pretty well-worn story for BP operations by this time. BP was assessed a fine of $87 million by the U.S. Occupational and Health Administration and another $50 million fine by the federal government for environmental crimes. Prudhoe Bay cost BP another $20 million in fines and a three-year probationary period.

Into this horrible picture, in May 2007, came the new CEO Hayward, who was put in place as the barely 60-year-old Browne was being forced out (for apparently being more concerned with his personal reputation than the reputation of the company he was leading). In the few years since Hayward took the helm, he had become well respected, even much liked by the analysts who saw his honest attempts at cleaning up a very bad safety record and adhering to the recommendations laid out by the OSHA and CSB in the wake of the Texas City disaster. Finally, 2009 looked to be a great year for BP with Hayward's stewardship and better hand on the tiller: BP shares made the biggest move upward during that year compared to every major competitor in the sector, all while providing investors with a fantastic and sector-leading dividend to boot. BP might even have been dreaming of moving up a rung from its no. 3 placement in market cap.

As I write this in the summer of 2010, it is so far entirely unclear what caused the massive oil spill from the deepwater Horizon well at Macondo, which was majority owned by BP (Anadarko Petroleum has a 25% interest) and leased by Transocean. In the first set of hearings in Washington trying to find the culprit, even engineers and deepwater specialists have so far been unable to adequately explain just what went on that day in April to cause the explosion and the death of 11 rig workers. If the disaster weren't so unbelievably terrible, those hearings would almost have been comical. BP representatives attempted to blame Transocean, and Transocean tried to blame the BP workers and Cameron, the company that manufactured the failed Blow-Out Preventer (an ironically named device, as it didn't prevent). For right now, it hardly matters. It is BP's rig, and therefore BP's responsibility to end the gushing oil from continuing to spill into the Gulf and then attempt to make right the environmental and human disaster that it leaves in its wake.

It looks to be a very long road. BP engineers, after failing to stop the flow of oil through both a so-called top kill procedure and then another junk shot procedure, have been left with trying to collect the spewing oil as best they can until a final solution relief well was drilled successfully in August. Only with a fresh pipe as access into the well was BP able to relieve the flowing oil pressure enough to force heavy mud and ultimately cement into the hole, killing the flow once and for all.

There have been two other offshore runaway wells to date of this type and magnitude to refer to for historical evidence: The Ixtoc spill in Mexico in 1979 and the more recent Timor sea spill by the Australian and Thai PTT Exploration company in 2009. In both cases, relief wells were the final solution, but in neither case did the first relief well precisely intersect and eliminate pressure enough to stop the flow of the primary well. In the Ixtoc spill, more than nine months elapsed before the final capping of the runaway. But even in the more modern 2009 Timor sea incident, a successful relief well was dug and made operational only on the fourth attempt. BP will never be the same company it was before this deepwater well spill began, that is clear. Besides accepting blame for the spill, there will be a flood of claims and lawsuits against the company for livelihoods lost, not only in the most obvious gulf states of Louisiana and Mississippi. Even with the $5 billion free cash flow per quarter and about a $10 billion dividend that BP ultimately suspended, the effects of this spill will cripple this company for years. And the government seems inclined to see that happen without much, if any remorse.

Within days of the failure of the top kill procedure and under political pressure to respond more forcefully, President Obama made several trips to the gulf and held several questions and answer sessions with the media. In each of these sessions, the President has made it very clear that he will use the full power of the U.S. government to first hold BP accountable for the deaths and injuries of the blown-up rig, but also for the injuries to life and property caused by the disruptions of the widening slick.

It's hard to imagine what that will ultimately entail, but I remember the Exxon Valdez oil spill in Alaska in 1989 when a captain ran a supertanker aground, dumping 11 million gallons of crude into Prince William Sound. In the aftermath of that disaster, Exxon paid out $1 billion in cleanup costs and another $2 billion in settlements. And this was in 1990 dollars in the Prince William Sound area of Alaska, where practically no one lives. The amount of oil already leaked into the gulf is only estimated at this date to be at least four times the amount leaked by the Exxon Valdez, with a soonest possible end of the leakage still a month and a half away. On top of this, the U.S. government originally leveled a $5 billion environmental fine at Exxon, at that time a larger figure than Exxon's 1989 full-year earnings. Subsequent appeals of that fine finally led to the Supreme Court in 2008—almost a full 20 years after the original disaster—when the Exxon fine was ultimately dropped to a mere $507 million.

This may be the only good news for BP, should it survive the cleanup costs—the Valdez case shows that only time really heals this kind of massive wound, both to the environment and to the outrage. Exxon asked for as many extensions to each case hearing as it could get, and then it appealed each ruling until it reached the ultimate court. It may not get you a moral outcome, but it will get you the

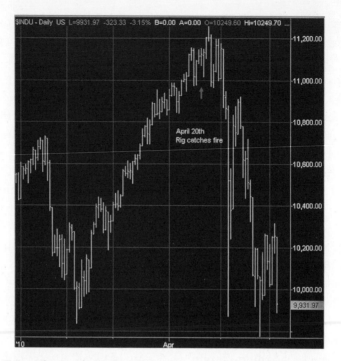

Figure E.1 The Stock Market Plummeted after BP's Oil Rig Caught Fire on April 20, 2010

smallest fine. "Appeal forever" is sure to be BP's motto for the next five years, replacing "beyond petroleum."

In the oil and stock markets, the Deepwater Horizon spill provided one of the most classic representations of the endless bid and the effects of an entirely financialized oil market moving prices, ignoring without regard the obvious fundamental affects of the Gulf coast spill. Figure E.1 is a daily chart of the stock market after the Deepwater Horizon rig caught fire on April 20, 2010 and the subsequent oil spill.

A similar picture is drawn by the Crude oil market (see Figure E.2), which we have become now accustomed to seeing move in tandem with stocks.

But the two charts, as similar as they are, painted a very easily interpreted picture. The immediate consequences and long-term effects of the rig fire on April 20 were not immediately apparent.

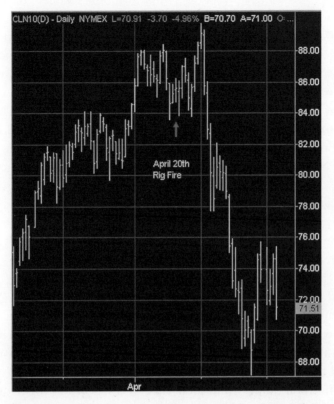

Figure E.2   The Crude Oil Market Plummeted after BP's Oil Rig Caught Fire on April 20, 2010

Indeed, President Obama took much criticism in his very slow reaction to the incident, but for that he needed not too much of an excuse—very few if any of us could see the reverberating results of that rig fire and subsequent oil leak. By early May 2010, with the flow unstaunched and the first confirmations of the vast amounts of oil that were flowing into the Gulf of Mexico, both the stock and oil markets had a much more firm and rigorous reaction—they crashed.

And they didn't crash equally. It became very clear where the brunt of selling was entering the market and moving the indexes—in energy. While the Dow Jones Industrial Average (DJIA) lost 11% of its value from its interim highs, the Standard & Poor's (S&P) Select Energy Spider Fund (a composite fund of energy stocks) backed off from an interim high of $62 to a low of just over $50, a retreat of close to 20%. Not surprisingly, crude oil itself fared even worse, backing off in the July contract almost 25%, and losing almost 30% in the spot June contract before it expired. This didn't make much logical sense: fully 24% of domestic U.S. oil supplies were being provided by the almost 4,000 offshore drilling rigs in the Gulf of Mexico, accounting for somewhere between 8% and 12% of total U.S. supply, depending on who was doing the counting. A disruption in this supply, even a small one, shouldn't have caused oil prices to go down; instead, they should have rallied. However, this entirely opposite reaction made the connection between financial players trading oil and hedging oil trades with oil stocks crystal clear. Without any regard to how the oil spill might play on current supply levels of oil coming into the United States through deepwater drilling in the gulf—a slightly bullish indicator—instead, the world wanted out of the oil trade all at once.

From a human perspective, it was a perfectly understandable response: Who wanted to have anything to do with oil with that live feed in the Gulf continuing to play? The image of the spewing pipe affected the psyche of investors with any exposure to energy (whether stocks or commodities), and their visceral reaction was to sell anything and everything that had anything to do with that offending picture.

The avalanche of selling came to the most obvious stocks first, to BP and to Anadarko and Transocean and Cameron, the four directly connected companies to the Deepwater Horizon rig. But it moved on into just about any issue that had connection to oil, hitting even the natural gas stocks that had only a passing interest in crude and the domestic pipeline companies that did little more than charge tolls for the use of their pipes in moving product. It was a total energy washout, despite the continued bleating of analysts in daily updates and industry notes that generational opportunities in energy issues unrelated to deepwater drilling, or even drilling at all were emerging. Nobody cared.

In the stock market rally from the lows of March 2009, the focus clearly was maintained on the banking sector, the object of such derision and bailout money. It was only because of the recovering health of the banks that the stock market managed such a robust and fast recovery, most analysts claimed. Now it was becoming clear that the fate of the equity markets hung in the balance of the energy sector—that spewing pipe in the Gulf had created a virus in virtually every energy stock, had put a 12-ton anchor around the index, and was threatening to take the entire economy down into a double-dip recession all by itself.

In energy equities, the picture seemed grim. However, in the oil markets, we began to see a bid forming—but it wasn't where you might have expected it, unless you understood the nature of the endless bid. The front months of the curve were tied (as always) to the stock market—in the endless bid, there is no differentiation between asset classes, they are all the same—money is either flowing in or flowing out and in front month oil contracts, like equities, it was definitely flowing out.

But the back months of crude were a different story. In the far backs, as far forward in time as 2018, a bid was definitely forming, driving the differential price between prompt crude and forward crude to dizzying levels. In less than two months after the Deepwater Horizon rig caught on fire, the spread between July 2010 and the December 2018 contract at the New York Mercantile Exchange (NYMEX) rose almost 100%, moving from an $11 differential to more than $21.

But there was much more to this than met the eye. We have seen that the West Texas Intermediate (WTI) contract for crude oil is a puny market in comparison to major asset markets, yet it is still burdened with being the benchmark pricing vehicle for oil. Even as puny as it is, it still manages to maintain about 350,000 open contracts in its spot, or first month and trade as much as 500,000 contracts a day—still a relatively tiny, but respectable turnover of $40 billion of oil. But move further back into the far back months of oil contracts, and that number of open contracts begins to tail off quite a lot. By the time you've moved into contracts more than a year into the future, open interest is down to a piddling 10,000 to 15,000 and are lucky to trade a few thousand contracts—not even a blip on the radar screens of most even moderately small fund managers.

Indeed, there's only one thing that could move these illiquid back-month contracts so quickly—swap bets being made over the counter by energy hedge funds. Which of course, makes perfect sense.

The President has been talking tough about offshore drilling and imposed a drilling moratorium. Offshore crude, before this incident, had been considered the most promising source for domestic energy growth over the next several years. The President had recently opened the Atlantic to deepwater drilling at the end of March, a move that surprised his followers, less than three weeks before the gulf disaster at Macondo. With the likelihood of increased regulation and other hurdles decreasing supply in both shallow and deepwater drilling, smart managers rushed to call their local investment bank and inquire about longer-term bets on the price of crude—not for today, when the risk of a double-dip recession still loomed, but for the next four, five, and even eight years from today, when decreased supply should have its greatest effect on price in a recovering economy.

While the thesis makes intuitive sense, the facts don't support it. Even a full-scale U.S. delay on new rigs, both in shallow and deep water, would result in a cut of approximately 500,000 barrels a day for domestic supply in 2013, energy analysts at Sanford Bernstein recently reported. In the global scheme of things, this is a piddling amount to lose—and there's every reason to believe that drilling will again resume to normal growth after this rig disaster is ultimately controlled. We are seeing a quick motion of money, not legitimate hedging—a desire to bet on the long-term future based on the results of a contemporary disaster.

These might be smart bets, or dumb bets, I don't know—but they are not insurance policies being taken out by energy end users afraid of what the price of oil might be a decade from now. They are speculative wagers on future prices, and their effect will be felt a lot sooner than five years from today. We are seeing another example of financial wagering creating a deeply sloped curve of prices and, as happened in 2008, it will do nothing but establish a floor that crude prices cannot get below—no matter how deep our supplies or weak our demand might be.

In other words, it is perceptions, and not realities, that are creating the oil prices we're all being forced to live with. The BP well disaster is only the latest event to have made that clear. Oil markets and oil prices continue to be rocked—not by legitimate changes in fundamental supply or industrial demands, but by the quick analysis of traders and investors looking to benefit from a well-placed bet. This is not good for anyone—not our economy and not for us as consumers of energy. Without change, Oil's Endless Bid looks capable of continuing to cripple our collective progress for decades to come.

APPENDIX A

A Brief Review of the History of Futures

The history of futures trading is long, extending back to the 1800s and the grain markets. The history of futures trading is also boring, and it has little to do with the modern uses of futures markets. Despite what you might hear from industry spokesmen (particularly when they are in front of congressional committees or CNBC cameras), the original purposes of futures markets have long been lost. Until relatively recently, futures markets were designed with the needs of real producers and end-users of raw commodities in mind. Now, however, the commodity markets merely represent a vehicle to another investment class, the assetization of oil (discussed in detail in Chapters 3 and 4), with little regard for the fundamentals of the underlying commodity and less regard for the most directly affected participants.

Understanding that change in the markets requires an overview of futures and their initially contemplated use. Follow me for the next several pages, and you will understand what so few experts on television seem to understand: the key differences between futures and other capital markets.

With a stock or a bond, a simple transaction takes place: A certificate representing a share of a company or a payment obligation with a lien on a company is exchanged for a money payment. Money in, product out. Like in the supermarket, you give the cashier your 59¢, and she bags up the can of DelMonte corn to take home. There is an exchange of tangible items on which you can at least try to place value.

Not so with futures. A futures contract, which is what changes hands on futures exchanges, does not represent anything tangible. It is nothing more than a promissory note, an obligation for a specific quantity of a very specific commodity, to be exchanged at a specific place at a specific time in the future.

Let's break this idea down because it is in this simple definition that most people miss understanding the price swings of oil or corn or interest rates. With any commodity futures contract, we have five variables we must deal with:

1. The exact specifications of the commodity: What are we trading?
2. A quantity: How much are we trading?
3. A venue where we can exchange this quantity of this specific commodity: for example, where is the supermarket located where I can give you the money for your can of corn?
4. There is a moment in time in the future when this exchange will take place (this is where a future contract becomes a derivative).
5. And finally, there is a price at which the commodity will be exchanged.

With all futures on regulated commodity exchanges, 4 of these 5 variables are made constant, and only price is left to be decided. In comparison, over-the-counter (OTC) derivatives can vary any and all of the other four constants as well as price, which makes them much more difficult to correctly price and certainly to understand than regulated futures. (Chapter 4 tells more about the OTC markets.) Let's use oil to better describe these five variables and how they are standardized to leave only price as the one left unknown.

Variable No. 1: What Are We Trading?

With oil, the contract that gained the vast majority of interest and volume on the New York Mercantile Exchange (NYMEX) is still West Texas Intermediate (WTI). WTI is one grade of sweet crudes drilled and pumped in the United States that represents only a fraction of all crude harvested in this country. Sweet grades of crude have a small sulfur content (for WTI, it's 0.34%), and this makes the sweet grades of crude more desirable because they are more easily refined into products we actually use, like heating oil and gasoline.

Why was WTI chosen? For whatever reasons, WTI became the grade of crude most easily traded on the futures market in the United States. It is the benchmark on which all other prices on most all other grades of crude that change hands is loosely based. So we have our first variable standardized: We will be trading WTI.

Variable No. 2: How Much Are We Trading?

The standardized quantity of a WTI contract traded on the NYMEX is 1,000 barrels, each barrel containing 42 gallons. [This number was chosen not only because it's easy to remember. When futures contracts are developed, an overwhelming goal is to create a contract that represents a useful vehicle for both commercial users and also for individual, liquidity-providing traders. In general, commercial users are better served with very large quantities, whereas individuals (with their limited bankrolls) are generally happier working with much smaller quantities and much lower single-contract price risk. Therefore, the choice of contract size is a very important balancing game for exchanges, and it can be the difference between a successful listing and one that flounders and is untradeable.]

With crude oil, a real-world hedger can use a real-world number of contracts to represent a real-world quantity of product: A standardized cargo is 100,000 barrels, or 100 crude contracts of 1,000 barrels each. For individual traders like me, the 1,000-barrel contract worked very well: In money terms, a 1,000-barrel contract translates to a $10 value for every 1¢ of price change per contract (1¢ per barrel x 1,000 barrels per contract). On-floor traders have very limited clearing costs so can practically discount commissions when thinking about risk. With a $10 threshold, a proper amount of risk for any individual trader can be achieved. You can see how traders referred to themselves and others as one-lot (contract) traders or 10-lot traders or 100-lot traders.

The history of crude oil proves that the NYMEX did an excellent job of finding the balance between individuals and commercial users of the contract, at least when the contract was first conceived. But as crude oil attracted more interested participants who needed much more exposure than any one trading individual might, the contract size proved entirely too small and inadequate, inspiring much more volatile price moves. For now, we've defined two key variables and have three more to go.

Variable No. 3: Where Are We Trading?

Although there are many supermarkets available to exchange money for crude oil in the real world, for the purposes of exchanges, the contracts mandate that exchange of product for money can only happen in one specific place. The NYMEX WTI crude contract defines its delivery point for sweet crude at Cushing, Oklahoma. Deliveries are ratable for every month, which means if you deliver, you can do it in equal quantities throughout the month or all at once at the beginning. Stocks can be swapped for money through any registered clearing firm. But a single and unique delivery point is an important and unique characteristic of futures.

Variable No. 4: When Will Our Trades Take Place?

We're ready for the fourth of our five variables: time. When will we meet in Cushing to exchange our 1,000 barrels of specific sulfur content sweet crude oil? For WTI, NYMEX has set up a monthly contract schedule. NYMEX lists 36 consecutive months for trade in crude oil, as well as other contracts that can extend years into the future (often the December contract).

Not all futures contracts are listed on a monthly basis, although this is far more often than not the standard listing schedule for most commodities; for example, metals contracts often have quarterly listings. The exchange can decide to list more or fewer contracts at its sole discretion, and the exchange is normally more than happy to list more, as long as they are in demand and trading. Every traded contract generates a fee for the exchange.

But here's the key point: Every month that is traded on the exchange is treated as an entirely independent issue, an entirely independent stock. There is nothing (besides the constant specifications that we have assigned with variables 1, 2, and 3) that forces the prices of each individual contract to match up with any other individual contract. Nothing. More money, among traders at least, is made and lost betting on the relationships between contracts as opposed to the outright price of any one contract. This is the essence of spread trading (described in Chapter 1), and the most common trade practice for professionals on any futures exchange. For now, let's start to put a little of this information to use by having a look at a standard price board:

	Mar	Apr	May
Last	48.00	49.00	50.00
2nd	47.90	48.90	49.90
3rd	47.80	48.80	49.80
Hi	48.00	49.00	50.00
Low	47.50	48.50	49.50
Open	47.50	48.50	49.50
Chg.	+100	+90	+80
Sett.	47.00	48.10	49.20

This is a very close representation to the boards we would see on the floor of the exchange every day. The top line indicates the contract month, last is the most recent traded price, followed by the second last and third last traded prices, from which you could get a gross trend of prices—in this example, going up. After those, you find the high price traded for the day, the low, and the first price traded after the start of trading that morning (the opening price). (All of these are important for some technical systems, but they were never really interesting to me.) Finally, you find the settlement price from the previous day and the daily change, which is simply the difference between the settlement price and the last traded price.

Notice that each monthly contract has separate and unique prices for all of these cells. Let's see what we can learn about today's action from what we see on the board:

- First, we notice that in general, the crude oil market is trading up on the day.
- March (the first month listed) is up 100 points, and because points represent cents per barrel, 100 points equates to $1 a barrel.
- We see that the March contract settled yesterday at $47 and last traded at $48.

In this fictitious board, March is the current first month listed and is also known as the spot month. It will be the next contract to reach delivery when exchange trading stops, and the remaining participants will have to deliver or receive delivery of product at Cushing. On the day prior to allocation of delivery, (sometime between the 18th and 20th of the preceding month, as directed by the exchange), the spot month will leave the board and push every other month down a slot. In our example, March will disappear and April will become the spot month.

When the media refers to what happened in the oil market on any single day, it invariably refers to the price action in the spot month. This makes some sense, because the spot market will be the first to converge into the cash market (where actual product changes hands); therefore, it will have the most effect on the actual price that product will be bought and sold. But you can often find market days where the spot month price will have moved in one direction while the rest of the listed months have moved in the opposite direction. In this case, is the motion of the spot month more important and more worthy of remarking on than the remaining entirety of the futures contracts? Most often, the answer is no. But be aware that when oil is quoted by the media looking for simplicity, the media will be referring to the price motion of the spot market.

You now know quite a bit more about the futures markets and the specifications of contracts than literally 90% of the people engaged in the trade and sale of futures. The reason for this is that most people involved in futures couldn't give a damn about the fixed aspects of commodity contracts. Contract specifications are for geeks and exchange administrators; no one who trades much cares about oil grades or delivery points or termination schedules. Most oil traders wouldn't be able to recognize the difference between a barrel of crude and a barrel of monkeys. No, the only thing that matters—to them, to their clients, and to their clearinghouses—is price.

And price is where all the fun begins.

Variable No. 5: What Price Are We Trading For?

Of all the five variables we need to try to understand in order to trade oil, we've managed to standardize (at least in theory) most (but not all) of the questions surrounding four of them: quality, quantity, time, and location. This leaves our one last and most interesting variable, price. We need to know the many factors working on price to understand oil trade, but even more important, we need to understand the participants and their motivations if we are to understand how prices are reached in the futures market.

Futures markets have many important differences from other capital markets, but they share with stocks the most common form of price discovery: the open-auction system.

In the open-auction system, interested parties will assemble (either in person or more recently in a virtual way, electronically) to enter their bids and offers to buy or sell issues. This can just as easily be stock certificates representing investment in companies, or in our case futures contracts, or regulated commodities on futures exchanges. For a large portion of my career as a trader on the NYMEX, the system of price discovery we used was very similar to the system across the street from us at the New York Stock Exchange (NYSE): Traders and brokers would assemble around a stand (or a bull ring for futures) and shout to each other their best bids and offers. For most stock exchanges during my career, stock trading was helped by the specialist or market-making system, where one specific individual was charged with the task of matching buyers and sellers. This often included entering their own competing bids and offers to make the market more tradable. I don't discuss the specialist system in detail in this book, except to say that it worked adequately well in providing liquidity while giving enormous power and advantage to those lucky enough to be stock specialists.

Our exchange, the NYMEX, didn't require a market-maker system, mostly because we had a total of 36 issues or contract months that were traded in crude, and of those, perhaps only five to seven of them were constantly active. [In addition, there were other energy contracts requiring somewhat less liquidity in heating oil and gasoline. When natural gas finally began trading and gained traction in the early 1990s, it derived its early liquidity from the traders in unleaded gasoline, whose dedicated pit was shared with natural gas when the contract was first introduced. (This was a common trick to give new contracts better chances for liquidity and therefore success: Even at the stock markets, you'd often see new stock issues be housed on the floor near other already well-established large-cap stock stands, where the interest and hopefully liquidity could bleed from the strong issues to the newer, weaker ones.) But by the time natural gas moved to its own dedicated pit, it had its own coterie of traders and didn't need any liquidity help; it soon dwarfed the unleaded gas from which it had emerged, in daily volume and open interest.]

In any event, the point I'm trying to make should be clear: With five or six really deep months of crude and three or four each of gasoline and heating oil and later natural gas, we were looking at 30 or 40 total contracts (at most) that required constant liquidity from traders. When you contrast that to the 10,000 stocks available for trade on the floor of the NYSE, you can see why a dedicated specialist system might have been a necessary addition to help the open-auction process at stock exchanges.

But for the NYMEX and the other large commodity exchanges in New York and Chicago, a market maker was an unnecessary liquidity device. As you'd expect in any open auction, adding active participants in a relatively small number of markets will close the gaps in price bids and offers. Just imagine EBay. Its great advantage is that it is the last remaining venue for internet auctioning. So whether you're looking to sell your old vacuum or looking to buy one used, your first thought will very likely be the same: Let's check out EBay. In the world of oil futures, the community of interested buyers and sellers was very, very small, but our advantage was similar: During those early years of financial oil, if you wanted to trade and you needed the most competitive and liquid market for trade, there was the NYMEX and little else. For oil price, there was (fortunately for us) nowhere else to go.

And this is important, because it underlines one of the most important factors to any successful commodity contract: exclusivity. Many similar contracts have competed for dominance of the same commodity over the history of trade. For example, the NYMEX saw early competition in oil from a competing contract introduced on the Chicago Board of Trade. But unlike the stock markets, where many exchanges have been successful offering trade in the same stocks, competing contracts for the same commodity have never been able to succeed side by side at competing exchanges. So although you have any number of choices in exchange venues if you want to trade Exxon/Mobil stock shares (particularly now with the advent of electronic communication networks [ECNs]), you still have only one lone venue for trading corn or soybean futures.

[As described in Chapter 5, the one recent and fascinating exception to this has been in the oil markets, where in 2003, the Intercontinental Exchange (ICE) introduced a West Texas crude contract to go with its already successful European grade Brent crude contract, which has so far competed successfully with the much better established NYMEX sweet crude contract.]

This kind of exclusivity was considered a necessary and enviable component to any contract's success. That is because from exclusivity naturally flows liquidity. Liquidity is a million-dollar finance word, but it simply refers to the sheer number of bids and offers for any security. And for the open-auction system to work well, more is always better. The more bids and offers you have, the closer the bids and offers will naturally get. The closer the bids and offers get, the more confident that both buyers and sellers will be that they are on the market—that is, getting a fair price. And the more confident you can make your clients on both sides of the market, the more trading you will see.

However, not every participant has an equally good feeling about liquidity. Exchanges will want as much liquidity as they can get without care for the people providing it, because more liquidity equals more trade and more exchange fees. Commercial participants will also yearn for deep liquidity, because a close gap between bid and offer should mean that they are not being taken advantage of by third-party exchanges in their entry and exit to derivative markets. On the other hand, independent traders (like I was) need liquidity too—but only when it suits them. Markets that are quoted wide—that is, where there is less liquidity and substantial gaps between the bid and offer—provide money-making opportunities for local traders close to the action. Chapter 6 discusses exactly how this is done, but we can again refer to our EBay example to see immediately why less liquidity in places can be a money making opportunity for a trader.

Let's say you wanted to buy a vacuum and you had only one place to go: EBay. You might log on and do a search on vacuum. Let's say that instead of the 11,384 results that I recently got with that search, you got only three. You can imagine that the sellers of those vacuums, without much competition to force their price lower, would be asking a pretty hefty premium for those three vacuums. If you are a buyer who really needs a vacuum (or maybe even more important, if you don't have any good reference of what a vacuum should cost), chances are you're going to be fodder for a vendor who's got a better handle on the market for vacuums. You're probably not going to get a very good deal.

In the futures market, it can work exactly the same way. Traders will want to quote wide—again, leave a large gap between bid and offer—whenever they can. By quoting a wide market, they can take advantage of customers who either must buy or sell contracts (for whatever reason), no matter the price or who are less sure what the value of the contracts really should be.

But traders don't often just quote markets wide. That would be an obvious indication that they were looking to take advantage and scare a customer away from trading the market. Much more often in the oil pits, you'd see traders giving contrived and even outright phony markets in illiquid contracts—they'd give a close, but fake bid and offer to a particular broker if they knew their customer was a more likely buyer or seller.

Let's take an example: If a broker had shown interest in an illiquid back month, a trader specializing in that month might first probe that broker with a fairly wide quote. If the broker then came in with a competing and higher bid than was originally quoted, the trader (knowing that the customer was more interested in buying) might now immediately beat that bid closing the market between bid and offer: He's trying to force the customer to pay up to his original high offer. The market now may give the impression to the customer of greater liquidity with the closeness of the new bid and offer. But in truth, nothing has changed much, because our trader isn't interested in buying anything with the bid he has entered; instead, he just wants to force the customer to trade. Liquidity traps like this were possible in rare contracts and more obscure month-to-month price relationships (known as spreads, which I described in Chapter 1) that attracted less attention from fewer participants, with very poor liquidity, mostly in the back months. However, in the front months that were closely traded by so many, liquidity was always necessarily deep. Everyone in the market relies on front-month depth, even traders able to quote wide in other spots. They also relied on the better liquidity in the front months to reduce risks and lock in profits. For everyone who trades, liquidity is the key, the lifeblood that fuels successful contracts.

Liquidity, as I have already said, leads to confidence and volume. Volume refers to the number of contracts traded, usually calculated on a daily basis. Volume can be a very important factor to price, although it's rarely thought of in that way. But growing volume is a clear and obvious indicator of growing interest. And growing interest is almost always indicative of rising prices. To people who measure statistics of markets (known as technicians) uncharacteristically large volume even on a single day is considered a strong indicator of a trend or change of trend.

Open Interest

Let's define one last characteristic entirely unique to futures before we start to talk about trading and considering putting our own hard-earned capital on the line with a bet on prices: open interest.

If you want to buy a house—that is, get long houses—you need to buy it from someone who has a house for sale. Similarly, if you want to buy a share of Citibank or Hewlett-Packard or Transocean, you also need to buy it from someone who owns a share already. I know this sounds simple and obvious, except that this rule doesn't apply to futures on commodities (more on this in Chapters 2 and 3).

Take a moment to consider this, because it goes against natural reasoning, but it deeply affects the way commodities trade differently than any other market. Most people who attempt to understand and trade commodities never seem to understand this absolutely critical difference. For example, stocks have an established and exact number of issued shares at any one time. Although a company can increase the number of publicly traded shares periodically or buy them back, these changes in the total number of shares are rare and a significant event in the calculation of share value.

In contrast, with commodities, there is never a standard number of contracts (shares) already established. So if you wanted to buy a contract of soybean oil for delivery in July, there are two equal sources you can go to get that contract: You could purchase it from someone who already owns a contract and is prepared to sell it for the current price. However, you could just as easily and equivalently buy the same contract from someone who doesn't own it at all and is willing to create a fresh contract for you both. It is an incredible concept when you think of it: Creating stock out of thin air. And we need to appreciate this characteristic fully to understand commodities as a unique asset class.

This is the idea of open interest: The number of contracts available for trading is a fluid number that is constantly changing. Contracts can be constantly created and retired. As contract months approach delivery, and as more and more of the participants are intending to take or make delivery (or are planning neither and need to cash in out of their bets, which is much more likely), the number of contracts that are open begins to contract. Only about 2% of the total number of open contracts in oil will remain in the end to be settled at delivery. Although this does not imply that 98% of the contracts traded are not legitimate hedges, it does show the constant and enormous variability in open-interest numbers. But as open interest recedes as contracts come close to delivery, other contract months can increase their number of contracts that are open.

What's important to remember is that the number of contracts available for trade in any one month and for the entire contract of all the listed and traded months is unlimited (at least theoretically). To be a buyer or a seller on the futures market, all you need to trade a contract is to find a willing partner. This has an enormous effect on pricing of commodities as compared to stocks (as we saw in Chapter 3).

At this point in the discussion on price, you may realize that I have diligently avoided any complicated talk of supply and demand. Most people might expect in any discussion of oil pricing to see references to OPEC, transport costs, peak oil arguments, refining capacity, emerging markets, and so on. Of course, I won't argue that fundamentals don't matter at all. There have been many important books written on the topic of fundamental growth and usage versus what is obviously a limited and slowly exhausting supply of a critical natural resource. But taking those fundamentals and translating them into price motion that anyone can understand is an impossible and ultimately useless task. For the purposes of this book, try to forget all of that. Even when Nobel-prize-winning economists and oil analysts have tried (and they constantly try) to price oil correctly using fundamental analysis, their estimations are almost always wrong. Flagrantly wrong.

Instead, let's think about the fundamentals of supply and demand as a trader might—as I did when I was trading, No one I ever knew deriving their livelihood from the daily trade of oil ever gave more than a passing thought about fundamentals, except in a key and critical way. For us, the fundamentals didn't matter. We didn't pay attention to the weekly change in storage numbers or rumors of OPEC production quotas. What mattered to us was how the perception of those fundamentals might affect the players in the oil market.

This may sound like the same thing, but it is not. I'll explain why the fundamentals matter less for commodities than any other capital asset and why the perception of those fundamentals matters more, so you can understand the key element to oil and the oil markets and how and why they move. I need to discuss this point more fully to realize how important, how paramount, the perception of the components acting on the market is to the participants engaged in it.

Again, let's draw on the capital market that most people know best: stocks. When stocks are priced, there are various fundamental but measurable metrics that we can draw on: earnings, growth, inventory, dividends (to name just a few). Into the question of price for stocks, we need to add risk factors, both of the company itself and for the stock market as a whole. And then, of course, these metrics aren't often dependably judged, and they can change and be interpreted differently.

But that's not the point. We can say that at least stocks have certain value relationships: We have confidence that a stock will represent a certain risk and value over time based on the numbers we can measure and that can translate directly to price. For example, if a company reports a sales increase, we will expect an increase in the share price. This is because there is an investment return to be expected in a stock when compared to a benchmark investment like a treasury bond. Although the variations in stock prices we see are large, they are all related to the predictions the investing community makes on measureable and established numbers.

Oil pricing (and for that matter, all hard commodities) does not operate in this way. The fundamental metrics that we relied on for stocks are fewer and less quantifiable, and it is difficult to apply sure values to them. Sure, we can take oil out of the ground, and that will cost a certain amount of money, so we know a bottom-line value for oil. But what more will we use to establish value? There is no return on oil, no sales to place a number on, no earnings. There is no theoretical limit to open interest, so we can't find a market cap for a contract for oil. Although an oil company certainly can have trucks and pipelines and refinery assets and a whole host of inventory and infrastructure items that we can measure as having value, an oil barrel has none of these things.

Also, oil isn't like stock in another key way. With stocks, one stock is just as good as any other, at least for investment purposes. You choose a stock based on earnings and dividends and other metrics which (if they match with other stocks), make your choice just one of convenience. In contrast, if we need oil, we can't substitute silver for it. One hard commodity isn't interchangeable with another, depending on its valuation. If we need gas to power our car, or if we need aluminum siding to keep our houses warm, we can't substitute one for the other.

So if there are no relative comparisons to help us come up with price, what can we use to figure out what a barrel of oil is worth?

Of course, it must all be about the people engaged in the making, buying, and selling of any specific commodity. Those are the people who must ultimately attach a value to our barrel of oil. This is how the commodity markets were conceived.

For example, a farmer is wondering whether to plant corn or whether to plant soybeans (or whether to give up farming and become a teacher). Whether he looks at the prompt cash market (which is where corn and soybeans are being bought and sold for cash) or whether he looks at the futures markets, he's going to see a community of participants far different from what he'd see in any other marketplace, certainly any other capital marketplace.

- In the prompt cash market, the buyers you'll see are the distributors, processors, transporters—that is, the feed companies, the cereal companies, and the vegetable companies. On the selling side, you'll see his fellow farmers, the grain elevators, and the local co-op.
- In the futures market, you will see the same players, except one more participant will be added: The speculator trader, who is adding liquidity and facilitating trade by making bets on the difference between the prices legitimate buyers and sellers are willing to pay.

Buyers in both the futures markets and cash markets will calculate costs of processing, transport, packaging, and advertisement among other costs and try to assess what they can sell their finished box of Corn Flakes for, before they engage in bidding on the cash and futures markets. On the other side, sellers will calculate cost of fertilizer and seed, the lease on the John Deere tractor, and their son's upcoming college tuition before entering an agreeable selling price into the market. When enough participants from both sides enter bid and offers with prices close enough to matching, we will begin to trade, because we have accomplished the task of attaching value to our bushel of corn, our ounce of silver, or our barrel of oil. It's a magical process, attaching value to something that really has none because it has no legitimate comparative benchmarks.

But this kind of price discovery sets commodity trading apart from any other kind of trading in any other capital market. And notice this key difference: Participants in the real growing, harvesting, processing, and sale of finished products of hard commodities are the legitimate creators of price. Or, to be more precise: Honest price discovery is only possible when those who participate in commodity markets have a primary need to engage in honest price discovery. It's a powerful, simple, and unique market idea. You want to know the price of oil? Put everyone who cannot find a substitute for it—both buyers and sellers—in a room and let them debate its worth, and you'll soon have your magical price. As long as the participants are real, the price will be too (or as real as anyone can make it). Price discovery has always been the primary role of futures markets—it legitimizes them. Because, while the participants in the markets will set the prices, the world will need to rely on them once they're set. It's a critical role, far more critical than price discovery in any other capital market.

We've discussed price, and we've happily avoided discussion of fundamentals, because we've learned it's much more important how the fundamentals of supply and demand are perceived by the market that counts. We don't really care as a trader anyway. Do you know what a barrel of oil looks like? Could you tell the difference between a transport ship carrying cargoes of raw crude from Nigeria or carrying cheap plastic toys from China? No? Perfect! We're exactly like every successful oil trader I ever met. Traders *want* to be ignorant in certain ways. We don't want to trade based on OPEC news; instead, we want to trade based on how Chevron will want to hedge their production estimates based on OPEC news. We don't care about Russian pipelines; instead, we only want to know if anyone needs to sell positions in the back months because the threat of a Russian oil glut when it comes online will cause all sorts of (unnecessary) selling. We'll concentrate on how open interest and volume and the relationships between the months and the various energy commodities are changing, because that helps tell us how the perceptions about the market are changing.

You're now armed with all the information and jargon I ever had entering the pits on any normal day of trading.

An Extreme Example of Intervention in the Futures Market

How Three Dallas Oil Tycoons Tried to Corner the Silver Market

T here has been one infamous example of rampant speculation in the futures market and the powerful effects of regulatory intervention to stop it: with the silver market in 1980. In 1979, the three Hunt brother descendants of Dallas oil tycoon H. L. Hunt embarked on a mission to corner the silver market. Led by oldest brother Nelson "Bunker" Hunt, the plan was two-fold, intending to first take control of the physical market and then using that control to help influence the underlying futures market. Bunker believed in the inflation protection of silver and in the ultimate collapse of paper currency, but his enthusiasm led to his and his brothers' bankruptcy.

Throughout late 1979, Bunker began purchasing physical silver and stockpiling it. When physical silver became less available in large quantities, Bunker began to use the futures market, buying up contracts on the COMEX exchange and surprising the market by taking the contracts to expiration, taking delivery, and storing those as well. In the early stages, Bunker managed to accumulate $1 billion of physical silver—which was enough to make a significant dent in stockpiles, but not nearly enough to destabilize and manipulate prices significantly.

But the fun had only started for Bunker in his quest to corner the market. The silver now in storage provided the collateral, along with the family reputation, to leverage the Hunt holdings into ever-larger positions in the futures markets. As the physical market continued to shrink from the continuous stockpiling by the Hunts, prices began to rocket higher, moving from about $6 an ounce at the start of 1979 to almost $50 an ounce in January of 1980.

The Hunts also elicited friends to join them in their silver quest, including Saudi investors. With huge stockpiles of physical metal off the market, and with the price skyrocketing, the Hunts were able to leverage loans for more and more futures contracts, no longer needing to demand delivery on all of them.

Because of their success in creating a physical spot squeeze on anyone who was short the futures, they could now afford to roll the vast majority of their futures positions, keeping upwards pressure on the futures market while retaining complete control of the physical market. At its height, the Hunt brothers controlled almost $5 billion of both physical and promised silver.

It was at this point that the U.S. government and the exchange took action.

In January 1980, the exchange instituted a liquidation-only restriction, which temporarily suspended the initiation of any new futures positions, both long and short, in the silver market. The only activity that would be permitted were trades that closed out already open positions—in other words, an investor could either sell contracts if he/she were already long, or an investor could buy contracts if he/she were already short.

The effect on the market was instantaneous. Without the ability to roll positions forward, the speculative long players would either be forced to find cash for delivery of prompt silver or would be forced to sell and close out the position. Those speculators who didn't have the resources to take delivery sold immediately, and the price of silver retreated $11 that day alone. The Hunt brothers, however, had deeper pockets than the average speculator, so they continued to try and hold on. So the exchange increased the pressure on the Hunts by increasing margin requirements, and the Federal Reserve made it clear to the banks that the Fed would look very poorly at any entity that would lend money (particularly to Arab interests) engaged in obvious speculative activity. Once the easy flow of cheap loans dried up, the Hunts and their silver goose were cooked.

A last-ditch effort by the Hunts to float bonds based on the physical silver stockpiles left in their possession was met with little interest: No one further cared to be against the government and on the side of the Saudis and the Hunt brothers. The failure of that final bond ploy caused the final collapse on what is known as Silver Thursday, March 27, 1980. Prices slid that day to $11 an ounce, down more than 77% from recent highs less than three months earlier. The Hunts were forced into bankruptcy, and it took them more than a decade to wind down their silver positions and pay the many fines that were imposed on them by the exchange and the courts for manipulating the market.

Two obvious lessons can be drawn from this one example. One, there is ample precedent for exchange and government intervention into a futures market that has been determined to be the victim of excessive speculation. And two, they have the tools to ably chase those interests out. All that is really required is the will to do it.

Index